MY '64

PENGUIN AFRICAN LIBRARY AP12

Edited by Ronald Segal

The Rise of the
South African Reich

BRIAN BUNTING

BRIAN BUNTING

The Rise of the
South African Reich

Penguin Books

Penguin Books Ltd, Harmondsworth, Middlesex
U.S.A.: Penguin Books Inc., 3300 Clipper Mill Road, Baltimore 11, Md
AUSTRALIA: Penguin Books Pty Ltd, 762 Whitehorse Road,
Mitcham, Victoria

First published 1964

Copyright © Brian Bunting, 1964

Made and printed in Great Britain by Cox & Wyman Ltd, London,
Fakenham and Reading
Set in Monotype Plantin

Contents

Acknowledgements

I would like to express my thanks to the many men and women in South Africa who helped me in the preparation of this book. In consequence of the situation which prevails in my unhappy country at the present time, I am unable to mention their names for fear that they may be victimized, but I would like them to know that their assistance has been most deeply appreciated and is hereby gratefully acknowledged.

This book is dedicated to all those in South Africa who are fighting against enormous odds to free their country from unendurable tyranny. Long terms of imprisonment and even the death penalty face opponents of the Nationalist government who fall foul of their oppressive laws. It is my hope that this book may help to mobilize public opinion in support of the growing international campaign to end the most vicious régime the world has known since the death of Hitler.

BRIAN BUNTING

'The history of the Afrikaner reveals a determination and a definiteness of purpose which make one feel that Afrikanerdom is not the work of man but a creation of God. We have a Divine right to be Afrikaners. Our history is the highest work of art of the Architect of the centuries.'

Dr D. F. Malan

'It was the Aryan alone who founded a superior type of humanity; therefore he represents the archetype of what we understand by the term: MAN.... It was not by mere chance that the first forms of civilization arose there where the Aryan came into contact with inferior races, subjugated them and forced them to obey his command.'

Adolf Hitler in *Mein Kampf*

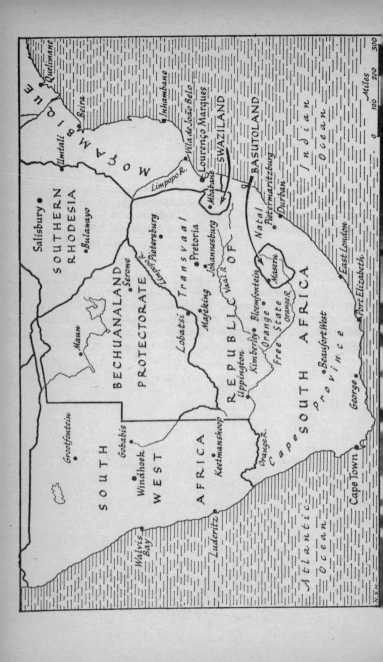

Editorial Foreword

Until recently South Africa was still hesitating at the frontier of terror. One civil liberty after the other had been ceremoniously killed, but a few legal safeguards survived to protect at least those citizens who were aware of them against persistent outrage. Africans were banished for years to desolate stretches of the country, and the more vigorous opponents of government policy, White as well as black banned from all gatherings, restricted to their magisterial districts, placed under house arrest, and prevented from communicating their views in speech or print. Yet, by comparison with consummate terrors like the German Third Reich, South Africa remained a mere approach. Africans, Indians, and Coloured were frequently beaten up in police cells, but the process was disliked, in the main, by authority, and policemen were occasionally prosecuted for assault. Those who were arrested and held by the police unduly could be released by a *habeas corpus* application, or at least charged and brought to trial in open court. Citizens were detained without charge or trial nevertheless, but only during a State of Emergency, a claim by the government of exceptional circumstances.

Then, with the General Law Amendment Act of May 1963, South Africa finally crossed the frontier of terror. The new law empowered the Minister of Justice to detain anyone he pleased, without charge or trial, for indefinitely recurring periods of ninety days, and to extend, till death if he so chose, the imprisonment of those who had already served their sentences. The new law – and this was its obvious intention – has outlawed law itself. For what meaning is left to legal procedure if, after trial and deliberate sentencing, a prisoner can be kept in gaol long after the set date

9

of his release? And what purpose can there be to a trial at all, if the Minister can simply ignore acquittal and imprison the accused from the court-room to the grave? There is now no longer in South Africa any legal protection against the Minister of Justice; he may imprison whom he pleases for as long as he likes.

Nor is this all. Those detained – and no one but the Minister need know who or how many they are – are kept in solitary confinement, with no visitors allowed except a magistrate, a carefully selected government employee, once a week. They are permitted no writing material and no books but the Bible – most African detainees have been denied even that – and are under the complete jurisdiction of the political police. Prisoners are shifted suddenly from one city to another, so that their relatives may be ignorant of their whereabouts and the circumstances of their custody concealed. Perhaps no recent report to have come from voluntary welfare workers in South Africa is more horrible than that of police throwing the clothes of African detainees upon the pavement, laughing while the relatives scramble to sort out the pieces, and speculating aloud to each other on who among the detainees is likely to hang. Increasingly the police want to feel – and display – their power.

One African detainee from Cape Town, Looksmart Solwandle Ngadle, is officially alleged to have committed suicide by hanging himself in his cell at a Pretoria gaol. Persistent rumour, however, suggests a different death, and notes smuggled out of gaol by detainees tell of constant assaults by the police, interrupted only by interrogation. An Indian, Ebrahim Siyanvala, was released from detention and then, on his way home, arrested for a minor traffic offence. He escaped from the police station, and two days later his body was found in a nearby river. Several confirmed cases of torture, including the use of electricity, together with reports of cells painted black and of lights left burning day and night, suggest why there has been at least one detainee who has found further police custody unendurable. More and more accused appear in South African courts with the marks of physical violence still upon them. The police, it seems, are not only brutal, they are carelessly so. And why should they not be careless? They have become the law.

Brian Bunting has studied the rise of the South African Reich, and events since he completed his study have confirmed its title. The South African Reich is no longer a possibility, it exists. Hundreds of thousands of White South Africans doubtless do not know what is happening in the police cells a mile or two from their homes, as hundreds of thousands of the very best Germans thought that the concentration camps were merely manufacturing soap. And if they do know? Millions of them, White as well as black, are afraid – the blacks of the Whites, though their fear only excites their resistance; the Whites of the blacks, of the world beyond, of each other and of themselves, though their fear only furthers their dedication to violence. Most of those who dislike the government are careful not to be discovered saying so. They behave as though the political police are watching them, waiting to trap them, all the time. For, in a police state, who is to know what the police are doing, or why? People are detained, even Whites in White South Africa, not because they are themselves politically suspect, but because they are closely related to other people who are. There are even sometimes mistakes, and mistakes take so long to be rectified. During the 1960 State of Emergency one White woman – no one knows how many Africans suffered similarly – was arrested and detained for several weeks in sheer error. And now, with the existence of the 1963 General Law Amendment Act, South Africa is in a constant State of Emergency. It is not civilization – White, Christian, Western, or anything else – that the South African Reich is attempting to secure with its policies. It is merely fear.

The parallel with the German Third Reich grows every day more evident. Is the record of connivance by the rest of the world to be repeated as well? At the United Nations Britain assails the South African government in careful phrases, calling its policies 'morally abominable, intellectually grotesque, and spiritually indefensible'. Yet, joined by most of its NATO allies, it strenuously opposes any action calculated to force a change in the policies it condemns. Opponents of international intervention, some of them well-meaning, cry that any attempt at compulsion, like economic sanctions, will cause more suffering to South Africa's subject population than to its rulers. One need not ask why so many who have never even lifted a tongue against the sufferings of South Africa's non-Whites should suddenly display concern whenever action is proposed that may succeed in bringing such sufferings to an end. It is sufficient that the non-Whites themselves, when possessed of any chance to express their views freely, entreat intervention, as offering an escape at last from an otherwise endless despair. Did the barbarities of Germany evaporate under the patient gaze of the outside world? Or did they swell till they spilt over the rim of the Reich and almost swamped humanity?

The appeasement of the South African Reich may yet lead to an end as cruel and destructive as the appeasement of its German model did. However passionately Britain or any other state may desire it, South Africa cannot go a lonely way, its human erosions sealed off at its frontiers. The very existence of White supremacy is an insult and an incitement to the peoples of the non-White world. Another racial massacre in South Africa – and who, since Sharpeville, does not expect one? – or a clash between the White forces of South Africa and the black forces of other African states may set off a colour conflict throughout the world. Doubtless the Munich mind dismisses the prospect as unprofitable. Is the world to be so wrong and so stupid again?

RONALD SEGAL

NOTE: Since this book was written the South African Foreign Minister, Mr Eric Louw, has announced his resignation and has been replaced by Dr H. Muller, former South African Ambassador in London.

1. The Birth of the Nationalist Party

Afrikaners generally trace the birth of their nation back to 1652, when the Dutch East India Company sent Jan van Riebeeck with a party of its servants to establish an outpost at the Cape. The purpose of the expedition was to establish not a permanent settlement or colony, but merely a refreshment station, which could victual the ships passing on the long voyage to and from India, and it was not until five years after van Riebeeck landed that permission was first given to some of the company's servants to set up as independent colonists.

Right from the outset the development of the colony was marked by two characteristics. The first was the hostility between the Dutch and the indigenous inhabitants, particularly the Khoi-Khoin, or Hottentots, to use the derisory term applied to them by the Whites. The second was the conflict between the colonists and the company, both competing for trade with the passing ships. By the very nature of their position the colonists felt themselves threatened on two sides – by authority in the shape of the company, which seized the lion's share of the shipping trade and insisted on a monopoly of trade with the Khoi-Khoin, and by the Khoi-Khoin, who resisted the intrusion of the Whites into their traditional grazing grounds and fought back when attempts were made to filch their cattle wealth. Later the importation of slaves from the East and from other territories in Africa was to complete a pattern of race relations which has persisted right up to the present day.

Slowly the colony expanded. The power of the Khoi-Khoin was broken, and their economy subordinated to that of the Whites. The colonists, their numbers augmented by natural increase and by immigration, spread out over the Cape Flats and crossed the Hottentots' Holland mountains into the interior. The conquest of southern Africa had commenced.

For 100 years after the landing of van Riebeeck, the colonists evolved their way of life in isolation. Often living on the level of bare subsistence, little different from that of the indigenous inhabitants, they developed powers of self-sufficiency and an independence of outlook which was contradicted only by their status as slave-owners. Their lives were on the whole a grim, unending struggle to survive in the face of a multitude of human and natural obstacles. The Bible was the fountain of their faith. An occasional visit to Cape Town, an occasional quarrel with authority, were the only diversions in an otherwise bleak existence.

Then there erupted into their experience two factors which were to shatter the basis of their whole society. The first was their meeting with the Bantu-speaking peoples of the Eastern Cape in the neighbourhood of the Fish River, about the middle of the eighteenth century. The second was the annexation of the Cape by the British in 1795 as a by-product of the Napoleonic wars. Conflict with the African peoples and with the British has been the core of Afrikaner consciousness ever since.

The resentment and resistance which the Dutch colonist had always displayed towards the 'interference' of the company in the old days was reinforced when the British all at once became the masters. For the British did not merely bring a foreign presence, they also brought with them foreign ideas – about government, about relations with the Africans, about the treatment of servants and slaves, about the independence of the magistracy, about language rights. The famous Great Trek of the 1830s had many causes, but not the least of them was Dutch hatred of British rule and racial policies.

The Dutch desire to be rid of British rule was not merely the manifestation of a spirit of national independence. It was also prompted by the wish to continue to own slaves, to be able to discriminate between White and non-White, to re-establish the patriarchal relationship between master and servant which had existed from the time of van Riebeeck and which now looked like being destroyed for ever. The new republics which were set up in the Orange Free State and the Transvaal enabled the Dutch to refashion for themselves their old way of life. A similar attempt in Natal was crushed by the British, who wanted to retain control of the port of Durban and the hinterland.

The Boer republics were seldom free of British harassment and intervention. From the time of their establishment to the end of the nineteenth century there were constant clashes, culminating in the outright annexation of the Transvaal in 1877 and what Afrikaners today call the First War of Independence in 1880, which resulted in the restoration of the territory to Boer control. But the respite was short-lived. The discovery of diamonds at Kimberley in 1867 and of gold on the Witwatersrand in 1886 transformed the imperialist attitude towards the South African interior. From being something of a liability and a burden, South Africa now became a land of opportunity and profit. Capital, adventurers, and entrepreneurs poured into the country from abroad and made their way to the diamond diggings and the goldfields. The railway line snaked north. Britain strengthened her military and political position on the flanks of the republics, and Rhodes began his machinations which culminated in the Jameson Raid of 1895.

War was now inevitable. Boer independence was incompatible with imperialist ambitions in Africa. The overt cause was the status and rights of the *uitlanders* – the foreigners – in the Transvaal to whom Kruger steadfastly refused to give the franchise. But no matter what concessions Kruger might have offered, the British were by this time determined on a show-down. The open clash broke out in 1899 and the peoples of South Africa were swept into the maelstrom.

For the Boers the war was the climax to 'a century of wrong', a century of British expansion, oppression, and meddling which had finally goaded them beyond the limits of endurance. There rose up before them as they fought the memory of the past, of the colony which had been annexed, of the slaves which had been freed, of the Slachter's Nek rebellion and its martyrs, of the battle of Majuba, of the thousand and one defeats and humiliations to which they had been subjected ever since the British presence established itself in South Africa. For a while they had been able to escape from British rule into the security of their own two republics, but now these too were threatened with destruction. Everything for which they had lived and struggled was endangered – their freedom, their language, their possessions, their racial supremacy, their very existence as an independent people with their God-given right to manage their affairs and their chattels as they pleased. The people of the two republics felt that the cup of their bitterness was too full to be borne. They threw themselves into the struggle feeling themselves ready to die rather than submit.

Imperialism had committed many atrocities in Africa before 1899, but the Boer War was widely considered throughout the civilized world to be amongst the worst – perhaps because the victims of aggression had white skins, not black; perhaps because, for once, the cause of the victims could be widely propagated abroad by their sympathizers and supporters; perhaps because of the blatant disparity in the relative strength of the two protagonists. It was never a fair fight. Against the might of the greatest imperial power in the world the Boers could pit no formal military apparatus whatsoever. They had no regular standing army. Their forces consisted of some thousands of volunteers hastily rounded up, poorly organized and equipped, and lacking discipline. After a few initial successes, the main Boer forces were crushingly defeated by British troops within a few months of the outbreak of war. Thereafter the Boer remnants carried on activity as guerrillas under the leadership of Smuts, Botha, and Hertzog for a further two years before they were compelled to acknowledge defeat at the Peace of Vereeniging.

The British won the war, but it was an expensive victory, as later history was to prove. In Britain itself it contributed towards the defeat of the Government and the advent of the Liberals to power. In South Africa the Boer War left an indelible scar. The Boer has since exacted his revenge, but he has still neither forgiven nor forgotten what was perpetrated against his people by the British during those years.

The occupation of the Free State and the Transvaal was completed only at the cost of the almost total destruction of the Boer communities which had formerly inhabited them. A scorched earth policy was adopted to flush out the elusive commandos; farms and homesteads were fired, crops and cattle impounded. To house the thousands of dispossessed women and children, the British resorted to the now notorious device of concentration camps.

At the end of the Boer War these camps housed 200,000 people, 120,000 Boers and (in separate encampments, naturally) 80,000 Africans. When the camps were first opened, conditions were primitive in the extreme, and the inmates were prey to the slightest infection. It is calculated that as many as 26,000 Boer women and children died in these camps – compared with a total of 6,000 Boers and 22,000 Britons killed on the battlefield. (A further 32,000 Boer soldiers were scattered in prisoner-of-war camps in the Cape and as far afield as the Bermudas, St Helena, and Ceylon.)

It was the camps which constituted the greatest outrage of the war.

Ramsay Macdonald wrote at the time:

I simply state the facts that hundreds of women fled before our columns for months and months, preferring the hardship of the veldt to the mercy of the camps. . . . We have to face this fact, which no one who knows the country dare dispute – that the camps were a profound mistake; that families on the veldt or in the caves fared better and suffered a lower mortality rate than those in the camps; that the appalling mortality of the camps lies at our door (one of the saddest things I have ever seen in my life was a camp graveyard with its tiny crowded crosses: it looked like a nursery of crosses); that the camps have created a fierce bitterness among the women and the young generation; that when every other memory of the war will have faded away, the nightmare shadows of the camps will still remain.

The British insisted that the disaster of the camps was accidental, due to factors beyond their control; that in fact their intention was humane – to provide for those who had been rendered homeless and destitute by the war. But it is not surprising that their enemies believed the mass deaths in the camps to have been deliberate, tantamount to planned genocide; that the British imperialists were trying by means of the camps to destroy the Afrikaner people. The British were accused of having poisoned the water supplies and having inserted fish-hooks and powdered glass into the food. It had all been part of the great anti-Afrikaner conspiracy.

It is easy to feel sympathy for the Boers in their gallant struggle to maintain their cherished independence. But one should not lose sight of the facts, and chief amongst these was that the Boer republics constituted an anachronism to the twentieth century. Their mode of government was incapable of adaptation to the requirements of the machine age, their code of conduct incompatible with the liberal philosophy of modern capitalism. In the Transvaal constitution it was written that there could be no equality between Black and White in Church or State. One of the most persuasive factors in Boer resistance was the desire to retain this bar in the face of cosmopolitan pressures from the rootless *uitlander*, who dominated the world of mining and finance and in whose interest the British ultimately resorted to force of arms.

One can feel sympathy with the Boer victim General Hertzog, for instance, whose own wife was one of the inmates of the camps for the duration of the war. But can one feel the same sympathy for the Boer leader, General Hertzog, who made it a matter of policy to have British African levies shot whenever they were captured, apparently in the belief that it was a cardinal sin for a black man to take up arms against a white?

After the war the Afrikaner nation, bruised and bleeding, rallied its strength to meet the danger which still faced it – that its language and culture would be submerged by those of the conqueror. Milner assiduously pushed his policy of Anglicization, and many an Afrikaner can still remember today how he was punished or humiliated at that time for speaking in his native language, Dutch. The Treaty of Vereeniging read: 'Both the English and the Dutch languages shall be taught in the public schools of the Transvaal and the Orange River Colony if the parents of the children demand it.' But, writes Hertzog's biographer C. M. van den Heever, the Afrikaners discovered 'that "parent's choice" was a dangerous principle, for ignorant parents were often influenced to take decisions which were not in the interests of their children'. Just as a large proportion of Afrikaners in the Cape had learnt during the nineteenth century to despise their own language and to absorb the culture of the Englishman, even to the point of having English spoken in their own church, so many Afrikaners after the Boer War decided to make their peace with the English, and allowed their children to be contaminated in their schools.

To the true Afrikaner nationalist, however, accommodation with Milnerism was impossible. The weaker ones amongst them might seek security in a spiritual surrender, but the majority were never reconciled. How could the camps and the devastation be forgotten? How could the memory of the lost republics be allowed to fade? How could the present policies of the British ever be accepted? 'The language of the conqueror in the mouth of the conquered is the language of slaves,' President Steyn of the Free State had said. Both in the Transvaal and in the Cape the Afrikaners established their own schools so that their children could be brought up in the ways of their fathers.

This division in the ranks of the Afrikaners had first revealed itself at Vereeniging, where Smuts and Botha had been keen, but Hertzog reluctant, to sign the peace treaty. Afterwards Smuts and Botha had taken the lead in seeking an accommodation with the British, while Hertzog remained resentful and suspicious. Nor was Hertzog an isolated individual. He stood for the majority of his people, as later events were to show.

C. M. van den Heever noted: 'The Afrikaner's feasts, his religious outlook, his family life clashed with this other civilization, and he retired into his shell at the ridicule that was poured upon him. He felt a stranger in his own land, and hatred and a sense of frustration welled within him.'

It was not just a question of culture. There was a fundamental difference over the treatment of the non-Whites. The British since 1854 had had a constitution overtly without colour bar in the Cape, and their attitudes were projected northwards immediately after the war. Hertzog 'was never to forget the scene in the Bloemfontein post office, where he saw his own people struggling with a strange language *among coloured persons and natives*' (my italics). Perhaps the greatest humiliation of their conquest for the Afrikaners was their enforced helplessness while attempts were made to break down the colour bar. True the attempts were not very vigorous. The British did nothing to extend political rights to the non-Whites after the war, and the extension of passes, the colour-bar franchise, job reservation on the mines, and anti-Indian legislation were features of their rule just as they were features of the Afrikaner's. Nevertheless, the tendency towards a fusion of cultures in an integrated society was something that the Hertzogites could not stomach.

Smuts was a more adaptable animal. He told Lord de Villiers on one occasion:

We who love South Africa as a whole, who have our ideals for it, who set a united South Africa in the place of the lost independence, who see in breadth of horizon and in wider and more inclusive statemanship the healing of many of our wounds and the only escape from our sorry trivialities and our troublesome past, we are prepared to sacrifice much for South Africa.

Smuts and Botha, with their supporters, having accepted the offer of the conqueror, turned their back on the republics and looked forward to the creation of a larger unity in South Africa, a comity in which both Boer and Briton would find an equal and honoured place. But for Hertzog the outlook was very different. 'He knew that a great nation could cooperate with a smaller without any sense of danger, but that the smaller could preserve itself only by vigilance, care, and if necessary, by isolation.' (Van den Heever.)

'If necessary, by isolation.' In this phrase lies the key to much of the subsequent history of the Afrikaner nationalist. Afraid of domination at first by the British, later by the African, the Afrikaner nationalist has tended always to seek safety in isolation. Seventy years earlier he could escape from his conflicts by embarking on the Great Trek. In the period following the Boer War, he could only retire into himself and wait for his opportunity. He sought comfort from his church. He founded organizations in which he felt the 'soul' of the Afrikaner nation could best find expression. In 1905 came the founding of the Afrikaanse Taalvereniging (Afrikaans Language Association) in Cape

Town, the Afrikaanse Taalgenootskap in Pretoria, and similar organizations in Potchefstroom and Bloemfontein. The S.A. Akademie voor Taal, Letterre en Kuns (S.A. Academy for Language, Literature, and Culture) was founded in 1909 to maintain and further both forms of the language – Dutch and Afrikaans – and to draw up spelling rules for Afrikaans. In this way the Second Language Movement which developed at this time can be considered a direct consequence of the Boer War, a form of compensation for defeat.

The bitter-enders among the Afrikaners never accepted the finality of defeat and looked forward to the time when, through internal schism or external intervention, they would be able to re-establish the Boer republics. A German journalist who interviewed Hertzog for the *Tagliche Rundschau* wrote: 'Hertzog believes that the fruit of the three-year struggle by the Boers is that their freedom, in the form of a general South African Republic, will fall into their laps as soon as England is involved in a war with a Continental power.' This provides a clue to Afrikaner nationalist thinking and action during both the First and Second World Wars.

The grant of responsible government to the Free State and Transvaal did much to persuade a section of the Afrikaner people that some sort of future could be worked out through cooperation with the British. And so the ground was carefully prepared for union, which came about at last in 1910. But it was a union without unity. Neither the die-hard north nor the relatively liberal south could be persuaded to drop their respective points of view on the colour question. The compromise which was eventually effected – a suffrage restricted to Whites in the Orange Free State and Transvaal, with the entrenchment of a qualified non-racial franchise in the Cape and, at least on paper, in Natal – has proved a source of friction and disagreement to this very day. The constitution accorded equal rights to the Dutch and English languages.

After union the Afrikaners found their political home in Die Nasionale Suid-Afrikaanse Party (S.A.P.) led by General Louis Botha – an amalgamation of Het Volk in the Transvaal, Die Afrikanerbond (Suid-Afrikaanse Party) in the Cape, the

Orangia-unie in the Orange Free State, and the Volksvereniging with a section of the English in Natal. This party was formally established in November 1911 after it had ruled for some time and had won the first election in 1910 with sixty-six seats, to thirty-seven for the Unionists (British jingo opposition), five for the Labour Party, and eleven Independents.

The first South African Cabinet drew its strength from both the Afrikaner and English sections of the population and consisted of Generals Botha and Smuts with H. C. Hull from the Transvaal, J. W. Sauer, H. Burton, F. S. Malan, and Sir de Villiers Graaff from the Cape, General Hertzog and Abraham Fischer from the Free State, and Sir F. R. Moor and Dr C. O. Grady Gubbins from Natal, under General Louis Botha as Prime Minister.

Five hundred and fifty delegates attended the inaugural conference of the S.A.P. at Bloemfontein – 'Het National Kongres' – and speeches were delivered by Generals Botha, Smuts, Hertzog, and de la Rey and President Steyn. In his chairman's address General Botha declared that it was a privilege 'to preside over so many moderate men'. The party would strive for the *samesmelting* (fusion) of the two sections, out of which one nation would be born.

The conference decided to scrap the word 'Nasionale' in the title of the party. One delegate said that the word 'nationalist' was 'unpopular with many in the country'. These remarks must have chilled the hearts of the real nationalists who were present, but for the moment they swallowed their pride and went forward with their associates.

There remained a fundamental difference of approach between the two wings of the S.A.P. General Botha and General Smuts believed that all efforts should now be devoted to eliminating racialism between the English and the Dutch, that both White groups should be reconciled in 'one stream'. Towards the British, therefore, Botha propounded a policy of conciliation, believing that both sides should be ready to compromise in the interests of a united nationhood.

Hertzog, on the other hand, believed in the so-called 'twin-stream' policy, whereby the English and Dutch were to develop separately side by side, with the rights of neither subordinated to those of the other. In Hertzog's view, Botha's policy could lead only to the destruction of the Afrikaner people. The English culture was dominant. English was the language of the courts and the civil service, the highest posts in which were held by Englishmen or English-speaking South Africans. The English were strongly entrenched in the leadership of industry, commerce, and high finance. The Boer War had resulted in the expulsion of no fewer than 10,000 Afrikaners from their land, and these men, demoralized by defeat and completely without training or experience of urban life, were to swell the ranks of the growing army of poor Whites in desperate competition with the non-Whites on the lower rungs of the economic ladder. For the Afrikaner to practise 'conciliation', Hertzog believed, would mean his permanent subordination to the English, an end to his dreams of State and nationhood.

The Botha Cabinet plodded along uneasily, outwardly united, inwardly divided, until 1912, when on 12 December at De Wildt, Hertzog gave utterance to his secret feelings in a manner which Botha could not overlook.

'Imperialism is only good for me in so far as it is useful to South Africa,' he declared, during a bitter attack on Unionist leader Sir Thomas Smartt, whom he described as a 'foreign fortune hunter'. 'When it comes in conflict with the interests of South Africa, I am a determined opponent of it. . . . I am not one of those who speaks of conciliation and loyalty, for those are idle words that deceive nobody. I have always said I don't know what this conciliation means . . . the people who speak most about loyalty know the least about it.' The language question was a weighty issue, he said, but it was only part of the greater problem, that of South African nationalism.

This speech, running counter as it did to government policy, provoked a storm and Botha asked Hertzog to resign. Hertzog refused, and so Botha resigned himself and formed a new cabinet without him. This brought about a breach in the ranks of Afrikanerdom which has persisted to this day. The basis had been laid for the emergence of Afrikaner nationalism as a fully-fledged political force in the arena of greater South African politics.

While the Botha–Smuts faction was greatly disconcerted by Hertzog's conduct, most Afrikaner nationalists were wild with enthusiasm. In support of Hertzog a mass meeting was held at Princess Park, Pretoria, on 28 December 1912, and 5,000 people attended. Hertzog was given a hero's welcome, and General de Wet, speaking from the top of a dunghill, declared that he would rather stand there with his own people than on a decorated platform amongst strangers.

When Parliament reassembled, Hertzog had six supporters in the House, and though he was now out of the Cabinet, he still remained a member of the S.A.P., hoping that the next conference of the party would declare itself in his favour. When the conference opened at Cape Town in 1913, Botha made an effort to hold the party together and called for reconciliation, but Hertzog replied that the rift was a matter of principle, not a difference of personalities, and that a superficial peacemaking would serve no purpose. A motion of confidence in Botha was passed by 131 votes to 90, and Hertzog, followed by his supporters, left the hall in dramatic fashion.

The logical next step was for Hertzog to gather his own supporters together and form his own party, and this he did at Bloemfontein from 7 to 9 January 1914, by a conference under Hertzog himself as chairman and De Wet as the vice-chairman. Some 450 delegates from all over the Union attended and decided to establish the Nationalist Party. Its programme of principles stated that the development of the national life should be on Christian-National lines, a phrase which was to become as significant in South African politics as National-Socialism in that of Germany. The 'native policy' of the party was to be 'the dominance of the European population in a spirit of Christian trusteeship, with the strictest avoidance of any attempt at race mixture'. These have remained the basic tenets of Afrikaner nationalism to this very day.

Despite occasional flights of opportunism, indeed, there has been a remarkable consistency about Nationalist Party policy throughout the fifty years of its existence. The Nationalists claim that this is because basically their policy has been forged from the experience of the volk ever since the days of van Riebeeck. The two pillars on which the party is based remain – apartheid between English and Afrikaans-speaking White South Africans; and apartheid between White and Black South Africans.

They are different sorts of apartheid, admittedly, but the underlying idea is the same. It is that the purity of the Afrikaner race will only be preserved by isolation from other White groups; and that the purity of the White race will only be preserved by isolation from the non-Whites.

At first the Afrikaner nationalist regarded the greatest threat to his existence as coming from the English-speaking section, associated as it was with the premier imperialist power of the day. The threat from the non-White could be contained more easily. The vast majority of non-Whites did not have the vote, were residentially segregated – with a large proportion sealed off in the Reserves – and had as yet no effective political or trade union organizations to speak for them. The Native National Congress had been in existence for two years before the Nationalist Party was formed, but had not yet developed into a movement of real significance.

Nevertheless, the potential threat of the Black man to White supremacy was clearly recognized by the Nationalist politicians. In Botha's Cabinet, Hertzog had been Minister of Native Affairs for a short while and had drafted a Bill which contained the essentials of his segregation policy. The government took it over from him and it became the basis of the 1913 Land Act, which made it impossible for Africans to acquire land ownership rights in most parts of the country, the so-called 'White areas'. It was in fact to counter the threat of this Act that the Native National Congress had been called into existence, a Black nationalism responding to the aggression of White nationalism.

In a speech reported in *The Star* on 14 October 1912, General Hertzog adumbrated a policy which bears remarkable similarities to the Bantustan policies of the Verwoerd government today. *The Star* reported:

He was convinced that segregation with the separation of Black and White as was done in the Transkeian territories was the only solution. ... The natives would not be allowed to have land in the White man's territory. ... They would place natives in those parts where there were already large masses of their compatriots. . . . His scheme meant nothing less than defining the respective spheres of Blacks and Whites. . . . Natives would be given the right to enter European territory in order to earn a living there.

And in a speech on the Land Bill in the Assembly on 16 May 1913, Hertzog filled out the picture:

The fact was that so far they had always seen to it and would always do so, that in practice, whatever his rights on paper, the native would not have these equal rights. . . . When they placed the native in a separate territory they gave him an opportunity of developing, and his position would become stronger and stronger, and he would be able even to have a continually growing measure of self-government within that territory. . . . Of course, if they had a certain amount of self-government, they would still stand under the control of this House.

It was a pipe dream then; it is a pipe dream now. But the Nationalists have clung to their tattered vision as if it were a revelation from on high, a divine guarantee that they will survive by expelling the Black man from their midst, while at the same time they develop an economy based on the careful exploitation of Black labour. The contradiction between their vision and reality has never been resolved.

The most striking feature of the Nationalist constitution at this period was the fact that it contained no reference to the desire of the Nationalists to convert South Africa into a republic. This, says van den Heever, was 'merely a matter of procedure'. But the opportunity to further the republican aim, at least for the more militant Nationalists, came with the outbreak of the First World War on 4 August 1914.

Parliament was summoned on 9 September, and General Botha announced that since South Africa was an integral part of the British Empire, she was automatically at war with the common enemy. The British Government had requested South Africa to undertake military operations against German South-West Africa, and Botha informed parliament that the Union government had agreed. General Hertzog immediately moved an amendment that all measures should be taken to defend South Africa if attacked, but that an attack on German territory would be 'in conflict with the interests of the Union and the

Empire'. He assured the House that the people would not support such a war. Hertzog's amendment, however, was defeated, and Botha's motion accepted by the margin of ninety-one votes to twelve.

General de la Rey, who had till then been a supporter of Botha and was a nominated Senator, opposed Botha on this point. He abstained from voting, declaring that he had conscientious objections, and on the same night left Cape Town by train for the north, to be seen off by his friend Botha at the station.

Clearly something was in the wind. A section of Nationalist Afrikanerdom was convinced that the hour had struck to stake their claim for the reconstitution of the Boer republics.

General Christiaan Beyers resigned as Commander-in-Chief of the Union Defence Force. He wrote: 'It is sad that the war is being waged against the "barbarism" of the Germans. We have forgiven but not forgotten all the barbarities committed in our own country during the South African War.' On the same day Beyers was visited in Pretoria by de la Rey, and after a discussion of half an hour or so the two left by road for Potchefstroom, where General Kemp was in charge of a training camp. What the generals had in mind is uncertain, but there is good reason to believe that de la Rey intended to discuss plans for the simultaneous resignation of leading army officers as a protest against the government's actions.

Disaster struck unexpectedly. On the road through Johannesburg de la Rey was shot while travelling in General Beyers's motor-car. It was an accident, caused by a ricocheting bullet from the gun of a police constable who was taking part in an intensive search for the Foster gang, responsible for a series of murders and robberies on the Reef. But in the eyes of Nationalist Afrikanerdom, the death of de la Rey had been engineered by agents of the government, and the whole incident caused a popular mood of shock and outrage. At the funeral Generals Beyers, de Wet, and Kemp had difficulty in restraining the feelings of the crowd, whose emotions had been worked to a pitch by the 'visions' of one 'Siener' van Rensburg, a Boer War veteran, who proclaimed that he saw, amongst other things, the figure fifteen and a clot of blood. Generals Botha and

27

Smuts attended the funeral to convey the sympathy of the government.

The declaration of war, followed so shortly by the killing of General de la Rey, provoked a widespread and hostile reaction amongst the Nationalists. Protest meetings were held against the conscription of soldiers, and there were widespread disturbances, culminating in rebellions in the Transvaal and the Orange Free State. General Manie Maritz, who was head of a commando of the Union forces on the border of South-West Africa, refused to obey an order to move against the Germans and joined them instead with the intention of setting up a 'free republic'.

In a proclamation issued on behalf of the 'provisional government', General Maritz announced: 'that the former South African Republic and Orange Free State as well as the Cape Province and Natal are proclaimed free from British control and independent, and every White inhabitant of the mentioned areas, of whatever nationality, are hereby called upon to take their weapons in their hands and realize the long-cherished ideal of a Free and Independent South Africa.'

Generals Beyers, de Wet, Kemp, Maritz, and Bezuidenhout were proclaimed heads of the new provisional government. Typical of the rebel attitude was the following paragraph from the proclamation of Maritz: 'It is known that on various occasions the enemy has armed natives and Coloureds to fight against us and since this is calculated to arouse contempt among the Black nations for the White man, therefore the warning is issued with emphasis that all Coloureds and natives who are captured with weapons, as well as their officers, will pay with their lives.'

Once again, as with Hertzog in the Boer War, the greatest crime was for a Black man to take up arms against a White. The fight for the republic was an exclusively European one.

Botha and Smuts struck back energetically against the rebels. Martial law was proclaimed on 14 October, and the Union forces quickly crushed the scattered forces of their opponents. General Maritz was defeated on 24 October and took refuge with the Germans. General Beyers was drowned in the Vaal River on 8 December. General de Wet was taken prisoner in

Bechuanaland, and General Kemp surrendered. The 'provisional government' was scattered to the winds, while the leading rebels were sentenced to long terms of imprisonment and heavily fined.

The rebellion added one more to the stock of Nationalist martyrs. This was Kommandant Jopie Fourie, who was forced to surrender on 16 December, immediately court-martialled, and sentenced to be shot. Dr Daniel François Malan, leading figure in the Dutch Reformed Church, happened to be in Pretoria at the time. He drew up a petition for a reprieve, obtained thousands of signatures, and was one of a deputation which tried to interview General Smuts on his farm at Irene, near Pretoria. The members of the deputation were told that General Smuts was walking on his farm, and they waited in the homestead for his return. But he did not reappear, and eventually the deputation departed, leaving the petition in the hands of an aide, Lt Louis Esselen. There was some suspicion that Smuts had deliberately avoided meeting the deputation. In any event, Smuts received the petition on the following morning. The sentence of death was confirmed, and Fourie was shot.

The episode made a deep and lasting impression on Nationalist Afrikanerdom. Dr Malan himself regarded it as a turning-point in his career.

With the collapse of the rebellion and the gathering momentum of pro-war propaganda, the Nationalist Party experienced many difficulties. Nationalist meetings were broken up by patriotic mobs, and several Nationalist leaders were manhandled. The party considered it politic to play down its republican aspirations. A statement by the Federal Council of the Nationalist Party said:

While the right of every individual to discuss the desirability of the republican form of government is acknowledged the Council is of the opinion that, as a result of the war, public feeling is at present running too high for a calm discussion of the matter on its merits, and for the time being it is not desirable that any steps should be taken to make active republican propaganda which would cause ill-feeling and embitter social relations and would create a wrong impression in the minds of the population or a section thereof.

The top Nationalist leaders were also careful to dissociate themselves from the rebellion, though their attitude towards it was, to say the least, equivocal. President Steyn and General Hertzog had been asked to repudiate the rebellion of General Maritz, but had refused to do so. On 27 January 1915, there was a meeting of the Die Raad van Kerke (the Assembly of Churches) in Bloemfontein, followed by a meeting of *predikante*. An appeal was made to the government to cease all executions and the Dutch Reformed Churches decided that no church punishment would be imposed on the rebels without the collection of complete evidence. On 4 August 1915, in a speech at Cradock, Dr Malan declared: 'We love freedom, but revolution is neither in our blood nor in our history nor in our religion.' He would have had some difficulty in proving the truth of any of those propositions.

At the same time, the rebellion served to consolidate all Nationalist Afrikaners round the newly-born Nationalist Party and brought it into the forefront of political activity. In July 1915, the first Nationalist daily paper, *Die Burger*, was established in Cape Town, and Dr Malan was persuaded to leave the ministry to become its first editor. Among those who had urged him to accept this post were General Christiaan de Wet and ninety-four other rebels in jail.

'In the awakening of our feeling for national unity lies our salvation,' stated the paper's first editorial.

On 4 August, 1915 6,000 women marched from Church Square to the Union Buildings in Pretoria to plead for the release of de Wet and the other rebels. They carried with them a petition signed by 63,000 women.

At the inaugural conference in Middelburg in September 1915, Dr Malan became the first Chairman of the Cape Nationalist Party. The manifesto and programme of action which were adopted declared that jingoism could no longer be tolerated, as it was creating division amongst the people. The government, the conference proclaimed, was embracing the jingo and alienating the Afrikaner, causing workers' strikes (1913 and 1914) and a rebellion, mismanaging the country's finances and education, and suppressing free speech. The conference pledged the party to work for national unity, equality of language, the development of independent universities, the segregation of the Africans in their own territories, and the transfer of African education to the Department of Native Affairs.

The tremendous strides which had been made by the Nationalist Party were registered at the Union's second general election on 21 October 1915. The Nationalists were returned as the third biggest party with twenty-seven seats (seven in the Cape, sixteen in the Orange Free State, and four in the Transvaal), to fifty-four seats for the S.A.P., thirty-nine for the Unionists, four for the Labour Party, and six Independents. For a party barely twenty months old, this was no small achievement.

The next opportunity which arose for pursuing the republican ideal was the peace conference at Versailles after the war. The Nationalists took at their face value the famous fourteen points of President Wilson and such pronouncements as that of Lloyd George, that 'no peace is possible until stolen rights and freedoms are restored and the principle of nationalities and the independent existence of small states is recognized'. An independence congress was held at Bloemfontein on 16 January 1919, and Hertzog declared: 'The aim of your coming together is the freedom of South Africa.' It was decided to send a deputation to Versailles to request complete independence for South Africa, or at least the restoration of freedom to the Transvaal and the Free State, with the Cape and Natal granted the right to self-determination.

'As a Free Stater I love the freedom of the Free State more than the subordination of the Union (to the Empire),' declared Hertzog. He said that if each of the four provinces could gain their independence, there was nothing to prevent their coming together again in freedom.

The congress declared: 'No true enduring peace and contentment is possible until not only the stolen rights are restored but also the whole Union is completely independent and separated from the British Empire, whereby alone full equality between the English and Dutch sections and a sound and friendly relationship between South Africa and the United Kingdom can be established and fostered.'

Generals de Wet and Hertzog, Dr Malan, F. W. Beyers, Senator A. D. W. Wolmarans, P. G. Grobler, A. T. Spies, and E. G. Jansen were chosen as delegates to put the Nationalist case to the British government and later to the peace conference. The South African government refused passports to General de Wet and Grobler, however, and their places were taken by N. C. Havenga and H. Reitz.

The delegation set off in high spirits, but met with a miserable reception everywhere. The crew of an English ship on which they had booked to leave refused to transport these 'traitors to the British Empire', and so on 4 March they were compelled to travel to New York by Dutch boat, thereafter transhipping to London. Attempts to see Lloyd George in Britain were unsuccessful, and at the Versailles conference itself the delegation was regarded as having little more than nuisance value. Who were these dissidents from the backveld to challenge the great prestige and authority of General Smuts, who had made his mark on the world stage during the war? Finally, managing to see Lloyd George on their return from the Continent, the delegation was given a sympathetic hearing, but firmly told that the British government was powerless to take any action except on the advice of the legally elected South African government. The homeward journey of the delegation was again by Dutch boat, via Spain, Egypt, Ceylon, Singapore, and Java to Durban.

The delegates themselves were given a hot welcome on their return home. It had at first been proposed that their followers should entertain them to dinner at an hotel, but because of a menacing mob the celebration was advanced to lunch-time. The mob, however, was not to be put off, and eventually the delegates had to be smuggled from the hotel by an unwatched sidedoor and packed off home while the crowd threw rotten eggs and sang 'God Save The King'. The high hopes of the independence congress had been drowned in the ridicule or indifference of the whole world.

Despite these wartime setbacks, however, the Nationalist Party continued to gain ground with the electorate, and there is no doubt that already it could claim to be rallying the majority of Afrikaners to its banner. At the third general election on 10

March 1920, the Nationalist Party was returned with the largest number of seats – forty-four, as against forty-one for the S.A.P., twenty-five for the Unionists, twenty-one for Labour and six independents – while the Nationalist vote had grown to 100,491, as against 89,843 for the S.A.P. Smuts, who had taken over the leadership of the S.A.P. after Botha's death, was in a dilemma, as he was unable to obtain a majority unless he contracted an alliance with one of the other parties. He at first proposed an all-party government, but Labour refused. Hertzog then proposed a Nationalist–S.A.P. coalition, but on the basis of 'South Africa first' Smuts refused. Finally in November 1920 the S.A.P. and the Unionists fused, with the new Cabinet containing three Unionists – Smartt, Patrick Duncan, and J. W. Jagger. At the fourth general election on 8 February 1921, the S.A.P., now incorporating the Unionists, swept home with seventy-nine seats. But the Nationalists had not lost ground – they won forty-five seats, one more than in the previous election – while Labour had nine and there was one Independent.

2. The First Nationalist Government

The next step in the advance of the Nationalists was to be made in association with the Labour Party. In the light of the Nationalist Party's subsequent history, of course, the two parties may seem to have been strange bedfellows, but at the time there were many points of contact between their respective policies. On the one hand the Nationalists, associating British imperialism with entrenched money interests in South Africa, tended to be vaguely anti-capitalist in their propaganda if not always in their practice. On the other hand, the Labour Party tended to match the Nationalists in its determination to maintain the colour bar as the only way of maintaining the standards of the White worker. As early as 1907 the Transvaal Afrikaner party Het Volk had had a private election arrangement with Labour against their common enemy, the imperialists. Now, in the turbulent days of the post-war depression, the paths of the two parties were to draw closer together again.

The Nationalists were not untouched by the revolutionary propaganda in circulation throughout the world as a result of the war and the Bolshevik revolution. The old order was tottering. Sympathy for the Bolsheviks (so long as they stayed in Russia) was widespread. Nationalists even found the idea of Bolshevism a handy weapon in their unceasing campaign against the British.

Addressing a Nationalist Party Congress at Pretoria in November 1919, General Hertzog 'warmly commended Bolshevism to the public'.

'I say that Bolshevism is the will of the people to be free,' he declared. 'Why do people want to oppress and kill Bolshevism? Because national freedom means death to capitalism and imperialism. Do not let us be afraid of Bolshevism. The idea in itself is excellent.'

His lieutenant, Dr Malan, was reported to have proclaimed at Vryburg on 23 January 1920: 'The aim of the Bolshevists was that Russians should manage their own affairs without interference from outside. That was the same policy that Nationalists would follow in South Africa. The Bolshevists stand for freedom, just like the Nationalist Party.'

An opportunity for the Nationalists to engage in some revolutionary activity of their own was to occur very soon, when the Rand was rocked by the 1922 strike of White miners in protest against a pay cut and an increase in the ratio of Black workers to White on the mines. The Chamber of Mines was determined to reduce production costs at the expense of the White mineworkers, about four fifths of whom were Afrikaners. In the event, the Nationalist politicians showed that they were neither willing nor able to defend the interests of the White workers, and that all their stirring demands for 'death to capitalism' and 'national freedom' were mere phrase-mongering.

The strike soon developed into an all-out struggle between the government and the mine-owners on the one hand and the workers on the other. At the end of January 1922 the Augmented Executive of the Mining Unions issued a communiqué: 'The attitude of the Prime Minister (Smuts) indicated that the government is backing the present attack by the employers on the White workers.' The statement called for the defeat of the government and invited negotiations with the Nationalist opposition.

In the early days of the strike, before martial law was declared and the shooting began, Nationalist politicians, headed by Transvaal Chairman Tielman Roos, frequently stood on the same platform as the strike leaders and mouthed the ambiguous strike slogan: 'Workers of the world unite and fight for a White South Africa.' The strikers were promised that they would be supported by the Nationalists and would be fed by the Afrikaner population of the countryside. Many of the strikers were organized in commandos on the Nationalist model.

A meeting of Nationalist and Labour Members of Parliament

called in Pretoria early in February to discuss the situation was even nicknamed 'Roos's Parliament'. No concrete decisions were taken but there is no doubt that Nationalist agitation played a considerable part in getting the strike under way. The judicial commission which investigated the subsequent disturbances attributed them, amongst other things, to the help that the strikers expected from the platteland, political incitement by certain Nationalists, and the desire of Nationalist-minded strikers to establish a republic.

A huge meeting of strikers was held in the Johannesburg Town Hall on Sunday 5 February, and at the height of the proceedings a carefully stage-managed entry was made by R. B. Waterston, a Labour M.P. and leader of the Brakpan commando. After a melodramatic speech, Waterston read a resolution demanding an end to domination by the Chamber of Mines and asking the Nationalists to proclaim a South African Republic and form a provisional government. It was carried in tumult, and Waterston hastened to Pretoria, accompanied by Shaw, Fisher, Kentridge, and others. But the Nationalist Party leaders received the deputation coldly and rejected its proposals altogether.

While the Nationalist leaders stood aside, however, the Nationalist rank and file continued to play a substantial part in the strike, organizing commandos on the Reef. As the struggle sharpened, these took on a more pronounced political character, and the commandants began to call themselves generals and to act in an independent manner. Strikers sang the 'Red Flag', the 'Marseillaise', and 'Die Volkslied', the old Transvaal republican anthem.

Smuts allowed the situation to develop and then, when all possibility of negotiation was past, struck back hard, using artillery and aeroplane bombardment against the strikers who were, for the most part, unarmed and at best in possession of a few rifles and small arms. Hundreds of strikers were killed, and when the fighting was over, hundreds more were rounded up and imprisoned on a charge of treason. Three of the strike leaders were hanged, and went to their deaths singing the 'Red Flag'.

The strike exposed the revolutionary pretensions of the Nationalist Party and revealed its leadership as representative of a reactionary land-owning class which had no interest in the cause of the workers as workers. The Nationalist leadership toyed with the strike only for as long as it appeared to hold out some prospect of advancement towards the cherished ideal of a republic. When the chances of victory for the strikers disappeared, the Nationalist politicians abandoned the workers to their fate and returned to the parliamentary arena, there to pursue their struggle 'on constitutional lines'. The Nationalist Party never at any stage aimed to overthrow the existing social order, but sought to advance itself opportunistically by any means that lay to hand. It was prepared to support any anti-Smuts movement. Its object was to obtain power, and the banner of 'freedom' which it raised was for Europeans only, preferably Afrikaners who supported its leadership.

The 1922 strike resulted in defeat for the White workers, but it was a Pyrrhic victory for Smuts and the mining magnates. Immediately after the strike a United Front was set up, supported by rank and file members of the Nationalist, Labour, and Communist Parties, with the aim of preventing further executions, procuring an amnesty for the imprisoned strikers, and defeating the Smuts government. For a time the United Front was active everywhere on the Reef, drawing its strength from the bitterness of feeling amongst the White workers and their desire to revenge themselves on the principal author of their misery, General Smuts. Hardship was widespread at the time. Already at the 1921 Congress of the Nationalist Party Malan had pointed out that the number of poor Whites had increased in the previous two years from 106,000 to 200,000. After the 1922 strike the lot of the White worker was even more precarious and, though his militancy had been sapped by the outcome of the fighting, he nevertheless remained determined to bring about a change.

The parties began to look towards the next elections, and Labour decided to withdraw from the United Front in order to clear the way for an alliance with the Nationalists. Behind the scenes the leaders began to negotiate.

Towards the end of 1922 the Federale Raad of the Nationalist Party declared that it was ready to lend its support to a joint struggle against the S.A.P. by voting either for Nationalist or for

Labour candidates 'in order to eliminate or reduce the domination of the mine magnates and their money power'. In 1923 the Nationalist–Labour pact became a reality. An exchange of correspondence between the Labour leader Colonel Creswell and General Hertzog pledged the Nationalists not to upset the existing constitutional relations between South Africa and the British Commonwealth (a tricky point for the Labour Party, based as it was almost exclusively on the English-speaking section of the working class), while retaining the right to propagandize for independence outside Parliament.

At the Cape Congress of the Nationalist Party in 1923, Dr Malan said that the Nationalist and Labour Parties were both 'squarely opposed to capitalistic and monopolistic domination and exploitation of the people. In the existing circumstances . . . cooperation between the Nationalist Party and the Labour Party is not only completely justified but is also a clear and urgent patriotic duty.'

After losing the Wakkerstroom and Oudtshoorn by-elections, Smuts decided to hold a general election in 1924. The voters performed their clear and urgent patriotic duty, and the S.A.P. suffered a resounding defeat, with Smuts losing his own constituency of Pretoria West to a Labour candidate. The Nationalist Party won sixty-three seats and the Labour Party eighteen, to fifty-three for the S.A.P. and one Independent. General Hertzog became Prime Minister and appointed two Labour members to his first Cabinet, Creswell and Boydell, increasing the number to three in 1925 when Creswell handed the Labour portfolio to Boydell and Madeley took over from the latter as Minister of Posts and Telegraphs.

In retrospect, the participation of the Labour Party in the coalition marked the beginning of the downfall of the Labour Party and the ascendancy of the Nationalists over the White (mainly Afrikaner) workers.

The advent of the Nationalist Party to power did a great deal to satisfy the Afrikaans ego. Hertzog's first act was symbolic – the release from prison of Manie Maritz and the remaining survivors of the 1914 rebellion. Afrikaans, the despised 'kitchen Dutch', was raised to official status beside English and Dutch, and the principle of bilingualism was pushed in the public service. The concept of Union citizenship was introduced, and the South African flag raised to equal status with the Union Jack. Above all, the constitution was amended to place on record the sovereignty and guidance of Providence over the Union – something which had been unaccountably overlooked by the fathers of Union in 1910.

Hertzog also took the opportunity to demand at the Imperial Prime Ministers' Conference of 1926 greater independence for the Dominions within the framework of the Empire. The result was the famous Balfour Declaration that the dominions 'are autonomous communities within the British Empire, equal in status, in no way subordinate to one another in any aspect of their domestic or external affairs, though united by a common allegiance to the Crown and freely associated as members of the British Commonwealth of Nations'. This declaration was incorporated in the 1934 Statute of Westminster, and was made a law of the Union by means of the 1934 Status of the Union Act.

Hertzog considered this achievement tantamount to the reconquest of the power which had been lost by the republics at the close of the Boer War. On his return to the Union he urged the abandonment of Clause 4 in the Nationalist Party constitution which aimed at independence, and in 1927 this was duly amended to note acceptance of the declaration of the Imperial Conference of 1926.

Dr Malan was even more enthusiastic. He declared in 1927: 'We no longer regard England today as a conqueror but as the mother of our freedom. With our whole heart we recognize the magnanimity of England, and the result will be a friendship between us and England such as never existed before. There is no longer a British Empire, only an alliance of free nations in which we want to remain owing to friendship and self-interest.'

In the light of the words which were to be bandied about in the Union a bare ten years later by these self-same Nationalist politicians, such utterances bear a peculiar significance indeed.

The most concrete achievement of the Nationalist–Labour government, however, was in the sphere of legislation to entrench and extend the colour bar. In the words of C. W. de

Kiewiet in his *History of South Africa* the Nationalist and Labour parties

were, in a manner of speaking, a White people's front against the natives. Only the passage of years revealed how thoroughly the change of government in 1924 had committed South Africa to policies conceived more resolutely than ever before in the interests of White society. It would be premature to speak henceforth of South Africa as a planned society. Yet there were manifest in government and legislation an increased unwillingness to leave the movement of society to chance, or to the unpredictable workings of economic or social laws. Better guarantees were sought for the development of a stable up-to-date White society. Means were more energetically sought to secure the political security of the White race as a whole and the economic security of its feeblest members.

The pact government, in other words, took the first tentative steps towards the creation of an authoritarian state based on that rigid race stratification which was to become such a feature of Nationalist rule after 1948. It was in 1924 that South Africa began to experience ever-increasing government intervention to ensure White supremacy and put an end to the *laissez-faire* policies of the S.A.P. and the mining magnates.

The mine-owners of 1922 had wanted to break down the colour bar within their labour force so as to increase the possibility of exploiting cheap Black labour and lessen their dependence on expensive articulate White workers. The Nationalist–Labour pact government responded by passing one law after another in the political, social, and economic spheres to halt African advancement and buttress the position of the Whites.

A Department of Labour was created whose main function was to cater for the labour needs of the Whites and protect them from any competition by the Blacks. A civilized labour policy was adopted whereby non-White unskilled workers on the railways and in other fields of State employment were replaced by poor Whites at 'civilized' rates of pay. The Mines and Works Act of 1926 restored the statutory colour bar on the mines, whereby certain categories of skilled and semi-skilled work were reserved for Whites alone. (The effect of previous legislation had been nullified by decisions of the Supreme Court.) In 1927 a law was passed prohibiting 'immorality' between Europeans and Africans.

In the sphere of the franchise an attack was launched against the non-Whites on two fronts. The relative strength of the non-White vote, limited already for all practical purposes to the Cape by the compromise agreement in the Act of Union, was further eroded by the enfranchisement of European women in 1930. Non-White women remained voteless, so that the strength of the European electorate was practically doubled. In 1931 the Whites of the Cape and Natal were granted adult suffrage, but for the non-Whites educational and property qualifications were retained. Thus the European electorate was expanded to its maximum, while the non-White electorate was pegged.

The second front of attack was represented by Hertzog's four Bills, introduced in 1926 but not finally passed until ten years later, and then in greatly modified form.

They set out:

(1) To abolish the common roll vote in the Cape which the Africans had enjoyed since representative government had been introduced there in 1853, and to substitute seven M.P.s and four Senators (Whites) elected on a communal roll. (2) To establish an African Representative Council. (3) To peg African land ownership. (4) To confirm the Coloured vote in the Cape and extend the same rights to Coloured men in the other provinces.

Bill No. 4 may cause some surprise, but it should be borne in mind that at this stage the Nationalists had to cater for a sizeable Coloured vote in the Cape, and in any event still hoped to use the Coloured people as allies in the fight against the Africans.

Whilst Hertzog preached segregation for the Africans, he showed himself differently disposed towards the Coloured, who 'had his origin and existence in our midst. He knows no other civilization than that of the White man. However often he may fall short of it, his outlook is essentially that of the Whites and not that of the natives, and his mother tongue is that of the White man. In his case there can be no talk of segregation.' (Quoted in van den Heever.)

Dr Malan was quite as forthright. Addressing the Malay Congress in 1925, as Minister of the Interior, he said: 'The

Nationalist Party is seeing to it that there shall be no colour bar for Coloured people and for the Malays. The government will always try to give the Malays a higher status than they possess, and that is – equal rights with the White man.'

When the Women's Enfranchisement Bill was before the Assembly, he pleaded for the inclusion of Coloured women in the voters' rolls, and in the joint session of Parliament he pressed for the extension of the franchise to the Coloured people in the northern provinces.

Yet Bill No. 4 was eventually dropped altogether. When the other Bills were finally passed in 1936, the number of M.P.s to be elected on a communal roll had been reduced to three (from the seven originally proposed) and the amount of land for African occupation pegged permanently at thirteen per cent of the total (for seventy per cent of the population; and even that thirteen per cent has not yet been fully bought by the Native Trust).

Hertzog's colour bar Bills caused widespread and vigorous agitation when they were first introduced, not least among the African people themselves. The meteoric rise of the Industrial and Commercial Workers' Union, which at one stage claimed 100,000 members, and the agitation of the Communist Party and other organizations, led the government to take further steps on that road of repression to which the world has grown so accustomed in Nationalist legislation since 1948. The Native Administration Act of 1927, re-enacting provisions of the old-type colonial legislation which stemmed from Natal (e.g. the Code of Native Law), and the 1930 amendment to the Riotous Assemblies Act of 1914, directing against 'agitators' for African rights the provisions of a law which had first been aimed at the White workers, both conferred enormous administrative powers on the government to interfere with the freedom of the individual and severely limit freedom of speech and assembly. Right from the outset the exercise of Nationalist power was marked by that combination of legislative and administrative restriction which so disfigures South African government policies today.

It is to the lasting disgrace of the Labour Party that, while preaching the brotherhood of man, it restricted that brotherhood to men with white skins only. Yet, as it turned out, it was on the reefs of colour that the Nationalist–Labour alliance eventually split. Cabinet Minister Madeley was expelled from the Cabinet for having received a deputation from the I.C.U. against the express instructions of General Hertzog himself. Creswell stood with Hertzog on this issue, but the majority of the Labour Party National Council backed Madeley, who also had the support of six M.P.s. The dispute cost the party dear. In the 1929 elections Labour lost ten seats, with the Creswellites gaining five and the Madeleyites three, to seventy-eight for the Nationalist Party, sixty-one for the S.A.P., and one Independent. For the first time the Nationalist Party could have ruled alone, since it enjoyed a majority over all the other parties combined. But Hertzog chose to maintain his alliance with the Labour right wing, and Creswell and Sampson were given seats in the Cabinet.

The Nationalist Party's 'Black menace' propaganda was proving popular with the electorate. But the mining magnates were shortly to make a come-back. In September 1931 Britain went off the gold standard. South Africa, whose economy was tied to that of Britain, would normally have followed suit, but General Hertzog chose to regard such action as derogating from the newly-won independence of the South African State, and the country stayed on gold. Farmers could not find an outlet for their products, and the numbers of the unemployed swelled spectacularly. Widespread political agitation arose to compel the government to abandon the gold standard. Tielman Roos, former Chairman of the Transvaal Nationalist Party, who had been desiccating quietly on the Appeal Court bench, announced on 22 December 1932, his return to politics and at the head of a new group joined the agitation against the gold standard. He called for a national government, and the combination of economic and political pressures assumed alarming proportions. £3 million left the country within three days. Panic reigned. Five days later on 27 December it was announced that the country had abandoned the gold standard.

The way was now prepared for a political realignment. Roos, a master of intrigue, had made considerable inroads into the ranks of the Nationalist Party, so that Hertzog was later frankly to admit that the party had become 'rotten'. In the eyes of the electorate the time had come for a change, and Hertzog was convinced that he would lose the next election. To stave off the threat from Roos, he entered into negotiations with Smuts. On 23 February 1933, the two leaders announced that they had reached agreement on a coalition, and by the month's end a new coalition Cabinet had been set up with Hertzog as Premier and Smuts as Deputy. In the face of Smuts's adamant refusal to countenance it, the alliance with Labour was quietly dropped.

The 1933 elections gave seventy-five seats to the Nationalist Party, sixty-one to the S.A.P., four to Labour, two to the Roos Party, two to the Home Rule group, and six seats to Independents. An uneasy peace supervened.

For a time the parties retained their separate identities in the coalition. But the internal logic of coalition, which was to create a strong united front among the Whites to deal with the economic problems of the depression and to settle once and for all the question of the 'Native Bills' (pending since 1926 because the government did not have the two-thirds majority required by the constitution) eventually drove them towards fusion. On 5 December 1934, the followers of Smuts and Hertzog met in Bloemfontein and formed the United South African National Party, better known simply as the United Party. For the Nationalist die-hards and their counterparts among the English-speaking section, this was to be the parting of the ways.

Coalition was one thing, fusion another. Coalition was a tactical necessity forced upon the Nationalist Party by the crisis through which the country was passing. But fusion was the destruction of the Nationalist Party itself, the end of the dream which the Afrikaner people had cherished ever since the Boer War – the restoration of independence and the supremacy of the volk. Fusion was in fact a complete negation of the 'two-stream' policy with which Hertzog had started his political career after Union, the very issue on which he had broken with Botha. Yet now Hertzog himself, the man who stood for the aspirations of Afrikanerdom in the eyes of his people, was entering into political union with Smuts and the English-speaking section in a bid to create one White nation.

In a speech at Paarl in 1934 condemning fusion, Dr Malan declared: 'Instead of bringing together those who belong together, we see everywhere that Afrikanerdom is dissolving and dissolution means death.' The hard core of the Nationalist Party, headed by Malan, refused to follow Hertzog into fusion and nineteen Members of Parliament remained on the opposition benches, after almost half the Cape Nationalists and three-quarters of the Free State Nationalists had followed Hertzog into the United Party. In the Transvaal J. G. Strijdom was the only Nationalist M.P. left in opposition. In the Free State there were four, led by C. R. Swart (now the State President). These were the leanest days of 'purified' Nationalism since the Party itself had been formed in 1914.

On the other side of the political spectrum, the jingo element within the English-speaking section found fusion equally unacceptable and in 1934 formed the Dominion Party, which stood for the maintenance of the closest bonds of Empire and the Thin Red Line.

Fusion, however, won the overwhelming endorsement of the electorate at the next election in 1938, and the United Party won 111 seats, to twenty-seven for the Nationalist Party, eight for the Dominion Party, three for Labour, and one Socialist.

The enormous majority of the United Party, however, was to prove illusory. Fusion brought no unity, either ideological or racial. When war eventually came, the party split into its component parts.

Hertzog's decision to join forces with Smuts was undoubtedly a betrayal of Nationalist policy and the surrender of principle to personal vanity by an opportunist. The ostensible reasons he gave for his action were fallacious: what weighed most with him was the desire to remain Prime Minister. There was a similar element of opportunism in Malan's decision to break with Hertzog. In the 1933 election the Malanites had been content to stand as coalition candidates. Did Malan break away because Hertzog dropped him from his Cabinet? Or did he refuse office? One may be excused for feeling that expediency played as important a role as principle in the decisions of the Nationalist leaders at this crucial stage in their history.

Hertzog taunted Malan with the prospect of an endless wandering in the wilderness, a permanently ineffectual opposition. But Malan turned back to the Afrikaner people for support. He felt that he was building on a surer foundation than Hertzog. Blood was thicker than water, and in time the appeal of naked racialism would show results. The Afrikaner people constituted the majority of the electorate, and if their national sentiment could be aroused, they would prove to be politically indestructible. Time was to prove him right, despite many disappointments. The tenacity with which the 'purified' Nationalists fought for their point of view from this moment of their lowest ebb until they were swept to power in 1948 constitutes one of the most remarkable features of recent South African political history.

3. The Broederbond

The character of the Nationalist Party underwent a considerable change during the years of wandering in the wilderness. It became more bitter, more exclusive, more aggressive – and it gained steadily in strength all the time. It began to appreciate that politics could not be confined to the parliamentary arena, and devoted more and more attention to extra-parliamentary activities, not only in the political, but also in the social and economic spheres. Attention was paid to the all-round development of the Afrikaner people, to Church affairs and social welfare work among the growing army of poor Whites, to education and sport, to culture, trade and industry. The Nationalist forces were intensely active on all fronts. The work of a small number of well-organized and dedicated cadres brought about a complete transformation in the national scene.

Guiding force in the rebirth of this nationalist spirit was the Afrikaner Broederbond (Association of Brothers), a secret society which has gradually come to assume a dominant position in the affairs of the *volk*. The Broederbond was formed in 1918 and maintained an open existence until 1924, when it went underground and its affairs became largely a matter for conjecture. An *élite* organization, its membership was stated in 1944 to be 2,672, of whom 8·6 per cent were public servants and 33·3 per cent teachers. In 1952 the Rev. V. de Vos, who had broken away from the Nederduitse Gereformeerde Kerk in 1944 and formed a Reconstituted Dutch Reformed Church because the N. G. Kerk, he alleged, was dominated by members of the Broederbond, gave the following breakdown of Broederbond membership – 357 clergymen, 2,039 teachers, 905 farmers, 159 lawyers, and 60 M.P.s Today the membership of the Broederbond is estimated to be in the region of 7,000. Its general mode of operation has been to coordinate activities among Afrikaners and to ensure that Broeders are placed in key positions which can then be utilized for the advancement of the volk.

In an article that appeared in the Johannesburg *Star* on 12 October 1948, a former Secretary of the Broederbond, L. J. du Plessis, described its early days of existence up to the time it went underground. He then wrote:

What happened since, I can only surmise when hearing of prominent members like Bosman becoming Manager of Volkskas[1] and Prof. L. J. du Plessis, Chairman; Erasmus, Secretary of the Transvaalse Onderwysers Vereniging;[2] Diederichs, Chief Organizer of the Reddingsdaadbond[3]; Albert Hertzog, 'protector' of the mine-workers; Rev. W. Nicol, Moderator of the Dutch Reformed Church for three consecutive synods: Klopper, head of the Afrikaanse Taal en Kultuur Vereniging[4]; and last but not least Dr Verwoerd, Editor-in-Chief of *Die Transvaler*.

In a circular issued by the Broederbond of 16 January 1934, the Chairman, Prof. J. C. van Rooy of Potchefstroom University, and the General Secretary, I. M. Lombard wrote: 'Let us focus attention on the fact that the primary consideration is: whether Afrikanerdom will reach its ultimate destiny of domination (*baasskap*) in South Africa. Brothers, our solution of South Africa's ailments is not whether one party or another shall obtain the whip hand, but that the Afrikaner-Broederbond shall govern South Africa.'

Neither of the two leading Afrikaners of their day, General Hertzog or General Smuts, were considered eligible for membership of the Broederbond, for their policy of cooperation with the English-speaking section of the population was felt to be inimical to the interests of the Afrikaner nation. But Hertzog was well aware of the machinations of the Broederbond behind the scenes, and in a trenchant attack on the organization in a speech

1 A large and powerful bank.

2 Transvaal Teachers' Association.

3 lit. Rescue-work Society, an association originally dedicated to rescuing Afrikaners from poor Whiteism and subsequently devoted to building Afrikaner capitalism and attacking the trade unions.

4 Association for the Afrikaans Language and Culture.

at Smithfield – reported in *The Star* of 7 November 1935 – he stigmatized the Broederbond as 'a grave menace to the rest and peace of our social community, even where it operates in the economic-cultural sphere'. Its members 'are sworn not to entertain any cooperation with the English-speaking population and thereby they stand in direct racial conflict with our fellow English Afrikaners, and are striving by way of domination on the part of the Afrikaans-speaking section to put their foot on the neck of English-speaking South Africa'.

Hertzog attacked Dr Malan for pursuing 'a course of national division and strife' through his opposition to fusion, and he claimed that this was due to Malan's having joined the Broederbond in 1934. In particular, he said, the Broederbond had acquired a dangerous hold over education in the Orange Free State. 'I know of few towns and villages in the Free State where the Broederbond has not established for itself a nest of five, six, or more Broeders to serve as a focal point for Bond propaganda, and I also know that there is hardly a single nest in which there isn't at least one teacher sitting as a hatcher.'

In a speech at Victoria West one week later, Dr Malan replied to this attack. The essence of the Broederbond was, he admitted, that it should consist of Afrikaans-speaking Afrikaners alone, but he claimed that there were at that time as many U.P. Members of Parliament in it as Nationalists. 'The Broederbond is nothing more than a non-political Afrikaans society which, where it is necessary, will take action for Afrikaans interests and will positively help up the Afrikaner, just as there are many other societies, each in its own sphere.'

He referred to Hertzog as a broken-down politician and renegade who was trying to whip up the race feeling of the English by making them afraid of Nationalist Afrikanerdom.

In 1944 General Smuts banned membership of the Broederbond to public servants, calling it 'a dangerous, cunning, political Fascist organization'.

Subsequent to Smuts's attack, I. M. Lombard wrote a series of articles for *Die Transvaler* (on 14, 20, and 30 December 1944, and 3 January 1945) in which he laid down the seven-fold ideal for which the Broederbond was striving: (1) the removal of everything in conflict with South Africa's full international independence; (2) the ending of the inferiority of the Afrikaans-speaking and of their language in the organization of the State; (3) separation of all non-White races in South Africa, leaving them free to independent development under the guardianship of the Whites; (4) putting a stop to the exploitation of the resources and population of South Africa by strangers, including the more intensive industrial development; (5) the rehabilitation of the farming community and the assurance of civilized self-support through work for all White citizens; (6) the nationalization of the money market and the systematic coordination of economic policies; (7) the Afrikanerization of public life and teaching and education in a Christian-National spirit, while leaving free the internal development of all sections in so far as it is not dangerous to the State.

'The Afrikaner Broederbond,' declared Lombard, 'is born from a deep conviction that the Afrikaner nation has been planted in this country by God's hand and is destined to remain here as a nation with its own character and its own mission.'

As will be seen later, these aims of the Broederbond bear a striking resemblance to the notorious draft constitution for a future South African Republic which was drawn up by Nationalist-orientated organizations during the war and the basic principles of which have underlain the policy and actions of the Nationalist Party ever since it came to power in 1948.

Controversy over the Broederbond continued to rage, and in 1949 the Dutch Reformed Church Council decided to conduct an investigation. The committee that was entrusted with the task came to the conclusion that the Broederbond was a healthy organization run on non-party political lines to further the interests of the Afrikaner nation. Among the subjects which had been discussed were immigration, usury, mother-tongue instruction, libraries – and the native question, which, it is the fond delusion of many South African parliamentarians, is a subject outside the confines of 'party politics'. Membership of the organization was open to Afrikaans-speaking Protestants of good character who regarded South Africa as their only fatherland. The names of members and the proceedings of the organization were secret, but anyone could reveal his membership if he pleased.

The report of the committee hardly satisfied the critics of the organization, for the Broederbond was supposed to be firmly in control of the Afrikaans churches, and would naturally have ensured a favourable verdict. The Minister of Lands in the Smuts government in 1946, Senator Conroy, spoke in Parliament of the 'hundreds of ministers of religion in the Dutch Reformed Church who had dragged politics into the Church' and claimed that ninety per cent of the Afrikaans churches had been brought under the influence of the Broederbond.

It is known that at least sixty members of the Broederbond stood as Nationalist Party candidates in the 1948 elections, amongst them Dr Malan himself, Dr Diederichs (now Minister of Economic Affairs), Dr Dönges (now Minister of Finance), Albert Hertzog, son of General Hertzog (now Minister of Posts and Telegraphs), Dr Jansen (later Governor-General), Prof. A. I. Malan, H. J. Klopper, and W. C. du Plessis. The last-named had been a senior official in the South African diplomatic service who was dismissed because he refused to resign from the Broederbond in terms of the order from General Smuts. He got his revenge in 1948, when he defeated General Smuts at Standerton in the general election which brought the Nationalists to power.

After becoming Prime Minister Dr Malan was pressed by the United Party opposition to investigate the affairs of the Broederbond, which was alleged to be ruling the nation from behind the scenes.

According to a report in the *Cape Times* on 7 September 1949, he said:

I belong to the Broederbond, and I have attended many of its meetings. All I can say to you is that all the matters which are discussed there are in the interests of the people. No enmity towards the other section of the community has been apparent at any of these meetings I attended. No pressure is brought to bear on the government of the country from the Broederbond. I have always been able to discuss these matters of importance to all aspects of the life of the people and I have come away from these meetings feeling a better man than before.

He offered to conduct an inquiry into the Broederbond, provided that a similar inquiry was also conducted into the affairs of the Sons of England.

Considering the number of Cabinet Ministers who are Broeders, Malan's testimony is unimpressive. And in recent times members of the Nationalist Party itself have joined the critics of the Broederbond. After a political row culminating in a court case that rocked the Free State town of Dewetsdorp in 1962, four people described as 'prominent Nationalists' told the *Sunday Times*:

We are good, sincere, life-long, and convinced democratic National- ists. As Nationalists of that order – the real substance of the party – we have come to share the view held by increasing thousands of our party members that the Broederbond secret society has become a menace to all that is most dear to the patriotic Nationalists and to the South African who loves his country.

In our view it has ceased to be Nationalist. It adopts the outrageous, insufferable attitude that it and its secret congregation are the cream of the Nationalist Party and we are the skimmed milk.

It skims the cream of benefit and privilege in our country while we, the true democratic and patriotic Nationalists, are in its cynical view merely here to ensure at election times that it is returned to power.

Here in this town and district the small coterie of Broederbonders, with their secret meetings, attempt to run our destinies. We, as the real Nationalists of South Africa, reject and refute them. (*Sunday Times*, 16 September 1962.)

There is little doubt that the Broederbond has been and still is one of the main driving forces behind the Nationalist Party. Most leading Nationalists are Broeders. So are the editors of most Nationalist newspapers, and the officials of the Afrikaans cul- tural societies, charitable associations, teachers' organizations, and financial institutions. Under the influence of the Broeder- bond, Afrikaners were encouraged to withdraw everywhere from organizations in which they mixed with the English- speaking section and to establish their own organizations run on their own lines instead.

True, the segregation of the Afrikaners in separate cultural organizations has a long background and, with the Kerk as its fulcrum, has been a prominent feature of Afrikaner national development ever since the nineteenth century. The S.A. Akademie voor Taal, Lettere en Kuns, was formed in 1909, the Afrikaanse Christelike Vrouevereniging in 1902, the first of the Afrikaner economic organizations (*Die Burger*, SASbank, K.W.V., the winegrowers' cooperative, and the burial society A.V.B.O.B., etc.) in the period 1915 to 1921. But the Broederbond gave this whole process of separatism a new impetus and perspective. The Broederbond was directly responsible for the establishment in 1929 of the Federasie van Afrikaanse Kultuur Vereenigings (whose committee members in 1946 included Prof. J. C. van Rooy as chairman and I. M. Lombard, both leading Broederbonders); the Reddingsdaadbond in 1939 (leading figure Dr Diederichs); the reform groups in the trade unions (leading figure, Dr Albert Hertzog); and the Ossewa Brandwag (led by Dr J. F. J. van Rensburg). In 1924 when the National Union of South African Students was formed it represented all students in all universities. It was partly the work of the Broederbond that it split in 1932, and the main body of Afrikaans students set up the rival Afrikaanse Nasionale Studentebond. Today parallel Afrikaans and English organizations exist in almost every sphere of life. The Voortrekkers are separate from the Scout movement, the Noodhulpliga from the St John's Ambulance, SABRA from the Institute of Race Relations. In the schools the Nationalist stands for mother-tongue instruction and separate schools for English and Afrikaans-speaking children wherever possible. There are separate Afrikaans universities and teachers' organizations. The Chambers of Commerce and Industry are paralleled by the Afrikaner Handelsinstituut. Even in sport the Afrikaner has his *volkspele* and *jukskei* from which the English-speaking are excluded, if not by regulation, at least by sentiment and tradition.

The Broederbond has thus sponsored a sort of spiritual Great Trek of the Afrikaners in the twentieth century, by which they have removed themselves from ' dangerous ' contact with other elements of the population and withdrawn into cultural isolation. Once behind the wall, they have become easy victims of the Nationalist virus.

4. The Followers of Hitler

> In standing guard against the Jew, I am defending the handiwork of the Lord.
>
> ADOLF HITLER in *Mein Kampf*

During the thirties many Nationalist Party leaders and wide sections of the Afrikaner people came strongly under the influence of the Nazi movement which dominated Germany from 1933. There were many reasons for this. Germany was the traditional enemy of Britain, and whoever opposed Britain appeared a friend of the Nationalists. Many Nationalists, moreover, believed that the opportunity to re-establish their lost republic would come with the defeat of the British Empire in the international arena. The more belligerent Hitler became, the further hopes rose that the day of Afrikanerdom was about to dawn.

This opportunistic attitude towards Germany paved the way for the gradual acceptance of many of the basic principles of Nazism itself. Hitler's successes in Germany evoked widespread Nationalist admiration. Partly under the direction of the Germans themselves, imitation Nazi organizations were founded in South Africa – the Greyshirts, the Boerenasie, and later the New Order – while anti-Semitism began to rear its head as well. Currents stirring the people soon enough washed the higher ranks of the Nationalist Party and even spread to the United Party itself.

There had been a strong infusion of German blood into the Afrikaner people from the earliest days of settlement, and many Afrikaners fancied a natural affinity between themselves and the German people. J. F. J. van Rensburg, later Kommandant-Generaal of the Ossewa Brandwag, notes in his autobiography: 'I started learning German: carefully, assiduously, gratefully . . . their language was the language of a kindred people, reeling in titanic battle for survival against most of the nations of the world.'

Another passionate Germanophile, himself of German origin, was Oswald Pirow, Hertzog's Minister of Justice and later Minister of Defence. Pirow made several trips to Europe, the most publicized being just after Munich, when he made a special point of paying his respects to Hitler, Goering, Mussolini, and Franco.

Pirow's daughter Else caused some consternation on her arrival in England on 6 June 1939, when she was interviewed by the *Daily Express*: '. . . my father was a boy in Germany, my grandparents on both sides are German. I have heaps of relatives there. At home we speak German . . . though I have never been there I feel Germany is "home".' Miss Pirow was on her way to train in a German women's camp. 'I am going to try my best to be a good German – for a year at least,' she said.

With war about to burst upon the world, such remarks hardly reassured those in England who looked to South Africa's support in any struggle against Germany.

But most prominent victim of the Nazi philosophy was General Hertzog himself. While still Secretary for Justice under the Hertzog régime, van Rensburg was offered the post of Administrator of the Orange Free State, but he was reluctant to accept because he believed that he was being edged out of his current job at the instance of General Smuts.

Van Rensburg told Hertzog, by way of excuse for turning down the offer: 'If I have to make a self-diagnosis, I could only call myself a race-conscious Afrikaner, with tendencies which many people today would regard as "fascistic".'

Hertzog smiled and replied: 'Well, well, possibly we have far more in common than most people would believe.'

Van Rensburg took the job.

Germany at this time was issuing a stream of strident propaganda for the return of her colonies, taken from her by the Treaty of Versailles, and Hertzog himself was one of Hitler's firmest supporters in the campaign. In 1935 he was reported to be trying to create a favourable atmosphere for the grant of colonial possessions to the Reich. Naturally reluctant to cede South-West Africa, he believed that Germany would be satisfied with a reasonable substitute, and he proposed Liberia as the most suitable sacrifice. Neither Liberia nor the United States thought much of the suggestion.

Another prominent Nationalist who gave his support to the German campaign for the restoration of their colonies was J. G. Strijdom, who told the Transvaal Congress of the Nationalist Party in 1937, that he would not move a finger to prevent the Germans from recovering South-West Africa.

Well-disposed though he was, Hertzog was eventually to be driven by the sheer extent of Nazi activities amongst the Germans in South-West Africa to take action against them. Provocative processions were being organized in the territory, and the Union flag had been hauled down from government buildings and replaced by the German flag. The Union Government appointed a commission of inquiry in 1936 which reported the existence of Nazi cells, Labour Front groups, Hitler Youth cadres and Winter Help centres, not only in South-West Africa but also in the Union. Acting on this report, the government declared the Nazi organization illegal.

Hertzog's sympathy for the Nazis did not, however, wane with time. According to his biographer, van den Heever, he became 'bitterly disappointed in the democratic system, with its capitalist foundations and Press influence, for he had cause to know that the voice of the majority is not always the voice of wisdom. . . . He was convinced that a new world order was on the way.' After his retirement or rather ejection from politics, he became more and more 'inclined towards National-Socialism, by which he meant the adaptation of the old Free State model republic to modern conditions, using the best from recent European experiments. . . . He regarded National-Socialism as suited to the moral and religious outlook of the Afrikaner; indeed, he considered that the constitution of the old Free State Republic was based on it.'

Hertzog's equation of National-Socialism with Christian-Nationalism did not go unnoticed by his admirers, least of all by those in the ranks of the Nationalist Party. The fact was that the Nazi doctrines of race and blood found a ready acceptance amongst wide sections of the White Supremacists in South Africa. No Nationalist, it is true, needed Hitler's urging to formulate a creed of White superiority over Black. But there is no doubt that the activity of the Nazis in Europe encouraged the appearance of the grosser forms of racialism amongst White South Africans, English as well as Afrikaans-speaking. During the thirties and forties the Nationalist Party itself was to adopt anti-Semitism as an official plank in its platform, and some of the most prominent Nationalist leaders have not managed to free themselves from anti-Semitism to this very day.

It had not always been like that. Jews had belonged to and played a prominent part in the Nationalist Party during the twenties, some of them holding official positions. Nationalist leaders had been cordial in their references to their Jewish fellow-citizens. In 1929 General Hertzog declared:

In their life in South Africa, these two sections of Afrikanerdom (the Jewish and the Afrikaans communities) have always been closely associated, no matter how much individuals might sometimes have left them in the lurch. Both are deeply imbued with the spirit of South African nationalism. . . . If ever there was a section that has been looked upon by the Afrikaners as fellow-Afrikaners, it is the Jewish section. . . . Where it concerned nationalism, love of people, hatred of oppression, the Jew and the Afrikaner always stood together.

Dr Malan himself proclaimed in 1930:

I think the people of South Africa, generally, belonging to all parties and sections, desire to give to the Jewish people in this country full equality in every respect, every opportunity which every other section enjoys, full participation in our national life, and I am glad to say that we are still in that position today in South Africa to appreciate, and appreciate very highly what the Jews have done for South Africa.

Yet Dr Malan's professed esteem for the Jews did not extend to the point where he wished to add to their number in South Africa. It was Dr Malan who, as Minister of the Interior, introduced the Immigration Quota Act which came into force on 1 May 1930. This placed a strict quota on immigrants of any race or creed born in countries other than those specified in the Act, and the specified did not include the countries of southern and eastern Europe from which most Jewish immigrants came. It was officially denied that the law was directed against Jewish immigrants, but a sharp drop in Jewish immigration resulted and Dr Malan years later admitted that this had in fact been its object.

Introducing the Quota Bill in Parliament, Dr Malan said that it was based on three principles: (1) the desire of every nation to maintain its basic racial composition; (2) the doctrine of assimilability; and (3) South Africa's desire to maintain its own type of civilization. The civilization of eastern and southern Europe was, to a large extent, different from that of Western Europe to which South Africa claimed to belong. He maintained that the new law, although not directed against the Jews, was in the interests of the South African Jewish community, because the steady flow of Jewish immigrants had created 'a nervousness among all sections of the population'.

The beginning of Nazi persecution led to an influx of Jewish refugees from Germany, which was not one of the restricted countries. In 1933, 624 immigrants came from Germany, of whom 204 were Jews. In 1934, the corresponding figures were 1,026 (452); in 1935, 996 (410); in 1936, 3,648 (2,549). Agitation by organizations like the Greyshirts reached unprecedented heights.

At first the Nationalist Party reacted unfavourably to the protests. *Die Burger* on 27 October 1933, said:

We are definitely of the opinion that such a racial struggle is absolutely undesirable and that all national leaders and all newspapers with a sense of responsibility must issue a serious warning against it. . . . There is not one single misdeed of which a Jew has been guilty that is not also to be found in wider circles. You cannot attribute any misdeed to the Jews as a group. . . . In our view a racial struggle of this sort would be harmful to the country and unjust to its Jewish citizens.

Even a year later, in October 1934, *Die Burger* could declare in an editorial: 'We believe that this party, generally known as the Greyshirts, under the cloak of an anti-Jewish movement, strives for a dangerous form of government in South Africa. The Greyshirts have as their aim to set up a dictator in South Africa.'

It was not very long, however, before the Nationalist Party itself succumbed to the virus and took the lead in anti-Jewish agitation. The government began to waver, and it was announced that new restrictions under the immigration laws would be introduced on 1 November 1936. To beat the ban, a boat was chartered, the S.S. *Stuttgart*, to bring 600 Jewish refugees from Germany to South Africa. The ship became the object of disgusting and degrading propaganda amongst the Nationalists and their allies in the various 'shirt' organizations.

The *Stuttgart* eventually arrived in Cape Town on 27 October, beating the ban by a few days. The night before it docked, the Greyshirts held a protest rally in Cape Town, reported to be the largest meeting they had ever held there, and afterwards the more militant amongst them braved the rain to stage a demonstration in the area of the docks. A similar Greyshirt meeting in Paarl was attended by 1,000 people.

Not to be outdone, the Paarl branch of the Nationalist Party held a protest meeting against Jewish immigration on the night of 4 November, a few days after the *Stuttgart* had arrived. It was addressed by, amongst others, Dr T. E. Dönges, now Minister of Finance, who said: 'The Jew is an insoluble element in every national life.' Dr H. F. Verwoerd, then a professor at Stellenbosch University, now Prime Minister, declared that the protest movement had been conceived at Stellenbosch long before the *Stuttgart* had even been chartered. In traditional style, he attacked the English Press for misrepresenting the situation and maintained that such immigration menaced the English-speaking South Africans far more than the Afrikaans-speaking. The meeting passed a resolution calling for an end to Jewish immigration on the grounds that the Jews were an unassimilable element.

During the same period Dr Verwoerd and five fellow professors from Stellenbosch went in deputation to the Smuts–Hertzog government to protest against the immigration of Jews from Nazi Germany. One year later Dr Verwoerd, then Editor of *Die Transvaler*, published a long article in his paper captioned: 'The Jewish problem regarded from the Nationalist point of view. A possible solution. Proportional distribution in trades and businesses the first great necessity.' Dr Verwoerd proposed a quota system for Jews in all occupations and pressed that Jews should be refused further trading licences until every section of the population had its proper share. (*Die Transvaler*, 1 October 1937.)

In response to all this agitation, the Hertzog government in 1937 introduced a new law known as the Aliens Act, in terms of which every alien immigrant would have to be screened by an Immigrants Selection Board. The Aliens Act specified 'assimilability' as one of the qualifications, but did not define it.

The Nationalists regarded this Bill as totally ineffective and moved an amendment in Parliament pleading for: (1) the prohibition of Jewish immigration; (2) the deletion of Yiddish as a recognized European language for immigration purposes; (3) no further naturalization of Jewish immigrants; (4) the closing of certain professions to Jews and other non-assimilable races; (5) a ban on the changing of names, retrospective to 1 May 1930; (9) electoral divisions to be delimitated on the basis of Union nationals (so excluding Jews not yet naturalized).

The Nationalists wanted 'alien' to be defined as 'a person not born a British subject or a Union national, and further includes all members of the Jewish faith living outside the Union' (i.e. whether British subjects or not).

In the course of moving his amendment, Dr Malan frankly admitted that he was discriminating against the Jews and said that this was because South Africa already had a Jewish problem. Anti-Semitism was growing stronger. Jews were getting the best jobs in business, and 'the Afrikaner is suffering in consequence'. It was undesirable that the Jews should hold the balance of political power in the country. 'Now the question arises with us, as a people, not only how we are going to keep them out in future, but how we are going to protect ourselves against those who are here.'

The good doctor claimed that when Jews amounted to more than four per cent of the population, there was trouble, and anti-Semitism arose. He claimed that the Jews in South Africa totalled six to seven per cent. (Dr Dönges at Paarl had also put the figure at seven per cent, though at a meeting in Parow a month later he said five per cent, a figure also mentioned by Eric Louw two years afterwards. The truth, according to figures quoted by Saron and Hotz in their book *The Jews in South*

Africa, is that Jews have never amounted to more than four and a half per cent of the White population of South Africa, a figure only reached as a result of the unusual immigration in 1936.)

Malan's amendment was defeated, but the Nationalist propaganda was not without its effect. The United Party government was put on the defensive and attempted to stem the flow of Jewish immigrants. In many instances entry permits which had been granted to the relatives of Jews already in South Africa were cancelled. Many German Jews who might therefore have found safety in South Africa were to perish in Hitler's death camps as a direct consequence of the agitation by the Nationalist Party and the cowardice of the Hertzog government. Yet Malan in his speech could claim 'I have no anti-Jewish animus' and speak hypocritically of 'my Jewish friends. . . .'

Despite the restrictions imposed by the Hertzog government, the Nationalists were not satisfied and returned to the attack in February 1939, when Eric Louw, South Africa's present Foreign Minister, introduced his Aliens (Amendment) and Immigration Bill as a private measure. Moving the second reading, he declared:

I am convinced that if it were possible to remove Jewish influence and Jewish pressure from the Press, and from the news agencies, the international outlook would be considerably brighter than it is to-day . . .

I, and those who feel with me, are worried about the extent to which a race, alien and unassimilable with the English- and Dutch-speaking population in South Africa, has during past years been securing control of business and industry and also of the professions. . . . I have gone through the telephone list very carefully in Johannesburg and Cape Town and have only taken those names which I am quite sure are Jewish. What do I find? That in Johannesburg sixty-five per cent of the attorney firms are Jewish, of the advocates forty-five per cent are Jewish. . . . I have here the results of the law certificate examinations in January this year. Forty-four per cent of the successful candidates in the law certificate examination were Jews.

While claiming that Jews were dominating the world of business, and hinting at the secrecy and dishonesty of their business deals, Louw at the same time alleged that most of the leaders of the Russian Bolsheviks were Jews and said: 'Communism has since its earliest days been linked with Jewry.'

Then came an exceedingly ugly threat. If the Jewish problem were not faced, he said, 'we will have in South Africa a repetition of the history that has taken place in the countries of Europe.'

His Bill specified that 'no applicant who is of Jewish parentage shall be deemed to be readily assimilable', with someone of Jewish parentage defined as 'that person whose father and mother are or were either wholly or partly Jews, whether or not they professed the Jewish religion'.

The Bill provided for the deportation of undesirable immigrants as well as for the control of businesses which might be carried on by aliens or in which aliens might be employed. It stipulated that Yiddish should not be regarded as a European language for the purposes of immigration.

'The attitude of the Nationalist Party is that the Jewish population of South Africa is already too large. It has exceeded the danger-point percentage. . . . We say that Jewish immigration must be stopped completely.'

The United Party government refused to accept Louw's Bill, and the Minister of the Interior, Stuttaford, remarked: 'When I read the Bill, I appreciated that it is racial in the extreme and reactionary, and it had the musty smell of the times of the Middle Ages. . . . The main object of the Bill, and the honourable member has not concealed it, is persecution of the Jews.'

J. H. Hofmeyr was even more forthright in his denunciation. 'The principles which lie at the foundation of this Bill,' he said, are 'unworthy and despicable'. One provision in it, he said, 'exceeds even the worst Nazi stipulations'.

Meanwhile relations between the Nationalist Party and the various 'shirt' organizations had become very close. On 25 October 1937, F. C. Erasmus, later Minister of Defence and Minister of Justice, at that time Secretary of the Nationalist Party, addressed a letter to the Greyshirts in which he said: 'My party is glad to give expression to the sincere appreciation of the useful work done by the Greyshirts in one important aspect, viz. that they have very pertinently drawn the attention of the people to the Jewish problem . . . we consider that a service has here been done to the nation which deserves recognition and perpetuation.'

By 1938 a number of Greyshirt officials announced that they had joined the Nationalist Party. Just prior to the 1938 elections Dr Malan openly appealed for Greyshirt support and afterwards acknowledged the help that his party had received from Greyshirt leader Weichardt and his Nazis. This alliance was to continue throughout the forties and after the war the Greyshirts were to merge altogether into the Nationalist Party. Their leader, Weichardt, is today a member of the Republican Senate.

Another organization with which the Nationalists found much in common during the thirties was the 'South African Gentile National Socialist Movement', headed by one Johannes von Strauss von Moltke, whose object was to combat and destroy the alleged 'perversive influence of the Jews in economics, culture, religion, ethics, and statecraft and to re-establish European Aryan control in South Africa for the welfare of the Christian peoples of South Africa'.

Von Moltke at one stage in his anti-Semitic career was ordered by the Supreme Court to pay £750 damages for defamation arising from the publication of a forged anti-Semitic document based on the 'Protocols of the Elders of Zion', which he claimed had been stolen from the Western Road Synagogue in Port Elizabeth.

Die Burger of 25 February 1938, carried a declaration by Von Moltke who, in pressing his followers to throw in their lot with the Nationalist Party, proclaimed: 'The Nationalist Party has unequivocally given proof that it is protecting the interests of the people and that it wants a race-pure Afrikaner nation which will rule in its own country.'

As a reward for his services, von Moltke was to become a Nationalist Member of Parliament and Chairman of the Nationalist Party in South-West Africa. Though he resigned from the latter position in 1961 on grounds of ill-health, he is still a Nationalist M.P.

One of von Moltke's companions in the Port Elizabeth synagogue episode, a certain Inch, was not so fortunate. In addition to paying £1,000 damages for defamation, he was later prosecuted for uttering a forged document, making false statements, perjury, and receiving stolen letters knowing them to have been stolen. He was sentenced to six years' imprisonment, later reduced to three years – a misfortune which no doubt accounts for the fact that he, too, is not included in the ranks of South Africa's legislators.

During the war the anti-Semitism of the Nationalists raged unabated, and the Transvaal Nationalist Party in 1940 actually incorporated in its constitution a provision debarring Jews from membership. The enemy was called not merely 'British imperialism', but 'British-Jewish imperialism', and the tattered canards of the Nazis waved and fluttered over rallies. In 1940 Dr Malan declared that Smuts had turned South Africa into a 'Jewish-imperialistic war machine'.

After the war was over, and the Nationalists began to woo the English-speaking voters, anti-Semitism slowly became unfashionable. Yet it is a vice which, once implanted, is very difficult to uproot. As late as 1946 the garrulous Eric Louw was to write:

If the Jews can manage to find a country of their own anywhere, we shall certainly place no difficulties in the way, provided that country is not too near South Africa! If any of South Africa's surplus Jews wish to go there, our best wishes will accompany them. I hope they will be so happy and successful there that they will never want to come back to South Africa again! We want to build up a population here who know only one loyalty: loyalty to South Africa and to the interests of our country. And this also concerns the English-speaking people in our country.

Six months before the 1948 election, Dr Malan issued a statement which, while denying that the Nationalist Party was anti-Semitic, reaffirmed that it stood for the cessation of Jewish immigration. He had modified his standpoint, however, since he indicated that an exception would be made on 'humanitarian' grounds for near relatives of Jews already in the country and those people required for the 'religious and cultural needs of the community'. Yet it had been against the immigration of precisely such categories of people that the Nationalists had agitated so vehemently during the thirties!

After coming to power in 1948 the Nationalists considered it politic to suppress all signs of formal anti-Semitism. Yet it continues to flow underground, a hidden current of racial antagonism that bursts to the surface every now and again in the heat of political battle.

On the one hand Nationalist leaders have made friendly gestures towards the Jews. The anti-Jewish clause in the Transvaal Nationalist Party constitution was repealed in 1951. In 1953 Dr Dönges, then Minister of the Interior, at a tea-party commemorating the golden jubilee of the Worcester Jewish congregation, said 'there was certainly a kinship between Jew and Afrikaner' and he praised the achievements of the Jews in Worcester. In the same year Dr Malan himself visited Israel and allowed his name to be inscribed in the Golden Book of the World Zionist Organization. Jewish business and Jewish immigration has been handled sympathetically by government departments. Such gestures have done a great deal to satisfy the Jewish Board of Deputies that the interests of South African Jewry are safe under the Nationalist régime.

On the other hand, the occasional ugly outbursts cannot be overlooked. On 18 June 1959, the *Cape Times* reported:

Two United Party M.P.s who launched a vigorous and well-documented attack on the farm labour scandal in the Assembly yesterday were made the target of the most violent anti-Semitic outburst heard on the Nationalist benches since the war days.

They were Mrs Helen Suzman (U.P. Houghton) and Dr Boris Wilson (U.P. Hospital). They were told by Nationalists members that, being Jews, they should be the last people to criticize farmers for ill-treating their African workers becuse of the number of Jewish farmers who had appeared in court in ill-treatment cases.

The most celebrated recent case of anti-Semitism, however, came from the Prime Minister, Dr Verwoerd, himself. Following Israel's vote at the United Nations against South Africa in 1961, the Prime Minister wrote a private letter to a Cape Town professional man declaring that Israel's attitude towards the Republic was 'a tragedy for Jewry in South Africa'. The fact that so many Jews had favoured the Progressive Party and so few the Nationalist Party in the last election had not passed unnoticed.

c

'South Africa did not want to oppress; she wanted to differentiate; and for that reason she believed in Israel. Now we begin to wonder if that support should not be withdrawn,' stated Dr Verwoerd.

The professional man had actually written to Dr Verwoerd deploring Israel's condemnation of South Africa, but was so shocked by the reply that he felt compelled to make it public. Not unnaturally, the Prime Minister's veiled threat to the Jews produced a strong reaction not only in South Africa but also in Israel. Even the Nationalist newspaper *Die Burger* commented that Verwoerd's remarks about the Progressive Party vote would have been best left unsaid.

Verwoerd himself was unrepentant and at a conference of the Nationalist Party Witwatersrand Executive defended his point of view.

'What is the value of the so-called threat contained in the letter?' he asked contemptuously. 'If I want to threaten the Jews of South Africa, I will threaten the whole lot of them.'

He went on to show the Jews clearly where their best interests lay: 'But I do not want to divide the White people of South Africa. I want to gather them in one group. This government has never been anti-Semitic, and I urge Nationalists not to allow the propaganda which resulted from the letter to drive them to anti-Semitism.'

Official Jewry was quick to draw the lesson. When Israel again voted against South Africa's apartheid policies at the 1962 session of the United Nations, the South African Board of Deputies immediately issued a statement deploring Israel's stand and affirming its loyalty to South Africa.

*

To comp ete the picture it should be mentioned that, while the Verwoerd régime has outlawed the Communist Party, the Pan-Africanist Congress, the African National Congress, and the Congress of Democrats, and is at the moment engaged in a frontal assault upon the Liberal Party, openly fascist and anti-Semitic organizations and individuals are allowed to continue with their activities unchecked. World Nazi organizations have branches in South Africa, where the political climate is regarded as being particularly favourable to them. South Africa was not spared in the world-wide outbreak of anti-Semitic incidents sparked off by the Cologne synagogue desecration of 1960. In January of the same year the Wolmarans Street Synagogue in Johannesburg was blasted by dynamite and sustained damage to the tune of £3,000. In June of the following year there was an explosion at the Jewish war memorial in the West Park Cemetery in Johannesburg. Anti-Semitic and fascist publications are freely circulated in the republic, despite stringent legislation which makes it an offence to incite racial hatred against any section of the population.

One of the most curious episodes was the visit to South Africa in September 1962 of William Webster, the 50-year-old envoy of British fascist leader Sir Oswald Mosley. Webster planned to raise £100,000 from sympathetic South African businessmen in order, he said, to put up 100 Mosleyite candidates in the next British elections and so split the Labour vote that the Conservatives would be returned to power for a further five years.

Webster's visit in itself would have been unremarkable were it not for the fact that he obtained an audience with J. F. W. Haak, Deputy Minister of Economic Affairs, who furnished Webster with the names of organizations from which he might obtain information on such South African exporters as were doing business with firms in the United Kingdom.

'The Nationalists have the right idea,' Webster told a reporter of the Johannesburg *Sunday Express*. 'They are much shrewder than you think. They are following the same path as Hitler did, but they will not be as hasty as he was. They are going very slowly now, but they will smash their enemies in the end.'

Asked who these enemies were, Webster replied: 'I don't have to tell you the Nazis went for the Jews and the Communists.'

Webster said that the Mosleyites were using the Black bogy in England too, and that the slogan of their campaign was: 'Beware of the Black man – he will steal your job, then your wife, and you will end up in his cooking-pot.'

Embarrassed by the publicity given to these rantings, Haak issued a statement stressing that the advice furnished by him to

67

Webster 'certainly cannot be interpreted as in any way associating myself with Webster's political activities'.

Yet the suspicion remains. Mosley himself has twice since the war visited South Africa and been received by Nationalist Ministers, including Verwoerd. What exactly is the connexion between the Mosley movement and the Nationalist government of South Africa? There is certainly an identity of outlook on many issues. The Mosley movement has largely abandoned its public anti-Semitism and is devoting its attention now to the problem of Black–White relations throughout the world. It campaigns to keep Britain 'White'. On 2 March 1960, Mosley called for the partition of the African continent into White- and Black-ruled areas. In this sphere of politics South Africa has not unnaturally replaced Nazi Germany as the fountain-head of inspiration for the world's racist organizations. If the great struggle today is regarded as being, not between Jew and Gentile, but between Black and White, then it is understandable that in the eyes of fascists the world over Verwoerd should be seen to have assumed the tattered mantle once worn by Hitler.

5. In the Shadow of War

The efforts of the Nationalist Party, inspired and aided by the Broederbond, were beginning to bear fruit. By regrouping itself after the Hertzog–Smuts fusion on the basis of a firm and agreed ideology, the party had immeasurably strengthened itself. As compared with the huge and amorphous United Party, it was compact, solid, united. The Nationalist cadres busied themselves amongst all sections of the Afrikaner people and made steady progress.

In 1936 the party felt sufficiently encouraged by the response it was getting from Afrikaners throughout the country to incorporate in its constitution the republican ideal for the first time.

'The Party is convinced,' read the constitutional provision which was adopted, 'that the republican form of State, separated from the British Crown, is best suited to the traditions, circumstances, and aspirations of the South African people, and therefore it will protect the republican ideal and strive to bring about a republic in South Africa.'

This was the first time since the Boer War that republicanism had been officially proclaimed by the Nationalist Party, and it was an indication of the rising militancy amongst the Afrikaner people. With the obvious signs of war preparations in Europe, more and more believed that the time was not far distant when the opportunity would arise for their deliverance from the Empire.

At the same time the Nationalist Party began to devote greater attention to the details of its 'native policy'. In preparation for the 1938 elections, it worked out a programme providing for: '(1) Separate living areas, trade organizations, and, as far as possible, also separate work places for White and non-White. (2) Job reservation in certain directions for White labour and/or accordingly a fixed and just quota for Whites and non-Whites. (3) Separate representation in our legislative bodies for enfranchised Cape Coloured. (4) The extension of the Immorality Act of 1927 to all non-Whites and the prohibition of mixed marriages.'

These points have remained basic to Nationalist policy ever since.

The Union Congress of the Nationalist Party in 1938 declared:

'This Congress regards the dominant position of the White race in the spirit of guardianship as of vital importance to the future and welfare of South Africa. It declares therefore that it must be the earnest and determined struggle of that race to preserve its racial purity, to ensure the creation of a sound relationship between it and the non-White races, and also to avoid its economic destruction.'

Dr Malan proclaimed at the Congress what was to become the basic slogan of the Nationalists: 'We want to make sure that South Africa remains a White man's country.'

In 1939 a 'colour petition' organized by the Nationalists and signed by 230,619 Whites was presented to Parliament but not discussed. It demanded: (1) a ban on all mixed marriages; (2) all blood-mixing of White and non-White to be punishable; (3) all *deurmekaarwonery* (living of the various races side by side) to be ended; and (4) economic and political segregation of White and non-White.

The success of this policy may be gauged by the result of the 1938 election. The United Party won a huge majority, it is true, obtaining 111 seats, but the Nationalist Party increased its own representation from the nineteen seats it had retained when it broke away in 1934 to twenty-seven. The proportion of Afrikaners voting for the Nationalist Party had substantially increased. For those who cared to interpret the political drift of events, this was a significant portent indeed.

The year 1938 was to see the whole Nationalist movement given a tremendous fillip by means of the Voortrekker centenary celebrations. These took the form of an ox-wagon procession from Cape Town more or less along the original routes used by the Voortrekkers and culminated in a gigantic celebration at Pretoria, where it was decided to erect a memorial to the Voortrekkers on a hill dominating the city. The arrival of the ox-wagon party was an historical event for Afrikaners in every little village and town on the way. Men and women dressed in Voortrekker costume – long trousers and an open-necked shirt with a knotted scarf round the throat for the men, and wide-sweeping Victorian dresses with the traditional kappies for the women. Such men as could develop them in time, wore beards. The whole affair was organized with brilliant insight and imagination – on the initiative, according to Prof. L. J. du Plessis, of the Broederbond itself. There was much speechifying and performance of traditional music and dances, with countless appeals to the glories of the past and calls for the renaissance of the Afrikaner volk, now scattered and disunited in the land of its birth and creation. Emotion flowed freely. Party politics ostensibly played little part in the celebrations, which were supposed to constitute rather a sort of vast national festival for all sections of the Afrikaner people.

But not all sections were welcomed. General Hertzog had been invited to lay the foundation stone of the Voortrekker monument in Pretoria, but there were objections and he withdrew. The greatest reunion of the Afrikaner volk since Union took place in the absence of the very man whose devotion to Afrikanerdom had led to the foundation of the Nationalist Party in 1914. Hertzog was too compromised in 1938, as leader of the United Party and a man pledged to cooperation with the English-speaking section. By the more extreme among the Nationalists, he was regarded as a renegade, almost on a par with Smuts.

Despite the notable abstentions, the Voortrekker celebrations resulted in a tremendous upsurge of national feelings among the Afrikaner people and shifted the balance of power substantially in the direction of the Nationalist Party. The Broederbond cadres were inspired and threw themselves into the task of re-uniting Afrikanerdom with renewed enthusiasm. Appeals were made to all Afrikaners to join together to achieve their national salvation.

The split in the ranks of Afrikanerdom represented by the

existence of the United Party remained the greatest obstacle to Afrikaner unity. There can be no doubt that it was one of the main aims of the Broederbond at this period to smash the United Party, to rescue the Afrikaner from the clutches of the Englishman, and to drive the Afrikaner people into one *laager*. But the Broederbond had to deal with individual political leaders as well as the mass of the people, and while many reconciliation attempts were to be launched during the succeeding ten years, one after the other was shipwrecked on the rocks of personal ambition.

One Broederbond-inspired initiative took place early in 1939 when Prof. A. C. Cilliers of Stellenbosch University produced a pamphlet entitled *Quo Vadis* and organized a reconciliation committee which in March 1939 issued a statement of objectives.

Coupled with the healing of the split in politics amongst the Afrikaans-speaking Afrikaners, [it] aimed at a united front which would include not only the entire Afrikaans-speaking community but also those English-speaking persons who had actually come to lay claim to South African citizenship and, in proof thereof, were prepared to collaborate on an equal footing with the former in putting into effect a clearly defined programme of principles and action.

Hertzog and Pirow were interested, but the Nationalist Party itself remained cool to the approach.

Two days before the publication of *Quo Vadis*, Hertzog's son Albert addressed an appeal for unity to his father in the form of a letter to the Nationalist newspaper *Die Burger*. Committees were formed with the name of 'Albert Hertzogkomitees' to forward reconciliation, but they were all on a basis which effectively ruled out English participation.

General Hertzog himself noted in reply to his son: 'On their basis the Afrikaans-speaking section of the population would be the only section of the South African population that would be regarded as a nation, and the English-speaking section of Afrikanerdom would not be considered as a part of the Afrikaner nation. The position of power must therefore be vested in the self-constituted Afrikaner nation.'

Hertzog added the prophetic commentary: 'Under no circumstances, I assure you, will I ever extend my collaboration in politics to persons who are not prepared to acknowledge and to accept the principle of absolute equality and equal rights for the Afrikaans and English-speaking sections of our people.'

The most powerful movement for forging unity amongst the Afrikaners at this period was, however, the Ossewa Brandwag (Oxwagon Sentinel), founded at Bloemfontein in October 1938 to embody and perpetuate the idealism to which the Voortrekker Centenary celebrations had given rise. The foundation members all came from Bloemfontein and its surrounding districts, and the first Chairman of the organization's Groot Raad (Grand Council) was the Rev. C. R. Kotze, a Bloemfontein *predikant*. Though ostensibly a 'cultural' body, the Ossewa Brandwag was organized on a commando basis, and its first units were recruited from the ranks of the South African armed forces. The first Kommandant-Generaal was Colonel J. C. Laas, an officer in the Permanent Force, and from its very inception the O.B. had a quasi-military character.

The aims of the Ossewa Brandwag as proclaimed by Laas were seemingly innocent. They were:

The perpetuation of the spirit of the ox-wagon in South Africa; maintaining, amplifying, and giving expression to the traditions and principles of the Dutch Afrikaner; fostering patriotism and national pride, and harnessing and uniting all Afrikaners, men as well as women, who endorse these principles and are prepared to make energetic endeavours to promote them. . . . The *modus operandi* is as follows: celebrating Afrikaans national festivals and our heroes' birthdays, erecting memorials, laying wreaths at monuments, locating and keeping in repair places of historical interest as well as the graves of Afrikaners who perished on the 'Pad van Suid-Afrika' (Path of South Africa); organizing gatherings such as target-practice, popinjay, and vulture shooting, playing jukskei, etc.; doing folk dances and singing folk songs, holding processions, regular gatherings of an educational and social nature, dramatic performances, lectures on our history, literature . . . debates, camps for men and women, etc.

The 'etc.' turned out to involve military drill and manoeuvres and a host of other activities which it would be extremely strained to classify as 'cultural'. Even before the outbreak of the war, Defence Minister Pirow found Laas's activities too much to swallow, and dismissed him from the force. Union Defence Force officers were forbidden to belong to the O.B.

Laas was a cloak-and-dagger character who surrounded his activities with an atmosphere of mystery and proved himself eventually as little able to satisfy his friends as his enemies. In September 1940 he was relieved of his command in the Ossewa Brandwag and replaced as Kommandant-Generaal by the former Administrator of the Orange Free State, J. F. J. van Rensburg, who was to bring about a drastic transformation in the character of the whole force.

Laas later came to life with a new organization, Die Boerenasie, but after a while abandoned that ship as well. Die Boerenasie rose to prominence for a short time under Manie Maritz (leader of the 1914 rebellion), but later sank back into obscurity, where it is now headed by one S. K. Rudman, of Natal, whose frenetic pronouncements on racial affairs occasionally figure in the columns of the Sunday Press.

Meanwhile the fortunes of the Nationalist Party had undergone a startling change, brought about by the outbreak of war in Europe. According to Colonel Denys Reitz in his book *No Outspan*, Hertzog had been anticipating this moment for some time, with plans to assume dictatorial powers and keep South Africa out of the war. Oswald Pirow, when Minister of Justice, had drawn up emergency regulations to be enforced as soon as war was declared, and under these regulations freedom of the Press and freedom of speech were to be severely curtailed.

'The last thing he (Hertzog) desired or expected was for the war to burst upon him whilst the House was sitting,' wrote Reitz. Yet that is precisely what occurred. War broke out in Europe on the Saturday, and Parliament was to meet on the following Monday. General Hertzog called his Cabinet together, but found that there was no unanimity. He himself, with the support of five Ministers, favoured neutrality, but Smuts and six others regarded a declaration of war against Germany as the only possible course for South Africa to take. Hertzog referred the matter to the Assembly, having taken the precaution of ascertaining beforehand that he could rely on the support of Dr Malan and the Nationalists, though without having presented the issue in the caucus of the United Party.

The Assembly debate was one of the most dramatic in the

history of the Union. For once the issues were not cut and dried beforehand, and the outcome of the vote depended on the weight which the members would attach to the speeches of their leaders. Hertzog was curiously wooden and in an unimpressive speech maintained that Hitler's invasion of Poland, after his annexation of Austria and Czechoslovakia, was no evidence that he aimed at world conquest. As a people who had themselves been oppressed, the Afrikaners knew what it meant to struggle for the right of self-determination and to face the hostility of the outside world. Germany's actions constituted no threat to the security of South Africa, and a policy of neutrality under the circumstances was the only logical course to adopt.

General Smuts replied that since the fate of South-West Africa would depend on the outcome of the war, South Africa's interests were vitally involved. Furthermore, South Africa was part of the Commonwealth, whose fate now hung in the balance, and to stand aside from the conflict would expose the whole civilized world to danger. Smuts's amendment to Hertzog's neutrality motion was carried by eighty votes to sixty-seven on 4 September 1939, and South Africa was formally at war. Hertzog resigned as Prime Minister at once, recommending that a general election be held to test the feeling of the electorate, but the Governor-General declined to follow his advice and called upon General Smuts to form a government.

Malan and his Nationalists had voted in the minority with Hertzog, and it seemed that the stroke of war had healed the breach in Afrikaner unity which had existed since the Smuts–Hertzog fusion of 1934. On 8 September there was an enormous gathering at Monumentkoppie in Pretoria, where a year before the Great Trek centenary had been celebrated. The supporters of Malan and Hertzog came together in their thousands to celebrate the recreation of *volkseenheid* (national unity). To the Malan-led Nationalists the war was a vindication of the policy that they had pursued since 1934. A real union with the English-speaking for which Hertzog stood had been proved illusory. Now at last the occasion had arrived for cementing the unity of the Afrikaner *volk*.

'An Afrikaner,' Dr Malan told the Nationalist Party Congress in November 1939, 'is one who, whether speaking the same language or attending the same church as myself or not, cherishes the same Nationalist ideas. That is why I willingly fight against General Smuts. I do not consider him an Afrikaner.'

An Afrikaner, in other words, was one who was prepared to accept the hegemony of the Nationalist Party. Was Hertzog such an Afrikaner? There were powerful figures within the Nationalist leadership who wanted no truck with Hertzog. They had regarded him as a renegade ever since 1934, and they saw no reason to change their opinion now. Hertzog was soon to feel a strong current of opposition to him following from the Swart–Strijdom faction in the Nationalist Party, who believed that the party should assert its claim to the leadership of all Afrikanerdom whether or not Hertzog saw fit to join it on its own terms.

On 23 November 1939, the Hertzogites and Malanites met in Pretoria to try and reach a basis of agreement, but they could not overcome their differences. The republican aim of the Nationalists constituted the main stumbling block. Hertzog felt that Afrikaner–English unity was a pre-requisite for the establishment of a republic. The Nationalists felt that there could be no unity until the republic had been established and the allegiance of the English to the 'mother country' constitutionally destroyed once and for all. The clash of personalities also played its part. Neither Malan nor Hertzog would give away to the other.

A Broederbond-inspired reconciliation committee set to work and produced a new formula for unity. Hertzog and Malan accepted it, but Strijdom with his following fought bitterly against it. Nevertheless, on 27 January 1940, a declaration appeared in the Press over the names of Malan and Hertzog announcing that the parliamentary caucuses of the two groups had reached a basis of agreement and that it was proposed to establish a Herenigde Nasionale of Volksparty (Reunited Nationalist or People's Party). The *hereniging* agreement was subsequently accepted by the provincial congresses of the two parties. Hertzog became official Leader of the Opposition and Malan Deputy-Leader.

Superficially the stage was now set for an all-out effort by Afrikaner Nationalism to gain political victory, but the *hereniging* proved to be almost as superficial as the fusion of Hertzog and Smuts in 1934. There was continual friction and backbiting within the Nationalist leadership, and scandalous rumours about Hertzog were circulated amongst the Nationalist rank and file. One of the more curious stories was that of the so-called Freemason's Letters. A cabinet-maker named Joubert, employed at the Bloemfontein Hospital, came to one of the Nationalist leaders in the Orange Free State and reported that he had accidentally found in a chest belonging to the Freemasons letters from General Hertzog and Mr Havenga (former Minister of Finance in Hertzog's government who had followed his leader into opposition on the war issue) which revealed that the authors were in league with General Smuts to turn South Africa into a republic within the 'Empire'. Despite a commission of inquiry which was subsequently set up, the source of the story was never properly established, but Hertzog himself firmly believed that the Swart faction in the Orange Free State Nationalist leadership had deliberately circulated the canard with a view to discrediting him in the eyes of Afrikanerdom.

Hertzog met with other deliberate affronts from some of the Nationalist leaders. After Hitler's May 1940 offensive and the capitulation of Norway, Holland, Belgium, and France, Hertzog on 19 July 1940 addressed a public letter to General Smuts and followed it with a manifesto signed by himself and Dr Malan protesting against South Africa's continued participation in the war and calling upon Nationalist Afrikanerdom to hold meetings and demonstrate in favour of peace.

Dr N. J. van der Merwe, a leader of the Nationalist Party in the Free State, called a mass Republican Rally in Bloemfontein for 20 July 'to take active and immediate measures, on constitutional lines, to bring about a republic'. Hertzog condemned the rally, but a crowd variously estimated at between 15,000 and 70,000 attended. It resolved that the time had come for the creation of a free and independent South African republic on the basis of Christian-Nationalism and the maintenance of White civilization, and a committee of action was appointed to implement the resolution. In his speech at the rally, Dr van der Merwe said that 'a certain British–Jewish influence which played an important part in the fashioning of fusion . . . is again at work', implying that it expected support from Hertzog and Havenga.

The divisions finally came to a head at the Orange Free State Congress of the Nationalist Party which opened on 5 November 1940, one of four provincial congresses called to consider the adoption of a programme for the Herenigde Nationalist Party. Two drafts were placed before the Congress, one sponsored by General Hertzog and the other by the Federale Raad (Federal Council) of the H.N.P. Hertzog's programme was voted down and that of the Federale Raad adopted. Hertzog felt that he could take no more. In a dramatic speech he pointed out that the programme of the Federale Raad did not guarantee full equality for the English-speaking section of the population, a principle to which he was pledged to adhere. Taking his hat, he stepped down from the platform and walked out of the hall. The Congress was stunned. Instinctively everyone realized that this was the parting of the ways, and that the old general was being driven out of politics after a life-time of service to the nation. The whole audience stood up as the general left. Swart jumped to the microphone and tried to produce some explanation for what had happened, but nobody listened. An epoch in the history of Afrikanerdom had ended.

Hertzog immediately resigned his leadership and membership of the H.N.P. in the Free State, and was followed by Havenga, Brebner, and Edwin Conroy. Then there was a slight pause while the two groups took stock. The Hertzogites numbered thirty-eight M.P.s at the time, to twenty-seven Malanites. But the Malanites had control of the powerful party machine, with the support of the entire Afrikaans Press except the *Vaderland*. If it should come to open battle, the outcome was a foregone conclusion. On 12 December 1940, Hertzog accepted the inevitable. He and Havenga resigned their parliamentary seats, maintaining that the Free State and the Transvaal had shown bad faith and that the party was now set on a course which would lead to the destruction of Afrikanerdom. For Hertzog it was the end of a political career; for Malan, the establishment of his supremacy as leader of Nationalist Afrikanerdom.

Hertzog's followers made an attempt to rally their strength. On 30 January 1941, General Conroy announced in the Assembly the formation of the Afrikaner Party in all four provinces, but of the thirty-seven M.P.s who had followed Hertzog into opposition in 1939, only ten joined the new party, and two of these later seceded to the United Party. The seats vacated by Hertzog and Havenga were captured by Malanites. The remaining twenty-five members stood fast by the H.N.P., finding new leaders in Kemp and Pirow.

6. Armed Struggle

As in 1914, the war appeared to many Afrikaners a golden opportunity to re-establish the Boer Republics. 'We are now ceaselessly on the road to our goal: the Republic of South Africa – the only status under which we can truly exercise the right to self-determination as a country,' said Dr Malan on 6 September 1939. True there was no outright rebellion as there had been in 1914. But this was not due to indifference by the anti-war section. The lesson of 1914 had been learnt. Precipitate action was to be avoided. The republican forces must only strike when the time was ripe.

Partly, too, the absence of rebellion on the 1914 pattern was due to the comparatively solid loyalty of the Defence Force and the foresight of the government. Smuts had also learned the lesson of 1914. On 14 September 1939, emergency regulations were promulgated empowering the government to intern without trial, while all firearms had to be surrendered. Right from the start, therefore, the anti-war section was deprived of many of its weapons and several of its leaders.

A third factor militating against rebellion was the constant disunity within the ranks of the opposition. Seldom was there clarity or agreement on either aims or tactics. The Hertzogites in the Afrikaner Party favoured a policy of strict neutrality and were opposed to the more extreme forms of opposition represented by the Nationalist Party and the Ossewa Brandwag. Havenga, who later assumed the leadership of the Afrikaner Party, declared on 3 December 1941: 'I think it is a crime against the people to tell them that the freedom which we enjoy, and which was once so highly praised by these same people, means nothing under the present form of government. We are as free as any people in the world. We were dragged into this war not because we are not free, but because the only constitutional authority which could speak for the people took a free decision. It was not England that declared war for us. We did it ourselves through our free Parliament.'

On 4 February 1942, General Conroy told the Assembly that the Afrikaner Party would neither help nor hinder the war effort. There is no doubt, however, that these sentiments belonged to a minority of those opposing the government. 'The republican section of our people,' wrote Dr J. F. J. van Rensburg of that period, 'again were of the opinion that England's wars were not our wars and further that there was a chance to win back the lost freedom if the war went badly for England. Also contributing hereto was a certain amount of goodwill towards the Germans who had never done us any harm.'

There were sharp differences between van Rensburg and Malan over the right course of action to be followed. Both believed that everything depended on the outcome of the war, but whereas Malan relied on negotiation with Germany to achieve his objectives, van Rensburg believed that at some stage freedom would have to be fought for and he made his preparations accordingly.

At first, however, relations between the Nationalist Party and the Ossewa Brandwag were cordial, with most members of the Ossewa Brandwag belonging to the party as well. At the higher levels, Nationalist Party leaders P. O. Sauer and F. Erasmus (later to be made Cabinet Ministers when Malan came to power) were Ossewa Brandwag generals. C. R. Swart, now South Africa's State President, was a member of the Groot Raad of the O.B., while Eric Louw, at present Foreign Minister, was also prominent in the organization.

Under the impact of the war and the dynamic leadership of van Rensburg, the Ossewa Brandwag soon grew into a significant force. From the semi-secret conspiratorial organization it had been under Laas, it was transformed into a mass movement whose membership, at its peak, was estimated to be anything between 200,000 and 400,000 members. In 1940 there was created inside the O.B. an *élite* organization known as the Stormjaers –

the storm troopers of Afrikanerdom. The Stormjaers were employed in a variety of operations ranging from the defence of Nationalist political platforms to outright sabotage, the dynamiting of post offices and railway lines, and the cutting of telephone wires. In the booklet *Vanwaar en Waarheen*, issued by the Kommandant-Generaal on the authority of the Groot Raad in 1942, van Rensburg wrote: 'The O.B. regards itself as the soldiery of the Republic . . . the O.B. is the political action front of Afrikanerdom.'

The ideologies of the Nazis were penetrating deep into the ranks of Afrikanerdom. In 1940, soon after the fall of France, Otto du Plessis (later to become Administrator of the Cape under the Nationalist régime) published a pamphlet – *The Revolution of the Twentieth Century* – in which he openly espoused the policy of totalitarianism. Oswald Pirow also publicly identified himself with National-Socialist doctrines in a pamphlet – *New Order in South Africa* – which ran through seven editions between December 1940 and May 1941. He even organized a New Order group inside the Nationalist Party from the ranks of the former Hertzogites who, having refrained from joining the Afrikaner Party, now looked to Pirow for leadership.

Van Rensburg himself had always been a professed National Socialist, and the ideas propagated by his organization had a pronounced Nazi tinge.

Afrikaans would be the only official language in a free, independent, Christian-National Republic. The English, as unassimilable and unnational elements, would be condemned to an inferior status.

Anti-Communism was an important plank of policy. Germany was the friend and Russia the foe. After the death of Mussolini ('this Caesarean figure', 'the greatest Italian of our age'), the O.B. held a memorial meeting in the Johannesburg City Hall. The Nuremberg sentences were described as pursuing the precedents of the Zulu Chiefs, Tshaka and Dingaan, and in the opinion of Dr van Rensburg represented the 'triumph of the ghetto'.

The emphasis was always on race and racial purity. Members were exhorted to 'think with your blood', and the creed of *blut und boden* was expounded in the O.B. Press. 'Family, blood, and native soil – that is, next to our religion and our love of freedom, our greatest and our most sacred national heritage.' (*Die O.B.*, 28 October 1942.)

The O.B. always displayed an exaggerated interest in physical culture and the need for discipline. ('As against the spirit of the French revolution which wanted to break away from every lord and master has come the new cry of urgency in the world: "Give us a master! Give us bonds which tie us to a stable way of life"' – van Rensburg in *Vanwaar en Waarheen*.)

While the leaders of the O.B. denied that they supported the German maxim of 'Kirche, Kinder, Küche', they proclaimed that the duty of the man was to work and fight, and the duty of the woman to create and tend the home and family.

The O.B. declared itself anti-capitalist and anti-imperialist and insisted upon the expropriation of the gold mines and other key industries controlled by 'British-Jewish' capital.

Right from the outset of the war ugly incidents took place between soldiers and anti-war civilians, most of them associated with the Ossewa Brandwag, while there was also conflict between soldiers and those policemen who refused to wear the red tab signifying that they were willing to serve anywhere in Africa. After a series of minor clashes, matters came to a head on the night of Friday 31 January 1941, when van Rensburg was due to hold a meeting at the Johannesburg City Hall. A riot broke out between the Stormjaers and soldiers who were determined not to allow van Rensburg a hearing. The Stormjaers were armed with sticks, lead piping, batons, knives, sjamboks, bicycle chains, and knuckle-dusters, while the soldiers were for the most part unarmed.

The battle raged for two days, into the early hours of Sunday morning. Armoured cars hurtled through the streets while enraged mobs of soldiers set fire to Nationalist newspaper offices and overturned and set alight police vans. Tear-gas bombs were hurled in all directions.

Before a commission of inquiry, Major A. L. D. Bold, a military police spokesman, testified that armed members of the Ossewa Brandwag had attacked unarmed soldiers and that the police had openly aided and abetted and in many instances led such assaults. Evidence was given that police had savagely kicked and batoned soldiers lying on the ground, and some police were alleged to have secretly supplied the O.B. with tear-gas bombs to use against the soldiers.

Chief Inspector D. Baillie of the South African Police defended the members of his force against these allegations, but admitted that when he forced his way into Voortrekker Building, the O.B. headquarters, he had found the place filled with armed men from top to basement. 'There were weapons of every description – sticks, lead piping, batons, sjamboks, and so on.'

One hundred and forty soldiers ended up in hospital as a result of the riots, and one man died from injuries caused by a baton. Giving evidence, van Rensburg himself boasted that it was only O.B. discipline and restraint which had prevented reinforcements in outlying areas from being brought into town and the scope of the battle from being thus vastly expanded!

During 1940 the Groot Raad of the Ossewa Brandwag had issued a statement of its principles in the course of which it had claimed that 'the O.B. as an organization does not aim at, nor does it tolerate, any undermining activities or any recourse to violence or underground revolutionary activities or injuring friendly political parties or organizations in their activities or in any way undermining them'. This high-sounding declaration was to be proved false in every particular.

Summing up the achievements of the Ossewa Brandwag, van Rensburg wrote in his autobiography, published after the war:

I fought (Smuts's) war effort and I fought it bitterly with all the means at my disposal – which were considerable. . . . There is no doubt that they (the O.B. members) seriously hampered the government's war effort. Hampered it because the government was forced to draw off considerable manpower to guard many strategic points and essential services. A not inconsiderable military element also had to be retained in South Africa as a strategic reserve for possible emergencies.

Thousands of members of the O.B. were interned for their activities during the war, and not because the government was prejudiced against their 'cultural' activities. Van Rensburg admits in his autobiography: 'We often broke the law – and broke it shatteringly.'

O.B. members were to be found in every branch of the public service, in the police, and on the railways, and everywhere they carried out their undermining activities. Smuts, however, handled a dangerous situation with care. Reluctant to ride his enemies too hard and thus goad them into open rebellion, he chose rather to pick off the activists and leave the leadership alone.

Here are a few newspaper items, quoted with unction by van Rensburg, from the period early in 1942 when Stormjaer activity was at its height:

CONSTABLE SHOT ON THE RAND

Johannesburg, Wednesday – Constable Steyn was shot shortly after eight o'clock this evening. It is learnt that he was killed resisting arrest. (*Die Burger*, 8 January 1942.)

POLICE CHIEF ON HUNDREDS OF ARRESTS

In the past few days 314 members of the South African Police have been relieved of their duties and placed under arrest. Apart from this number there are already seventeen N.C.O.s and eighteen constables against whom a charge of high treason is being investigated.

Further, fifty-nine railway constables are under arrest. (*Die Vaderland*, 21 January 1942.)

NUMEROUS EXPLOSIONS OVER LARGE AREA

Mines at Klerksdorp Idle.

Punctually at 1.30 this morning violent explosions at Vereeniging, Delmas, and Potchefstroom blew up power lines, ten of them carrying 80,000 volts and two of 132,000 volts. (*Die Vaderland*, 29 January 1942.)

All telegraph and telephone communication between Bloemfontein and the rest of the Union was dislocated in the early hours of the morning yesterday. Also, railway telegraph and telephone lines in various parts of the Free State have been destroyed.

The authorities are of opinion that the plan was carefully prepared and that it was executed by numerous saboteurs. (*The Star*, 2 February 1942.)

SABOTAGE IN ALL FOUR PROVINCES

Communications cut in Free State. Plan prepared on a large scale. (*Die Burger*, 2 February 1942.)

The implication of the police in sabotage activity deeply shocked most of the nation and led to a public distrust of the force which has not yet been finally eradicated. Fifty-eight Stormjaers were eventually charged with high treason, and a quantity of hand grenades provided exhibits in the case. Van Rensburg later wrote:

'That meant, I pondered, that one could subtract those sixty to eighty from the eight to nine thousand which formed the total arsenal.'

The case collapsed when the main Crown witness disappeared.

To meet this wave of sabotage, an emergency regulation was promulgated in February 1942 which made the possession of explosives with the intention of committing sabotage a capital offence. Seven days later Stormjaers blew up two telephone poles behind the Pretoria Central Jail, but were never captured.

Two other Stormjaers, Visser and van Blerk, were not so lucky. Convicted of implication in a bomb outrage at the Benoni Post Office, as a result of which an innocent bystander was killed, they were both sentenced to death. The Nationalist Party campaigned for their reprieve, claiming that they had been misled by those who had taken advantage of their honest nationalism. The sentence was commuted to life imprisonment.

A half-dozen or so other members of the O.B. were shot while trying to escape from internment camps or jails, the most celebrated incident of this kind being the dramatic pursuit of the 'People's Wrestler' and O.B. General, Johannes van der Walt, who was shot while on the run near Krugersdorp.

Van Rensburg later justified the violent activities of his supporters by proclaiming: 'The men whose actions necessitated this (the keeping of troops in the country to deal with the Ossewa Brandwag) did what they did, not to "help the Nazis", as their opponents so bitterly alleged . . . they voiced the protest of the Nationalist Afrikaner element, which felt that it was being discriminated against and being trodden under in its own fatherland.'

The Nazis themselves, however, saw the activities of the Ossewa Brandwag in a different light. Van Rensburg was played up over Zeesen radio as the real leader of the Afrikaner people. In June 1941 the notorious Robey Leibbrandt was landed from a German yacht on the Namaqualand coast with 10,000 dollars, a radio transmitter, and instructions to make contact with van Rensburg and investigate the possibilities of joint action.

Leibbrandt was a South African prizefighter who had once fought Max Schmeling in Hamburg and later become a fervent Nazi. He had joined the German army and was reported to have taken part in the invasion of Crete as a paratrooper. In South Africa he soon made contact with the Stormjaers and was brought to Pretoria to see van Rensburg.

Nothing, however, came of the negotiations. Leibbrandt's megalomania was enough to deter anyone from cooperating with him, and van Rensburg refused to be drawn. At the same time Leibbrandt's fanaticism attracted a number of members of the Ossewa Brandwag over to his side, and within a short while Leibbrandt was leading his own group, whose members were bound to one another by a blood oath reading in part:

'All my fight and striving is for the freedom and independence of the Afrikaner people of South Africa and for the building up of a National Socialist State in accordance with the ideas of Adolf Hitler.'

The armed truce between Leibbrandt and van Rensburg quickly developed into open enmity. Leibbrandt, disappointed at his reception and the relative failure of his mission, began to attack van Rensburg as an agent of Smuts. This was probably enough to seal his fate. After a few months in South Africa he was arrested, together with a number of leading Stormjaers. Placed on trial he was sentenced to death for treason, but once again the sentence was commuted to life imprisonment after much Nationalist agitation.

Prominent in the Ossewa Brandwag throughout the war and immediate post-war period was Balthazar Johannes Vorster, South Africa's present Minister of Justice and author of the 1962 Sabotage Act. Like many others he regarded the war as an opportunity to get rid of the hated domination of England and welcomed the Nazis as allies in the fight. The adventurism of the Ossewa Brandwag appealed to him more than the comparative respectability of the Nationalist Party, and while South African troops were helping to make the world safe from Hitlerism, Vorster was appointed a general in the O.B. for the Port Elizabeth district.

'We stand for Christian Nationalism which is an ally of National Socialism,' he said in 1942. 'You can call this anti-democratic principle dictatorship if you wish. In Italy it is called Fascism, in Germany German National Socialism, and in South Africa Christian Nationalism.'

Arrested under the emergency regulations in September 1942, Vorster went on hunger strike after two months and was transferred as a result to Koffiefontein internment camp where he was prisoner No. 2229/42 in Hut 48, Camp 1. While in the camp Vorster gave lectures in law to his fellow detainees and himself studied genetics, sociology, and philosophy. Since his teachers were possessed of ideas as warped as his own, it is not surprising that he derived no permanent benefit from his studies.

Vorster was released on parole in January 1944 and placed under house arrest in Robertson. During this period he lived by permit, even requiring a permit to meet his wife when she came down from the Transvaal to join him. He had to have a special permit when he wanted to visit Cape Town 'on business'. (He actually came to speak to the Minister of Justice, Dr Colin Steyn, about his friends still interned at Koffiefontein, but was thrown out of the office.)

What was done to Vorster in war-time he is now doing to others in peace-time, on the excuse that he is 'at war with the enemies of the *volk*'.

After the war, Vorster again became involved in politics. The Ossewa Brandwag was absorbed into the Afrikaner Party of Havenga, and Vorster was nominated for Brakpan in the 1948 elections. Ironically enough, at that time the Nationalist Party, joined with the Afrikaner Party in an electoral alliance, attempted to veto Vorster's nomination on the grounds that his war record made him unacceptable to the electorate. But Vorster eventually got the nomination, to be defeated by two votes (increased to four after a recount) by his present colleague in the Cabinet, Labour Minister Trollip, at that time a member of the United Party. Such are the ins and outs of South African politics.

If the Ossewa Brandwag provided the fireworks, it was nevertheless the Nationalist Party which remained throughout the war the real arsenal of opposition to South Africa's war effort. This was recognized from the start by the Nazis themselves, who made an attempt, early in 1940, to enlist the services of Nationalist Party leaders in an attempt to get South Africa out of the war.

According to German documents captured by the Allies after the war, a certain Mrs Denk, acting on the instructions of her husband, a known German agent stationed at the time in Lourenço Marques, sought and obtained an interview with Dr Malan in January 1940. She conveyed to him a message originating from the Nazi Foreign Minister, von Ribbentrop, that it was in the interest of South Africa to make peace with Germany at once.

The documents reported that Mrs Denk had transmitted to Malan the view that Germany wanted to live in friendship with the Afrikaner people. The Reich government regarded it as a matter of course that her former colonies would be returned to her without further ado – i.e. South Africa would have to give up the mandate over South-West Africa – but promised in return that the three British Protectorates of Swaziland, Bechuanaland, and Basutoland would be allocated to the Union government. Germany would not mind if South Africa extended her territory to include Southern Rhodesia and regarded South Africa as the 'leading white state in the South African living space'.

One of the documents stated that Mrs Denk had found Malan to be 'a fighter'. Nazi agent Denk reported: 'Dr Malan was extremely grateful for the news he received, and asked my wife to convey his sincerest thanks to me.' Malan said that he would talk to General Hertzog and other Nationalists to influence them in the speeches they would deliver in Parliament. 'He gave the assurance that he would build up and work entirely on the lines suggested by us.'

This was just before the start of the 1940 session of Parliament.

Five days later the Nationalist Party proposed a motion in the Assembly pressing for a separate peace.

When these documents were disclosed to Parliament by the Minister of Justice, H. G. Lawrence, in May 1946, they caused a sensation, and a select committee was appointed to investigate the allegations contained in them. Both Mrs Denk and Dr Malan gave evidence before the committee.

The select committee report, which was unanimous, did not find that Mrs Denk was an enemy agent, since there was no evidence that she knew the business on which her husband was engaged! It also found no connexion between the interview with Dr Malan and the separate peace motion introduced by the Nationalists in Parliament. Dr Malan had said that he did not report the incident because he had regarded it as a possible trap, and also because it had made no impression on him! The select committee found these reasons adequate.

As for the long reply which Dr Malan was reported to have made, both he and Mrs Denk denied that he had said anything at all. There was one peculiar discrepancy in the evidence, however. Dr Malan himself stated that he had understood the message to have come from Mrs Denk's husband and not direct from the German government. In fact Mrs Denk had indicated to him a channel of communication through which he could make contact with her husband if he wished. He had thought so little about the matter that he forgot what he had done with the address.

Mrs Denk, in her evidence, denied having given Dr Malan an address at all. She stated that Dr Malan had said nothing and that she had been very disappointed in his attitude. Asked whether the arrangement had been that if she got an answer she should communicate it to her husband, Mrs Denk replied that she would rather not say.

Advocate L. de V. van Winsen, who appeared for the government, was denied the right to cross-examine as such and could only ask questions through the chairman of the committee.

On 19 June General Smuts moved the adoption of the select committee report, saying that the whole House would be satisfied with the results and he himself did not wish to take the matter any further. It was left to the Dominion Party leader Colonel Stallard to move an amendment, stating that he could not accept the select committee's findings and asking for a commission of inquiry into the subversive activities of agents in South Africa. General Smuts rejected the amendment, and there the matter ended.

Whatever the truth of the affair may be, the fact remains that the Nationalist Party and Dr Malan as its leader were convinced that the outcome of the war would determine the fate of Afrikanerdom, that Germany would win the war, and that at some stage or other they would have to negotiate with her.

Speaking at a Nationalist Party Congress in Bloemfontein on 5 November 1940, B. J. Schoeman, then Nationalist M.P. for Fordsburg and at present Minister of Railways, said: 'The whole future of Afrikanerdom is dependent upon a German victory. . . . If Germany wins the war we shall be able to negotiate with her, and in that way ensure the establishment of an independent republic in South Africa.'

And Eric Louw declared on 20 August 1942, at Fraserburg: 'If Germany wins, Dr Malan will have the majority and Hitler will then negotiate with the one who has the majority, and the heaviest burden will be laid on those who pushed on the war.'

These were the expectations of the entire Nationalist leadership, and they were to have a profound effect on the policies pursued by the party during the war. It was not enough to be passively anti-war. A good Nationalist had also to be positively anti-democratic if he were to qualify for admission into the political kingdom that was to come. Nationalist Party policy became aggressively xenophobic. Not only was the British connexion to be broken once and for all, but the influence of un-Afrikaans elements in South Africa was also to be eliminated or at least severely curtailed.

At Fauresmith on 17 March 1941, Dr Malan said: 'As regards obtaining a republic, Mr Havenga interprets this as "the broad will of the people", so that a majority will have to be obtained amongst the English and the Jews. . . . I do not agree that in our country we are going to grant the right of veto to decide about a republic to any section which is not imbued with the real Afrikaner spirit.'

For good measure he proclaimed a week later at Stellenbosch: 'When the republic is established, you can only give a say in affairs to people who have identified themselves with the *volk*, and who have had enough time to do so.'

Lest it be thought that these were regrettable lapses uttered in the heat of the moment, the Federal Council of the Nationalist Party published in March 1941 a brochure entitled *Die Republikeinse Orde* which stated unambiguously: 'When we have the republic, the say of the inimical and un-national elements in our national affairs will be obliterated. Those portions of the Press which still wish to plead for foreign interests, who want to support doing away with the republic and the restitution of the British connexion, will be regarded as taking part in undermining and treacherous activities.'

Here are other gems from this brochure: 'The British parliamentary system as applied in our country must be swept away, because it has been a failure.' 'A large portion of the population of the Union is the "fifth column" of an overseas nation.' 'Is not the time ripe for us to base our national way of life upon another foundation by breaking away from democracy?'

This whole line of policy was considered necessary at the time, not merely to satisfy the aspirations of the *volk* at home, but also to convince the German conqueror that it was possible to negotiate with the Nationalist Party when the opportunity arose to do so.

In aspiring for leadership of the Afrikaner people, the Nationalist Party eventually found that it had a formidable rival in the Ossewa Brandwag. But at first cooperation between the O.B. and the Nationalist Party was close, with leading members of each organization holding prominent positions in the other. Dr Malan felt that, so long as the ascendancy of the party in the political sphere was recognized, the O.B. could be given a free hand in the broadly defined 'cultural' sphere to which it had dedicated itself in terms of Colonel Laas's original pronouncements. Laas, it is true, was forced to resign on 30 October 1940, but this did not immediately alter the situation, since his successor had not yet been appointed; and in fact on the very day of Laas's resignation, Dr Malan, after meeting the leaders of the O.B. in Bloemfontein, made a declaration in a speech at Cradock which became known as the 'Cradock Agreement', defining the respective spheres of the two organizations. Each organization undertook not to meddle in the affairs of the other. The Nationalist Party was to do the work of Afrikanerdom in the party-political sphere, while the Ossewa Brandwag was to operate on the other fronts of the *volk*.

For some months there was the closest cooperation between the two organizations. Even the appointment of Dr van Rensburg as Kommandant-Generaal of the O.B. in January 1941 did not immediately alter the situation, though the methods of the O.B. were to undergo a drastic transformation under van Rensburg's leadership, and it soon became apparent that he had ambitions for his organization and for himself as its leader which could not easily be reconciled with the roles which had been assigned to them under the 'Cradock Agreement'.

As the Ossewa Brandwag became more deeply involved in its work of subversion, so the Smuts government responded with a more intensive policy of internment. There was even talk that the government might ban the organization altogether.

Dr Malan sprang to the defence of the Ossewa Brandwag. In a speech on 5 March 1941, he said:

The Ossewa Brandwag has been accused of lending itself to subversive activities and also of encouraging them. Now I say: Carry out your threat. Ban it. Prevent it and prevent its meetings. If the Ossewa Brandwag decides to be passively disobedient and refuses to be dissolved . . . I shall share the consequences with the Ossewa Brandwag. At this stage I am prepared to say to you that if the government decides upon that act and the Ossewa Brandwag decides not to submit, I shall keep my pledge.

What action was contemplated by the O.B. in the event of its being banned was not clear, so that the Doctor's pledge could be made with a fair amount of security, since it did not immediately commit him to anything. However, it was at least a sign that unity in the ranks of Afrikanerdom was as complete as at almost any stage since the outbreak of the war.

7. The Draft Constitution

The Broederbond wanted to put it all down on paper. A Provisional Committee of National Unity (Voorlopige Volkseenheidskomitee) which had existed since 1939 under the chairmanship of Prof. L. J. du Plessis and with representatives from the F.A.K. (the Federation of Afrikaans Cultural Associations), the R.D.B. (Reddingsdaadbond), the O.B., and the three Dutch Reformed Churches, came forward at this stage with a plan designed to create a united all-embracing 'Afrikaner Front'. After preparing a draft constitution and programme based exclusively on Christian-National principles, they issued a 'Declaration on behalf of People's Organizations' (Verklaring namens Volksorganisasies) in which the common objective was stated to be 'a free, independent, republican, Christian-National state, based upon the word of God, eschewing all foreign models ... with a Christian-National educational system ... and the strongest emphasis upon the effective disciplining of the people. ...'

This declaration was signed by I. M. Lombard, as Chairman of the F.A.K.; J. F. J. van Rensburg, as Kommandant-Generaal of the O.B.; L. J. du Plessis as Chairman of the Economic Institute of the F.A.K.; N. Diederichs, as organizational leader of the R.D.B.; Rev. J. P. van der Spuy, Chairman of the Church Council; Rev. I. D. Kruger, Chairman of the Inter-Church Commission of the Dutch Reformed Churches; and Rev. D. F. Erasmus, Vice-Chairman of the Calvinist Association. The three D.R.C. ministers signed in their personal capacities.

The declaration was accepted by the Nationalist Party at its Union Congress which opened on 3 June 1941, and *Die Transvaler* of 13 June reported that it had been received by Dr Malan with enthusiasm. The Provisional Committee (which later became the Afrikaner Unity Committee) including this time, in addition to representatives of the above organizations, representatives of the Nationalist Party as well, met again on 9 June and decided to take steps to promote both the declaration and the draft constitution. The time had come to announce the basis on which the future South African Republic was to be established.

As it happened, the manner in which the announcement was made served to bring about the first serious rift between the O.B. and the Nationalist Party. The Ossewa Brandwag, regarding the decision of the Provisional Committee (at which Dr Malan had been present) as a mandate for publication, on 3 July issued a circular containing the principles together with certain details of the constitution and showered 100,000 copies on the country. Dr Malan was furious, regarding the act as a clear invasion of Nationalist Party territory and a violation of the 'Cradock Agreement'. Constitutions belonged to the party-political field and were to be handled by the Nationalist Party alone. By issuing its circular, the O.B. was trying to steal a march on the Nationalist Party and oust it in the eyes of the people as the main architect of the new constitution. The Nationalist Party itself did not issue the constitution until 1942, when it was published simultaneously in *Die Transvaler* and *Die Burger* on 22 and 23 January.

After referring disparagingly to 'the unauthorized use which has formerly been made of portions of it', the Nationalist Press declared:

It will be understood that the acceptance of this Draft Constitution as a guide still leaves an opening for amendments on certain special points. On the other hand, a thorough comparison of this article and the Party's Programme and Principles of Action, as well as between this article and Dr Malan's republican motion (in Parliament), will show very plainly that the Party and its chief leader have accepted the scheme in its principles and its broad outline.

This explanation is most interesting in the light of attempts which Nationalist leaders have since made to insist that this draft constitution was never officially Nationalist Party policy.

The Constitution for the Republic of South Africa is an out-and-out fascist and out-and-out racist document. Article 1 reads:

In obedience to God Almighty and His Holy Word, the Afrikaans people acknowledge their national destination, as embodied in their Voortrekker past, for the Christian development of South Africa, and for that reason accept the Republican Constitution which follows, to take the place of all the existing regulations in law which are in conflict with it, and especially with the total abolition of the British Kingship over the British subjects within the Republic.

As will be seen, the constitution is only intended for the Afrikaners; the English are to play a subordinate role.

Article 2 (ii) reads:

The Republic is grounded on a Christian-National foundation and therefore acknowledges, as the standard of the government of the State, in the first place the principles of justice of the Holy Scriptures; secondly, the clearest direction of the development of the national history; and thirdly, the necessary reformation of the modern government of states, especially with an eye to the circumstances of South Africa.

Article 2 (iv) states that the national flag shall be the Vierkleur of the old South African Republic and the national anthem *Die Stem van Suid-Afrika*.

Article 2 (v) reads:

Afrikaans, as the language of the original white inhabitants of the country, will be the first official language. English will be regarded as a second or supplementary official language which will be treated on an equal footing and will enjoy equal rights, freedom, and privileges with the first official language, everywhere and whenever such treatment is judged by the State authority to be in the best interests of the State and its inhabitants.

In other words, both languages will be equal, but Afrikaans will be more equal than English.

Citizenship will be accorded to those subjects 'of whom it can be expected that they will act as builders up of the nation', and they will be called 'burgers'.

The State will have the power to make sure that 'individual citizens, as well as the organs of public opinion, such as the existence of parties, the radio, the Press, and the cinema, whilst their rightful freedom of expression, including criticism of government policy, will be protected, shall not be allowed, by their actions, to undermine the public order or good morale of the Republic internally or externally.'

At the head of the State will be the State President, who will be elected by the registered burgers. 'The State President is further directly and only responsible to God and over against the people for his deeds in fulfilment of his duties . . . he is altogether independent of any vote in Parliament. . . . The State President decides on all laws, which can only become valid by his personal signature.'

The Prime Minister is appointed by the State President, who may also summon or prorogue or dismiss Parliament.

The people will be represented in (a) a Parliament of not more than 150 members, and (b) a Community Council, in which the spiritual, cultural, economic, and social interests of the community and of groups within the community will be represented in an advisory capacity. The members of the Community Council shall consist of 'fifteen persons appointed by the President-in-Council, on account of their knowledge and experience in connexion with the treatment of important problems of the country, such as the poor White (White poverty) question, the interests of the Coloured people, the government of the natives, the Indian penetration, and the surplus Jewish population with excessive economic powers; and thirty-five members chosen by suitable organizations. . . .'

Every coloured group of races, Coloured, natives, Asiatics, Indians, etc. will be segregated, not only as regards the place of dwelling or the neighbourhoods dwelt in by them, but also with regard to the spheres of work. The members of such groups can, however, be allowed to enter White territories under proper lawful control for the increase of working power and also for the necessary increase of their own incomes.

To each of such segregated race groups of coloured subjects of the Republic, self-government will be granted within their own territory under the central management of the general government of the country, in accordance with the fitness of the group for the carrying

D

out of such self-government for which they will have to be systematically trained.

Mixing of the blood between Whites and non-Whites is forbidden.

Non-Europeans educated for any of the professional callings, and non-European trades, are shut out from practice or trade among White people. . . . White employees may not be employed by non-European employers.

The public tone of life of the Republic is Christian-National. . . . The propagation of any State policy and the existence of any political organization which is in strife with the fulfilling of this Christian-National vocation of the life of the people is forbidden.

The constitution envisages strict State control over the economy of the country and also over employers' and employees' organizations and trade unions.

It is the right and also the duty of the State government to take the control and coordination of the economic and social life under its supervision, beginning with the agricultural basis of the national life, with the object of keeping the balance between the different population groups in the different callings and trades, and between capital and labour, and to protect against agricultural, industrial and commercial undertakings of a parasitic nature or undertakings which come into conflict with the interests of the community as a whole.

Country-wide group organizations for employers and employees in the various trades and callings must receive the recognition of the State, which can also call them into being or reform them, in accordance with the object of organizing them for self-government, by the official licensing of suitable persons for undertaking the work and by linking them up with the say of such groups in the governing of the State by means of the Community Council.

The currency of the country must bear a purely indigenous character. . . .

While some of the cruder provisions in this constitution have had to be dropped in the course of time, it is nevertheless astonishing to see how much of subsequent Nationalist government policy derives from the draft prepared during the war on the expectation of a Nazi victory over the forces of democracy. The

Immorality and Mixed Marriages Acts, the establishment of Bantustans and the Coloured Advisory Council, job reservation, decimal coinage, Press control and censorship, the Suppression of Communism Act, bannings, Group Areas, control of trade unions – all these and more are foreshadowed in the draft constitution. Moreover, the direction of present government policy in many spheres can be gauged by reference to this draft. For the government is still actively engaged in trying to put the principles of this constitution into effect, despite all disclaimers that it was ever official Nationalist Party policy. There is no doubt whatsoever that the draft constitution embodied the quintessence of Nationalist Party thinking during the war period, and subsequent events have shown that that thinking has not undergone any basic change in the intervening period. Tactics have altered from time to time, but the grand strategy has remained the same.

The constitution was prepared because Nationalist Afrikanerdom believed that the moment was at hand when it could be put into force. But almost as soon as the Provisional Committee agreed on its terms, a split developed within the leadership which was to become more and more pronounced as time passed.

In part this was due to a clash of personalities, in part to disagreement over the methods by which the republic was to be attained. Van Rensburg, at the head of what *Die Vaderland* had called 'the greatest Afrikaans organization outside of the Church' (1 January 1941), was not inclined to play second fiddle to Malan, whom he despised as a hide-bound constitutionalist. Malan, in turn, was having trouble inside the Nationalist Party with Pirow, who had established a separate apparatus of his own for disseminating the principles of the 'New Order'. There was more than one claimant to the role of Quisling in South Africa. If Hitler should win, who would negotiate with him in the name of Afrikanerdom? Whose principles would prevail in the establishment of the South African Republic?

Malan decided to put his own house in order first, and a campaign was mounted in the Nationalist Party to bring the New Order group to heel. Pirow responded by placing a motion on the order paper for the Transvaal Congress of the Nationalist Party in August 1941, upholding the right of the New Order to continue propagandizing within the Party.

Then, on the eve of the congress, van Rensburg, in a major policy speech, declared that no matter what the policies of other organizations might be, in the Ossewa Brandwag there was room for all Afrikaners, irrespective of their political beliefs. 'As far as we in the Ossewa Brandwag are concerned, National Socialists are also welcome,' he proclaimed. This was another direct slap in the face for the Nationalist Party, and relations between Malan and van Rensburg deteriorated still further.

At the Transvaal congress of the Nationalist Party on 12 and 13 August 1941, Dr Malan opposed the motion to allow continuation of New Order propaganda. Eighty-five per cent of the New Order programme was already incorporated in the principles of the Nationalist Party, and he did not consider a separate propaganda apparatus to be necessary. In any event, the Nationalist Party could not approve the one-party system, he said. Pirow's motion was defeated.

An interesting sidelight of the congress was the discussion on certain resolutions in favour of only one language for South Africa. The leader of the party in the Transvaal, J. G. Strijdom, said that he agreed with the purpose of the resolutions, but that for tactical reasons it should not be laid down in black and white. The resolutions were shelved.

The Transvaal Congress effectively put paid to the account of Pirow. On 16 August he and seventeen other M.P.s formally constituted themselves as a New Order group and announced their intention of defying the ban on their propaganda. But while they were able to retain their seats in Parliament, they were driven out of the counsels of the party. At last, on 14 January 1942, Pirow was forced to bow to reality by announcing that those in the New Order group would no longer attend Nationalist Party caucus meetings, though they still considered themselves members of the party. For all practical purposes, however, the two groups operated as separate entities from that time onwards, while the breach between Malan and Pirow was never healed.

Emboldened by his success in dealing with the Pirowites, Dr Malan next turned his attention to the Ossewa Brandwag and demanded that the O.B. cease to interfere in the party-political sphere which had been clearly demarcated for the Nationalist Party by the 'Cradock Agreement'. The Afrikaner Unity Committee rushed in to try and patch up a compromise, but the two leaders bickered and bargained without reaching agreement. Malan refused to withdraw his ultimatum, and in face of the conflict, the Chairman of the O.B. Groot Raad, the Rev. Kotze, resigned his position on 4 September. Other Nationalist leaders like Strijdom, Kemp, and Sauer withdrew from the O.B. altogether, while the O.B. itself expelled Eric Louw. In October the Nationalist Party called on its members to resign from the Ossewa Brandwag, while all Nationalist Party office-holders were forbidden to belong to it. By a curious coincidence, it was in October as well that the government prohibited certain classes of civil servants from belonging to the O.B.

Thus from the position of complete accord which had been reached in June, the two leading organizations of Afrikanerdom had drifted apart to the point where they were open enemies. Where but a few months before Dr Malan had promised to stand by the O.B. if it were attacked by the government, by December 1941 he was reported in the Press to have declared at a meeting in Paarl: 'The O.B. leaders were openly talking about attaining a republic by rebellion, and storm troopers had been told to be prepared for it. There were whisperings throughout the country that the storm troopers had rifles, cannons, and even aeroplanes. The O.B. was responsible for Afrikaners being interned.'

Then suddenly Zeesen radio took a hand in the dispute. From 5 September onwards it backed van Rensburg's stand, doubtless feeling that it could place greater reliance on the Stormjaers than on Malan's parliamentary cohorts. It hinted that Malan was playing the game of General Smuts and presented van Rensburg to its listeners as the saviour of oppressed Afrikanerdom.

The curious case of the Ossewa Brandwag general and wrestler-hero Johannes van der Walt illustrates the depths of real hatred to which this dispute, and the divisions caused by the war, moved the participants. Arrested on 17 December 1941 on the comparatively trivial charge of being in possession of an unlicensed pistol and bullets, van der Walt managed to escape from the cells at Marshall Square, Johannesburg, only a few days later, on 23 December. While he was on the run, on 2 February 1942, Dr Malan dropped a bombshell in the House of Assembly. He read an affidavit by Johannes van der Walt alleging that the Kommandant-Generaal of the O.B., Dr van Rensburg, and one of his leading lieutenants, Advocate Jerling, had taken an oath, sealed with fingerprints in blood, that they would not surrender an Afrikaner to the enemy (i.e. the government), even if he were not a member of the Ossewa Brandwag. Nevertheless, stated van der Walt, he believed that Jerling and other Ossewa Brandwag leaders had given to the government the names of people whom they wanted to have interned, while Jerling himself had instructed a subordinate that Leibbrandt should be surrendered to the police. Van der Walt also alleged in his affidavit that he had been ordered by Jerling to murder a certain advocate and that Jerling had embezzled O.B. funds.

Whether there was any truth in those allegations there is no means of knowing as they were never investigated. They were, of course emphatically denied by Jerling himself. But the whole episode casts a lurid light, not only on the activities of the O.B. during the war period, but also on the enmity which now existed between the O.B. and the Nationalist Party. A few months before it would have been inconceivable that Dr Malan should produce such a document in the House. Now he exhibited an overmastering desire to destroy van Rensburg and the organization which he headed.

Van der Walt's own position was never cleared up either. Had he turned traitor to the O.B.? And for what motive had he signed such a damning affidavit against his former comrades? The whole episode remains shrouded in mystery. A bare three weeks later van der Walt himself was given away. On 23 February 1942, a police cordon was thrown round the farmhouse in the Krugersdorp district where he was in hiding, and he was shot while trying to make his escape through a window. Partially paralysed, he lingered for over a year before eventually succumbing to his injuries and was buried on 28 March 1943.

Part of the reason for the discord between the Nationalist Party and the Ossewa Brandwag was a difference of opinion over the methods to be used in achieving the republic. Part was due to a clash of personalities between van Rensburg and Malan. But the main reason was undoubtedly the determination of Dr Malan himself not to yield the pre-eminence of the Nationalist Party in the political field because he believed a German victory to be imminent. When the war was over, there was to be only one candidate for the job of negotiating with Hitler, and that man was to be Dr Malan.

This idea had been in Dr Malan's mind ever since the outbreak of the war. As early as the Transvaal congress of the Nationalist Party in September 1939, he had said that if the war ended in Germany's favour, 'we would have to have an understanding with her over the future of South-West Africa, and it would have to be timely by means of negotiation'. The Nazi plunge through Europe in 1940, the attack on the Soviet Union in 1941 and the swift penetration of the German forces to the neighbourhood of Moscow, made it seem as though the war was all over bar the shouting. Dr Malan wanted to be in unquestioned command of Afrikanerdom when the time came for talking. Van Rensburg's challenge to his leadership had to be faced full on and defeated. In this grim struggle for internal power and influence, Dr Malan drew on every resource available to the Nationalist Party.

Already at the 1941 congress of the Nationalist Party in Bloemfontein Dr Malan had been given extraordinary, even dictatorial powers to handle the party's affairs. He could act on his own without reference to any of the leading committees of the party if he thought fit, and was accountable only to the party congress for anything he might do in the party's name. J. A. Smith, then a deputy leader of the Ossewa Brandwag, gave Dr Malan a sjambok as a symbol of his power to keep his followers under control.

Commenting on Malan's assumption of the new title of *Volksleier* (People's Leader), *Die Transvaler* declared that it was necessary for him to occupy the same position in South Africa as Hitler occupied in Germany.

The United Party newspaper *The Friend* described the congress somewhat less enthusiastically as 'a realistic rehearsal of Reichstag procedure in which only the leaders had the say. All resolutions were proposed and seconded from the platform, and according to the programme no debates ensued. Dr Malan spoke for two hours at the opening of the proceedings giving a consummate exposition of how it was proposed to adapt a democratic republic to National Socialism (Nazism)'.

As the quarrel with van Rensburg sharpened, so Dr Malan took the initiative in attempts to create a new Volksfront under his leadership. In the last quarter of 1941 he busied himself in negotiating for the establishment of a National Committee, a sort of shadow cabinet which would be able to take over power at once if necessary.

Hitler's victory, however, was unaccountably delayed and these attempts came to nothing. Party politics had to continue. Shortly before the 1942 congress of the Nationalist Party a campaign was launched in which party members were urged to contribute half-crowns ('silver bullets') to the fight against British–Jewish imperialism. At the congress, 'rejecting equally dictatorship on the one hand and British Imperialism on the other, Malan pointed the way to a Christian-National Republic in which the English might have a part, but in which the Afrikaner would enjoy a position of ascendancy.' (*The South African Opposition*, by Michael Roberts and A. E. G. Trollip.)

With the battle of Stalingrad approaching, Malan's plenary powers were renewed.

Meanwhile Dr Malan made an attempt to elicit from the Germans a more definite indication of their intentions towards South Africa. On 2 June 1942, in Johannesburg, he declared:

If the people will clearly take up the attitude that we refuse cooperation of any kind in the war, then we may expect at a suitable time an authoritative statement from Germany and Italy as to what they intend to do with South Africa. We expect a declaration whether the plan is that we stand under German or Italian authority. We want very much to know where we stand.

Whether any direct approach was made to the Axis powers we do not know. But a few months later Dr Malan appeared to have obtained some sort of answer to his query. On 17 August 1942, *Die Burger* reported a speech given by Dr Malan at Burgersdorp:

The German radio had given a clear and indubitable answer to his request for a declaration as to what Germany intended to do with us. This was the answer: 'Germany wants to see South Africa free and independent, but then it must be a really, truly free South Africa, which is not being ruled in the interests of foreigners. Just for that reason Germany takes no interest in the form of government which the people will choose for themselves. Provided the form of government represents the will of the South African people, Germany will not be offended or hurt by it.'

Despite the number of German pledges which had been dishonoured in the preceding years, Dr Malan was highly elated at the response.

If this could be said more authoritatively, for instance by the Minister of Foreign Affairs, it would be good enough for the speaker, although for the present he was accepting the above mentioned declaration.

This was as far as Dr Malan ever got to negotiation with the Germans – negotiation by radio. Zeesen promised South Africa independence and Malan declared himself satisfied.

Then came the battle of Stalingrad, and Malan's dreams rapidly faded.

The identification of the Nationalist Party with the cause of the Nazis was well illustrated by a court case involving Dr H. F. Verwoerd, who was Editor-in-Chief of the Nationalist Party newspaper *Die Transvaler* throughout the war period.

In consequence of the manner in which he conducted the affairs of his paper, the Johannesburg evening newspaper, *The Star* published in October 1941 an article entitled 'Speaking up for Hitler', which accused *Die Transvaler* of falsifying news in support of Nazi propaganda and generally acting as a tool of the enemy.

Dr Verwoerd decided to sue the editor, proprietors, and

publishers of *The Star* for damages, and the case came before Justice Millin, husband of the well-known novelist Sarah Gertrude Millin.

The Star claimed that what it had said about *Die Transvaler* was true and that publication had been in the public interest – the standard legal defence against an accusation of libel. It supported its argument by producing numerous examples from Dr Verwoerd's paper to show how closely *Die Transvaler* had followed the Nazi propaganda line.

Verwoerd lost the case, which dragged on for a considerable time before Justice Millin gave judgement on 13 July 1943, to find not the slightest doubt that Verwoerd had in fact furthered Nazi propaganda in his paper. The 25,000 word judgement concluded:

It is not necessary for the defendants (*The Star*) to establish that *Die Transvaler* propaganda agreed in every respect with that of Zeesen. What they have proved is that the plaintiff (Dr Verwoerd) caused to be published a large body of matter which was on the same general lines as matter coming to the Union in the Afrikaans transmissions from Zeesen and which was calculated to make the Germans look upon *Die Transvaler* as a most useful adjunct to this propaganda service.

The plaintiff cannot really deny this.

He says it is not his fault. He appeals to the principles of free speech and a free Press in a democratic country. . . . He argues that if he had to consider whether what he said would be useful to the Germans the effect would be to silence him; and the law does not compel him to be silent.

But the question in this case is not whether the plaintiff should be silenced. His legal right to publish what he did is not in question. The question is whether . . . he is entitled to complain if it is said of him that what he writes supports Nazi propaganda and makes his paper a tool of the Nazis.

On the evidence he is not entitled to complain. He did support Nazi propaganda, he did make his paper a tool of the Nazis in South Africa, and he knew it.

The result is that there must be judgement for the defendants, with the general costs of the three actions.

The immediate cause of *The Star* article had been *Die Trans-*

valer's handling of a statement issued by the government's Bureau of Information. This government statement had given the text of a Zeesen broadcast declaring that the Nazis 'did not want to force their state form on other countries'. The government Bureau of Information had then pointed out that this Nazi claim was 'belied by what is happening in Europe'. Verwoerd had printed the statement, but had deliberately excluded the Bureau's comment.

About this Justice Millin said:

The plaintiff is a very intelligent person. He must know as well as anyone else that no government carrying on a war can be expected to authorize the publication of enemy propaganda addressed to its own people without seeking to refute the propaganda. . . . The whole object of the introduction (by the Bureau) was to make an opportunity for warning the public not to believe the enemy statement. In suppressing this warning statement by the Bureau I think he (Verwoerd) can properly be said to have falsified current news. He presented what was said by the Bureau as news and he presented it falsely. . . . The effect was to support, or help on, German propaganda. Certainly the Germans could have found nothing more convenient for their purpose than what the plaintiff did.'

Justice Millin went on to deal with a number of instances given by *The Star* of false reports by *Die Transvaler* which were pro-Nazi in their effect. The judge said:

The conclusion is inevitable, that the plaintiff (Dr Verwoerd) when he published these false statements as current news was quite reckless whether they were true or false. He thus exposed himself to the imputation that he falsified current news. The result, as he admitted, might have been most harmful to recruiting for the armed forces. . . . It cannot be questioned that the publication . . . was in fact, if not in clear intention, valuable support to the enemy in the propaganda he was then making (as appeared from the evidence) to weaken the war effort of the Union.

Die Transvaler had suggested, in July 1940, that South African forces had suffered a serious military defeat against the Italians, and that the government had deliberately suppressed information of this and the accompanying heavy casualties. Justice Millin found the suggestion to have been completely false.

It has been shown to be false and the plaintiff, who was willing to adopt it when he saw it in the paper, does not pretend that he thought it was true. It is therefore correct to say that this is a falsification of current news which was approved by the plaintiff. It was calculated to cause alarm and despondency and it is not open to doubt that it was of great service to the enemy in the way of supporting his propaganda for the damaging of the war effort of the Union.

Verwoerd was sufficiently impressed by the judgement not to take it on appeal. Years later, taunted with this in Parliament, he was to say that a Nationalist could not have expected impartiality from the courts as they had then been constituted. And he was even to hint that the judgement in this particular instance had gone against him because the judge had been a Jew!

It would be wrong to create the impression that the whole of Afrikanerdom followed the leadership of Malan and Verwoerd during the war period. The majority of those serving in the South African armed forces were Afrikaners, and they played their part in the defence of their country as loyally as any other section of the population. The Afrikaner in uniform, moreover, had no easy time in his own country. He was regarded by the hard-core Nationalist as a renegade, and was often ostracized by his own community. There were even instances where Dutch Reformed Church ministers refused to allow soldiers in uniform to attend services in their churches.

When the soldier went north, cut off from the pressures of Church, Press, and party, he became subject to liberalizing influences and frequently changed his outlook. A survey conducted by the Army Education Service revealed that thinking on political and social problems amongst the soldiers – Afrikaner and English alike – was considerably in advance of the civilian community back home.

In South Africa, however, the Nationalist Party steadily strengthened its grip on the key institutions of the Afrikaner community, with Dr Malan's own leadership during this turbulent period revealing him to be a master of tactical manoeuvre. Not only was he able to stave off the challenge of rival organizations like the O.B. and the New Order, but he was even able, in the teeth of pro-war sentiment and the overwhelming propaganda of the government, to strengthen his political position. The grand strategy of White apartheid worked out by the Broederbond during the twenties and thirties was beginning to pay dividends. Sealed off from all external contacts in the various *volksorganisasies*, the civilian Afrikaner, unlike his military counterpart, was insulated from the liberalizing currents prevalent during the war period. Ideas of reform, of new deals, of making the world safe for democracy, the genuine idealism which enabled the Allies to mobilize millions of people the whole world over and lead them in the great crusade which defeated the Axis powers – all this passed the Afrikaner by. Instead, he was subjected to a concentrated indoctrination designed to lead him in the opposite direction. His leaders made the enemy's cause their own. With some, of course, this was merely opportunism, a belief that the Germans would win the war and give the Afrikaner the chance to establish his republic. The innermost Nationalist cadres, however, drank deep at the fountain of Nazism and found in the Nuremberg laws confirmation and rationalization of the racist doctrines which they had traditionally espoused in South Africa.

The O.B. staked all on a German victory, and lost. After the battle of Stalingrad and the entry of the United States into the war, when it became clear that Hitler could no longer win, its influence gradually waned, though it remained a powerful force for many years. Malan himself was more astute. He also entertained the prospect of coming to power as the result of a German victory, but he had the foresight to keep his escape lines open and never loosened his grip on the Nationalist forces in the parliamentary field. Van Rensburg, contemptuous of democracy and convinced that he would be able to seize power by unconstitutional means, refused to accept nomination for parliament throughout the war period and after. At first this had greatly enhanced his reputation in the eyes of a people daily expecting a Nazi victory. But in the later years it was the solid weight of Malan's parliamentary support which proved more substantial. The membership of the O.B. might wax and wane, but the ranks of the Nationalist opposition in Parliament never wavered.

As the prospect of an Axis victory faded, so too did the O.B.

leadership's hopes of ever attaining power. But with Malan it became just a question of fighting on another front, that was all. The fight might take a little longer, but the end result would be the same.

In this conviction, the Nationalists threw themselves into the preparations for the 1943 general elections with as much vigour and enthusiasm as ever. Basically their policy was the same as it had been before – the demand for a republic separated from the British Crown, independent of any foreign power, based on no foreign model but built in accordance with the Afrikaner people's nature and traditions and on the principles of people's government as embodied in the two former South African republics. While Christian-National in spirit and character, it would be based on true consideration of the equal political, language, and cultural rights of both sections of the White population. The White race and 'civilization' as a whole were to be safeguarded by means of the trusteeship principle.

The Nationalist election manifesto, however, was much milder than it would have been, say, two years earlier. The approach to the English-speaking voter was cautious and correct, while the more extreme objectives embodied in the 'draft constitution' for the future republic were carefully concealed.

Malan knew that he had no hope of winning the election, and he therefore carefully avoided entering into any election alliances with either the O.B. or the New Order group which might have bolstered his parliamentary strength but would at the same time have weakened his control of political Afrikanerdom and forced him to share the leadership with his rivals. The election results proved his strategy correct.

On the surface, the election result appeared to be a tremendous triumph for the Smuts government. The strength of the United Party was increased from seventy to eighty-five and the total strength of the coalition government from eighty-seven to 105 (Labour Party nine and Dominion Party seven). Including the native representatives and two Independents, the government could accordingly rely on 110 votes in the Assembly. On the other hand, the parliamentary opposition had been reduced to forty-three (compared with the sixty-seven who had voted against war in the 1939 debate and subsequently opposed the new Smuts government). The government's war policy had received the overwhelming endorsement of the electorate.

A closer analysis of the results, however, revealed a consolidation of the Afrikaner vote under Nationalist Party leadership. As compared with the twenty-seven seats it had won in the 1938 elections, the Nationalist tally was now forty-three – a substantial increase by any standards. Moreover, the Nationalist Party was now the sole representative of the opposition in Parliament. True to its beliefs, the O.B. had scorned the elections and made no effort to win any seats. The Afrikaner Party, however, had put up twenty-four candidates, every one of whom had been defeated. Moreover, the Afrikaner Party candidates had polled only 14,759 votes, revealing that by and large they had negligible support in the community. The New Order had nominated no official candidates, but several members had stood as Volkseenheidskandidate or Independents and got nowhere.

The government parties had polled 640,000 votes or sixty-four per cent of the total; the opposition parties, 362,000 or thirty-six per cent. According to calculations made by Roberts and Trollip in their book *The South African Opposition*, the U.P. had increased its vote by 82,000, but the Nationalist Party's increase had been 71,000, so that the ratio between the two parties had dropped from 184:100 in 1938 to 160:100 in 1943. In 1938, moreover, the Hertzogites had still been members of the United Party. The percentage of Afrikaners voting for the government had thus dropped from forty to thirty-two.

Malan could sit back quietly confident of the future. He was in sole political charge of Nationalist-minded Afrikanerdom. His rivals were scattered to the wind. His strength was steadily increasing. Despite the unfavourable turn of the war, he had every reason to be satisfied. In the Provincial elections which followed in October, the Nationalist Party forged still further ahead, gaining forty-eight seats. The Afrikaner Party, chastened by its showing in the general elections, had put up no candidates at all.

During the five years before the next general election, the Nationalist Party, while retaining its basic policies, changed its approach to the electorate with a view especially to winning support from the English-speaking voters. Even before the end of the war, democracy became fashionable once more, and nothing was heard of the need to establish a new State form which would inspire confidence in the enemy when the time came to negotiate. For of course by 1944 it had become clear that the Allies were fast headed for victory.

Malan outlined the 'new look' programme of his party in a speech at Stellenbosch on 9 November 1943, when he promised equal rights for English and Afrikaans and declared that the Nationalist Party aimed at a republic inside the Commonwealth. But it took some time to get the whole party lined up on this issue. At more or less the same time the irrepressible Eric Louw in a speech inveighed against a 'Smuts Republic' and pointed out that if South Africa remained inside the Commonwealth, she would be 'hindered by British Liberalism in our efforts to solve the colour problem and the Jewish question'. Old habits die hard!

In a bid to break out of its self-imposed isolation and carry its policy to the English-speaking section, the Nationalist Party established in February 1945 an English weekly newspaper called *The New Era*, edited by Dr E. G. Jansen, who was later to become Minister of Native Affairs and then Governor-General. What impact this paper made on the English-speaking voters it is difficult to say, but it was probably very little. Certainly the paper did not survive for long, and since coming to power the Nationalists have made no effort to resuscitate it.

Later in 1945, after the war was over, the Nationalist Party decided to make an assault on the English-speaking citadel of Johannesburg and staged its congress in the City Hall. This proved to be more than Johannesburg would stomach at that early stage. An ex-serviceman's organization, the Springbok Legion, called a mass meeting of protest on the City Hall steps to coincide with the opening of the congress. When the meeting ended, the crowd surged round the corner in a fury and attempted to break into the Nationalist congress. A strong force of police held the crowd at bay by means of repeated baton charges, but the battle raged fiercely throughout the night. Next day, as the ex-soldiers rallied their forces, the police advised the Nationalist Party to abandon its conference, since they could not guarantee the safety of participants. Malan and other top leaders were hustled out of the City Hall through a side-door, and the congress came to an end.

The approach to the English-speaking section had not got off to a very promising start, and in fact it is doubtful if many English votes were cast for the Nationalists in the 1948 election. Where Malan did make progress, however, was in winning ever greater support from the Afrikaners. The Afrikaans-speaking ex-serviceman, who probably voted for Smuts during the war, was soon brought back into the fold after demobilization, when he was once more subjected to pressure from Church, party, Press, and the hundred and one *volksorganisasies* with which he came into contact.

Malan also took steps to regularize his relations with the other Afrikaans political organizations. With the Ossewa Brandwag he still refused to have any truck, and in September 1944 the Transvaal Nationalist congress declared that membership of the O.B. was incompatible with membership of the Nationalist Party. But he entered into negotiations with the Afrikaner Party, led by N. C. Havenga, and by March 1947 the two parties had reached agreement to fight the 1948 elections as a united team. Malan thus abandoned the isolated stand he had adopted in 1943, no doubt considering that the moderation of the Afrikaner Party would help to win over a considerable proportion of those Afrikaners still supporting the United Party, while conceivably appealing as well to some English-speaking voters.

Meanwhile, the character of the Afrikaner Party had itself undergone a great change since the war. Members of the Ossewa Brandwag, barred from the Nationalist Party, had been advised to make the Afrikaner Party their home in the territory of party politics, and by 1948 it was estimated that some eighty per cent of Afrikaner Party members were also members of the Ossewa Brandwag, while van Rensburg himself was on the party's Executive Committee. The 'moderate' Afrikaner Party was thus little more than a parliamentary front for the Ossewa Brandwag.

Malan appeared to be driving the devil out of one side of his house and admitting him through the other.

Further to the right the discredited remnants of the New Order, the Greyshirts, and the Boerenasie in 1944 attempted to form a National Socialist Front. With the defeat of Hitler, however, their appeal had vanished and they gained no ground, though they threw their weight behind the Nationalist-Afrikaner Party alliance in the 1948 elections.

The main gimmick produced by the Nationalist Party for the general elections of 1948 was a new colour policy – the doctrine of apartheid. This was the work of a special commission which had been appointed by the party and was proclaimed in a pamphlet issued by the Head Office of the Nationalist Party shortly before the end of 1947. It said:

The policy of our country should encourage total apartheid as the ultimate goal of a natural process of separate development.

It is the primary task and calling of the State to seek the welfare of South Africa, and to promote the happiness and well-being of its citizens, non-White as well as White. Realizing that such a task can best be accomplished by preserving and safeguarding the White race, the Nationalist Party professes this as the fundamental guiding principle of its policy.

The pamphlet further declared that:

the Bantu in the urban areas should be regarded as migratory citizens not entitled to political or social rights equal to those of the Whites. The process of detribilization should be arrested.

The party proposed that apartheid should also be applied to the Coloureds, while the Indians were offered only the prospect of repatriation to India. The party regarded the Indians as an unassimilable element in South Africa.

There is no doubt that in its policy of apartheid the Nationalist Party had hit upon an election winner. To understand why, one has to consider what had been happening in the sphere of race relations under the Smuts Government.

The war had brought about a tremendous increase in industrialization and consequently in the demand for African labour. In the ten years up to 1943-4 the volume of output of manufacturing industry increased by 127·6 per cent, while industrial employment increased by 96·6 per cent, with particular expansion of the non-White labour force. For every 1,000 non-Whites employed in secondary industry in 1935, some 2,100 were employed in 1946, while the comparable figure for Whites was only 1,350.

The bulk of the increase in the non-White labour force was provided by African workers, and the consequent growth in the number of urban Africans created a variety of social problems, not the least of which was provided by the increased competition between them and the poor Whites, the bulk of whom were Afrikaners.

The more progressive-minded elements in the United Party attempted to make an adjustment, mental as well as physical, to cope with these problems. Speaking at a meeting of the Institute of Race Relations in the Cape Town City Hall in January 1942, General Smuts made the weighty pronouncement that the traditional segregation policy had been a failure. To segregation he opposed the idea of trusteeship, not for the benefit of the trustee but for the benefit of the ward.

There is a death-rate among the children, a sickness rate among the adults, which we cannot tolerate. . . .

When people ask what is the population of South Africa, I never say 2,000,000 (then the total White population). I think it is an outrage to say 2,000,000. This country has a population of over 10,000,000, and that outlook which regards the natives as not worth counting is the ghastliest mistake possible. . . . The native is carrying this country on his back.

In the same year Colonel Denys Reitz, Minister of Native Affairs, proposed the recognition of African trade unions, while Minister of Finance J. H. Hofmeyr proclaimed that henceforth White and Black should learn to live 'as common citizens of a common country'.

The government made some timid efforts to give effect to this new outlook, and a few social security measures for Africans, such as unemployment insurance and school-feeding allowances, were introduced. It also appointed the Fagan Commission to inquire into the situation arising from the increased African migration to the towns, and the Commission reported: that more than half the African population lived outside the Reserves in the European areas, on the farms and in the towns: that the Reserves were incapable of supporting the whole African population; that the urbanization of the Africans in the European areas was an irreversible trend which had to be accepted; and that it was impossible to confine the Africans to migratory labour.

Smuts had also set up a Social and Economic Planning Council to map out a programme for the future development of the country, and its Report No. 13, on the 'Economic and Social Conditions of the Racial Groups in South Africa', published in 1948, noted:

The townward movement which has characterized all the racial groups, but which is now becoming particularly marked among the natives, is therefore a natural response to economic pressure. From an economic point of view it is generally to be welcomed, since it usually implies a movement of labour to much more productive employment and hence to an increase in the national income. The movement must, of course, give rise to severe social stresses. But in the Council's view it would be wrong to try to eliminate these stresses by a futile attempt to stem the townward drift, since this would mean retarding economic development. Rather should the adjustment to the urban environment be assisted by positive measures such as the provision of adequate housing facilities and social services.

As we have seen, this ran directly counter to the apartheid policy of the Nationalist Party enunciated in 1947, which demanded that the townward drift of the Africans should be halted and labour maintained on a migratory basis. Fundamentally the differences between the two parties was due to the difference in their class basis. The United Party was the mouthpiece of the mining, financial, and industrial interests, mainly English and Jewish in composition, who stood to benefit from the industrial revolution through which the country was passing and were prepared to accept some of its social consequences. The Nationalist Party, on the other hand, was deeply rooted in the countryside, and while its advance guard was beginning to make incursions into the realms of finance and industry, it was still largely dominated by the outlook and needs of the farmer.

But it was not only the Nationalists who were alarmed by the urbanization of the African. A considerable portion of the United Party, especially that group with rural roots, was not prepared to take the road mapped out by the Fagan Commission and the Social and Economic Planning Council, and this division within the government was undoubtedly one of the factors responsible for the paucity of progressive legislation during the war and immediate post-war periods.

The result was that the problems accumulated – and nothing was done about them. Africans swarmed into the towns, many of them living in slums cheek by jowl with the poor Whites. In the African townships themselves overcrowding was intense, and the overflow spilled out into the surrounding areas where families squatted in conditions of indescribable squalor.

Pressing for improvements, the non-White organizations, trade unions, and the Communist Party launched militant campaigns of protest. In 1946, a total of 75,000 African miners came out on strike demanding a wage of 10s. a day. Smuts sent his police and troops to quell the strike, and thirteen Africans were shot dead and a large number injured in clashes on the Reef. Afterwards two trials were staged: one against members of the Johannesburg District Committee of the Communist Party and a number of other people who were eventually found guilty of assisting the continuation of a strike; the second, a charge of sedition against the members of the Central Committee of the Communist Party which dragged on for two years before being quashed in the Supreme Court.

The year 1946 also saw a great passive resistance campaign by South African Indians against the provisions of a law enacted by the Smuts government to peg property deals with Asians, who in return were given the right to elect three Whites to represent them in Parliament. The Indians rejected both portions of the Act and carried their fight right to the United Nations, where they succeeded in laying the basis for the mounting international condemnation of South Africa's apartheid policies.

Capitalizing on the troubles through which the country was passing and blaming them all on the integration policy of the United Party, the Nationalists warned that white civilization was in danger and fought to retain South Africa's traditional policy of *baasskap* (mastership).

The Transvaal leader of the Nationalist Party, J. G. Strijdom, had said at an earlier period:

Our policy is that the Europeans must stand their ground and must remain *baas* in South Africa. If we reject the *herrenvolk* idea and the principle that the white man cannot remain *baas*, if the franchise is to be extended to the non-Europeans, and if the non-Europeans are given representation and the vote and the non-Europeans are developed on the same basis as the Europeans, how can the European remain *baas*? . . . Our view is that in every sphere the European must retain the right to rule the country and to keep it a white man's country.

The official apartheid policy was couched in more polite language. The only alternatives before the country, the special commission of the Nationalist Party had reported, were apartheid or complete equality. The United Party was following the latter course. Only apartheid could save the country from the ultimate disaster of miscegenation.

It (apartheid) envisages the maintenance and protection of the indigenous racial groups as separate ethnological groups with possibilities to develop in their own territories into self-reliant national units. . . . National policy must be framed in such a way that it promotes the ideal of eventual total apartheid in a natural way.

On 14 July 1947, Strijdom told the Nasionale Jeugbond (Nationalist Youth Association) at Bloemfontein:

The only alternative is the policy of the Nationalist Party of separation and apartheid in the sense that the natives must stay in their own territories and should come to the cities only temporarily as workers.

Integration or apartheid – that was the issue put to the voters in the 1948 elections. Nobody could be quite sure as yet what apartheid meant, but at least everybody was quite clear what it did not mean. It did not mean equality; it did not mean race mixing; it did not mean integration and the extension of rights to the non-Whites. Fundamentally the Nationalist Party stood for *baasskap*, and everybody knew what *baasskap* meant.

The results of the 1948 general elections were: the Nationalist Party – seventy seats; the United Party – sixty-five seats; the Afrikaner Party – nine seats; the Labour Party – six seats; Native Representatives – three seats.

The Nationalist-Afrikaner Party coalition accordingly had seventy-nine seats to a total of seventy-four for their opponents. The Smuts government had been defeated, with General Smuts even losing his own seat of Standerton.

Though they had polled 140,000 votes fewer than their opponents, the Nationalist-Afrikaner Party combination was now in power. A stunned country listened to the results as they were broadcast over the radio throughout the night. Not even the Nationalists had expected such a landslide – a gain of thirty-six seats as compared with the 1943 elections. Many an ex-serviceman thought to himself: Was this the fruit of victory, that the admirers of Hitler should come to power?

As for Dr Malan, he was naturally triumphant.

'Today,' he said, 'South Africa belongs to us once more. For the first time since Union, South Africa is our own. May God grant that it will always remain our own.'

8. Making Power Secure

At the time of the 1948 elections those still serving sentences for war-time offences were Leibbrandt, Visser, and Van Blerk, with Holm (the South African Lord Haw Haw who broadcast from Germany), Strauss, and Pienaar imprisoned for having committed treason in Germany. All were released on the advent of the Nationalist government to power, the Minister of Justice, C. R. Swart, stating that it was necessary to heal the wounds created by the war.

The wounds of which he spoke were not those suffered by the men and women who had fought in the armed services against the Hitlerites, or by the near relatives of the many South Africans who had sacrificed their lives. They were the spiritual wounds of Nationalist Afrikanerdom, certain of whose 'soldiers' had been punished for offences against the State during war-time. The new government's action created an uproar, but since this was not reflected in Nationalist ranks it was ignored.

On his release Leibbrandt immediately announced his intention of establishing an 'anti-communist front' on military lines to support the Nationalist government. For this, however, the country was not yet ready, and after pressure had been brought to bear on him Leibbrandt announced that he was abandoning the plan to avoid embarrassing the Nationalist government. Years later, when former Ossewa Brandwag general B. J. Vorster was made Minister of Justice, Leibbrant was to revive his plan; and this time the Minister would declare his willingness to receive help in the struggle against Communism no matter from what quarter it came.

From the moment that it came to power, the Nationalist government was acutely aware that it represented a minority of the electorate, and it immediately took action to strengthen its position. This took the form of (*a*) legislative and other steps to increase its representation in parliament and undermine the electoral basis of the opposition; (*b*) the establishment of effective control over the army and police force, civil service and railways, etc; and (*c*) the implementation of the basic apartheid laws so as to fragment the population and make Nationalist Afrikanerdom the dominant national group in a multi-national country.

There has been nothing haphazard or *laissez-faire* about Nationalist rule, in striking contrast to previous régimes. Operating on the basis of a preconceived ideology which has undergone very little change in the last fifteen years, the Nationalists have planned their strategy with care and worked step by step towards their goal. Nothing has been left to chance.

When Malan became Prime Minister he enjoyed a majority of only five in the House of Assembly, and once the Speaker and the Chairman of Committees had been appointed, his majority was reduced to four in the full Assembly and three in committee. In the Senate the government was actually in a minority, and even after the reconstitution of the Senate as provided by law the government and the opposition were equal. The seat of one opposition Senator, a native Representative, was, however, vacant during the first sitting, so that the government enjoyed a working majority of one. Nevertheless, the position of the government could only be described as precarious; the slightest mischance, and its slender majority might disappear. Its power hung by a thread.

Step by step the government increased its majority. In March 1949 Senator J. M. van Brink was put out of the opposition caucus because he found that he was not opposed to apartheid. Eventually the Nationalists elected P. W. Joint in his place. In the Assembly, Rood (United Party) resigned, and Loock was elected for the Nationalist Party by sixteen votes to represent Vereeniging. The Nationalists had accordingly gained two seats, but still the gap between them and the opposition remained too narrow for comfort.

In the 1949 session of Parliament the Nationalists placed the issue beyond any doubt by the passage of a Bill giving South-West Africa representation in the Union Parliament by six elected M.P.s and four Senators, one of whom was to be nominated by the government for his knowledge of 'the reasonable wants and wishes' of the 'Coloured races' of the territory. The Bill was something of a legislative masterstroke. On the one hand it was a formal step towards the incorporation of the territory in the Union of South Africa, despite the demand of the United Nations that South-West Africa be handed over to the U.N. Trusteeship Committee like all the other former mandated territories. Since General Smuts before him had also defied the United Nations on this issue, Dr Malan was sure of widespread popular support for his proposal, any opposition to which could easily be dismissed as unpatriotic. At the same time, the passage of the Act was a piece of blatant constitutional juggling in the interests of the Nationalist Party, which was assured of support not only from the majority of Afrikaners in the territory but also from the Germans, still smarting from their treatment by Smuts during and immediately after the war, when it had been proposed to deport several hundred of those regarded as hard-core Nazis.

The representation granted to South-West Africa was out of all proportion to the electorate, which numbered only 24,000 Whites at the time. In South Africa proper a constituency varied in size between just under 9,000 and just over 12,000 voters. Under the South-West Africa Act, however, the size of a constituency became a mere 4,000. In the event, all six seats have been won by the Nationalists ever since the first elections for the territory in 1950. The four Senators have likewise all been Nationalists.

Thus in South-West Africa, which handles its own budget, the White minority gets representation in the South African Parliament without taxation; whereas in South Africa as a whole the non-White majority gets taxation without representation in Parliament. Such is the logic of apartheid.

The next step taken by the Nationalist Party to strengthen its position was at the expense of its ally, the Afrikaner Party. This took the form of an announcement on 25 June 1951, that the two parties were uniting into one which would be known as the Nasionale Party. The statement declared that the name had been chosen because it 'formerly described the political home of both our cooperating parties, and also included all nationally-minded Afrikaners from both language groups'. Through co-operation, the statement added, 'Afrikanerdom has risen out of the condition of disunity, impotence, and mortification in which it found itself ... regained its self-respect and has actually reached a climax of unity and power'.

For the Afrikaner Party this was the kiss of death. The result of the merger was the elimination of all former parliamentary members of the Afrikaner Party with the exception of its leader, N. C. Havenga himself. The remaining Afrikaner Party M.P.s were rejected as Nationalist candidates for the 1953 elections, and Afrikaner Party influence within Nationalist ranks simply disappeared. From this time onwards the Nationalist Party has been the sole representative of 'Afrikanerdom' in the political field. Groups of Nationalist dissidents which have attempted to form themselves from time to time have been pulverized by the Nationalist Party machine.

A further legislative measure taken by the Nationalist government to strengthen its position amongst the White voters was the passage of the Electoral Laws Amendment Act of 1958, whereby the vote was extended to White persons of eighteen years and over (the previous age limit had been twenty-one). The opposition strongly attacked the new measure, pointing out that people legally unable to conduct their affairs without the assistance of a parent or guardian were now being granted a say in the running of the State. But argument proved useless, as most of the newcomers to the voters' roll would be Afrikaners, and hence mostly Nationalists. By 1951 the Afrikaner birth-rate was one third higher than the English, with the median Afrikaner age being twenty-three compared with thirty for the English-speaking group.

More serious were the steps taken by the Nationalist government to restrict or eliminate altogether the non-White franchise – Indian, Coloured, and African – since most of the non-Whites were inevitably anti-Nationalist. Only a small minority in each non-White group ever supported apartheid, and they were generally condemned by their communities as government stooges. The vast bulk of non-Whites are and always have been opposed to apartheid and, if possessed of the vote, could be expected to use it solidly against the Nationalist government.

A more deep-seated reason for disfranchising the non-Whites lay in the traditional attitude of the Nationalists to the franchise as the preserve of Whites alone. 'The Volk desires to permit of no equality between Coloured and White inhabitants in Church or State,' declared the Transvaal Grondwet (constitution) of 1858. It was one of the coincidences of history that round about the same period, in 1853, the grant of representative government to the Cape should have produced a franchise which, while laying down certain property and educational qualifications, placed no restriction on any voter because of race or colour. When Union came into being in 1910, the Cape's non-racial franchise was retained, but was not extended to the other provinces, and Nationalist Afrikanerdom has ever since fought strenuously to eliminate the non-White vote and restore the constitutional colour bar of the Boer republics.

In the very first session of Parliament after its advent to power in 1948, the Nationalist government passed two laws to restrict even further the already limited franchise of the non-Whites. The first was the Asiatic Laws Amendment Act, withdrawing the representation in Parliament and the Natal Provincial Council which had been granted to the Indians by the Smuts government in 1946 as a *quid pro quo* for the Pegging Act. True, the Indians, conducting a passive resistance campaign against the Act, had rejected the franchise, and no elections had ever been held. But the Malan government felt it necessary to place the issue beyond doubt by deleting the franchise clauses from the Act altogether.

The second measure was the Electoral Law Amendment Act, which provided that the application form of a Coloured voter should be witnessed and completed in the presence of an electoral officer, a magistrate, or a police officer of a rank not below that of a second-class sergeant, or police officer in charge of a police post or his deputy. Previously a voter could complete his form without supervision, and all that was required was its lodgement with the electoral officer.

'If this amendment is carried,' commented H. G. Lawrence, former Minister of Justice, expressing the opposition viewpoint in the House, 'it will in practice make it virtually impossible for any qualified Coloured persons to be registered.'

His warning proved to be justified. Though approximately 120,000 Coloured persons are estimated to be eligible, the number of voters on the roll has never risen as far as 50,000. Difficulty of registration is not, of course, the only factor preventing Coloureds from enrolling themselves. There has always been widespread apathy towards the White-controlled elections, and a section of the Coloured people has even conducted a bitter boycott campaign against them, while the placing at last of the Coloured voters on a separate roll effectively killed Coloured interest in the parliamentary battle. According to figures given by the Minister of the Interior in 1959, the number of Coloured voters on 30 June 1948 was 46,051; on 2 May 1953, 47,849; on 3 April 1958, 19,128; and on 17 December 1958, 23,822. These figures must be compared with a European electorate of 1,800,748 at the time of the republican referendum in 1960.

What frightened the Nationalist government was not the actual strength of the Coloured vote in 1948, but the potential strength of the whole non-White vote if the principle of a non-White franchise were permitted to survive and educational opportunities were extended to all sections of the population. The non-Whites, after all, constituted the majority. So long as they were allowed to belong to the same body politic as the Whites, the day would surely dawn when they would predominate and govern the Whites instead. The answer was obvious. Only the White man should be represented in parliament.

Abolition of African representation in parliament had been part of the Nationalist Party programme in the 1948 elections, but the Afrikaner Party leader N. C. Havenga felt obliged to honour the 1936 agreement to which he had been a party, and when the Afrikaner Party merged with the Nationalists in 1951, it was tacitly agreed to shelve the question of the African franchise for the time being. Instead, all attention was concentrated on the Coloured vote.

The history of the Separate Representation of Voters Bill from the time that it was introduced in 1951 until it became law in 1956 showed that the Nationalist government would go to any lengths to twist the constitution to its purposes. Everything that was done was done lawfully, it is true. But in the process the whole tradition of parliamentary government was trampled in the dust.

The Separate Representation of Voters Bill proposed to remove the Coloured voters from the common roll in the fifty-five Cape constituencies and place them on a separate roll instead which would then elect four Whites to the House of Assembly at regular five-yearly intervals, though not at general elections. The value of this exchange can be gauged from the fact that the Coloured vote was significant in about half of the Cape constituencies, and decisive in seven. Removal of the Coloured vote from the common roll would thus be of immediate benefit to the Nationalist Party, quite apart from the ideological considerations.

The Bill was passed first by the Assembly and then by the Senate, sitting separately, in spite of the opposition argument that the franchise rights of the Coloured people were entrenched in the constitution and could therefore only be altered by a two-thirds majority vote of the two Houses of Parliament sitting together. The legislation was then tested in the courts, and the Appellate Division handed down a unanimous judgement on 20 March 1952, declaring that the entrenched clauses of the Act of Union were still in force and that the Separate Representation Act was null and void because it had not been passed in the manner prescribed by the constitution.

Dr Verwoerd, then Minister of Native Affairs, had declared on 7 June 1951, that if the courts rejected the Bill, Parliament would immediately reverse the decision, and as soon as the judgement had been delivered, Dr Malan stated that it had produced an unacceptable constitutional position, drawing the courts into the political sphere and endangering the legislative supremacy of Parliament. The government, he said, would take steps to ensure that this sort of thing did not happen again. Government fury at the Appeal Court knew no bounds. One Cabinet Minister referred to the judges as the 'handful of old man in Bloemfontein' (the seat of the Appeal Court). Another called them 'a bunch of liberals'. The thin line separating the judicial from the executive power became obvious to all, and the country awaited the government's next step in a mood of some apprehension.

In the 1952 session of parliament, the government introduced the High Court of Parliament Bill 'to vest in the democratically elected representatives of the electors, as representing the will of the people, the power to adjudicate finally on the validity of laws passed by Parliament'. This measure provided that a Special Committee of the Union Parliament, composed of its members and called the High Court of Parliament, should have the power to review any judgement of the Appeal Court which invalidated any Act. This new High Court was expressly declared to be a court of law, and its decisions were to be final and binding in the same way as those of the Supreme Court.

The attitude of the Nationalist Party to this flimsy device was illustrated by S. M. Loubser who said in the debate: 'The United Party comes and whines, "the constitution". Anyone would think that the constitution was of greater importance to them than the maintenance of White civilization in our country.'

At the committee stage of the Bill the opposition refused to participate further, on the grounds that the Bill was a fraud and that they wished to waste no time in discussing the details. Then, early in August, the Cape Provincial Division of the Supreme Court temporarily barred the removal of Coloured voters from the common roll pending a decision of the courts on the High Court of Parliament Act. Late in the same month the High Court of Parliament met in Pretoria. The Court comprised only the Nationalist Members of Parliament, since the opposition refused to have any truck with it, but it felt itself competent to reverse the Appeal Court decision on the Separate Representation of Voters Act none the less, and on 28 August issued its 'verdict'. The true verdict, however, was pronounced on the following day by the Cape Supreme Court, which declared the Act invalid, a decision unanimously upheld in November by the Appeal Court.

Malan now decided to comply with the requirements of the constitution and the courts and, after the 1953 elections, submitted the Separate Representation of Voters Act to a joint session of the Assembly and the Senate, but he failed to secure the necessary two-thirds majority. He then directly threatened the Appeal Court by introducing an Appellate Division Bill to provide for a Court of Constitutional Appeals which would become the only court competent to hear appeals relating to Acts of Parliament. Using this as a big stick, he belaboured the opposition parties, trying to win the support of sufficient conservative United Party members to achieve his elusive majority and so place the Coloured voters on a separate roll constitutionally. His tactics were not entirely misdirected. In the period from 1953 to 1955, six members of the United Party were expelled from the caucus and formed themselves into the Conservative Party; while one, Dr Bernard Friedman, hived off to the left and ultimately joined the Progressive Party.

Believing that he had made significant progress in undermining the opposition, Malan withdrew the Appellate Division Bill and placed a Separate Representation of Voters Validation and Amendment Bill before another joint session of the Assembly and Senate during 1954. But this, too, failed to secure a two-thirds majority.

In November 1954, Dr Malan suddenly resigned as Prime Minister. To this day nobody outside the inner circles of the Nationalist Party really knows why. Perhaps he had balked at the next necessary step in the struggle over the Coloured vote, though Nationalist politicians have never been remarkable for squeamishness in the attack on non-White rights. He had wanted Havenga to succeed him and made it plain where his preference for the leadership lay. But Transvaal strong-man J. G. Strijdom allowed himself to be nominated and was duly elected Prime Minister. Havenga retired completely from the political scene – the last of the Hertzogites, broken by the extremist faction in the Nationalist Party.

Strijdom proceeded to attack both the Appellate Division and the Senate. He (a) appointed five new judges to the Appellate Division – presumably judges in whom he reposed complete confidence; (b) in May 1955 had Parliament pass the Appellate Division Quorum Act, raising to eleven the number of judges required to sit in any case involving the validity of an Act of Parliament; (c) in June 1955 propelled through Parliament a Senate Act to enlarge the Senate from forty-eight to eighty-nine members, elected on a basis which ensured that the Nationalists would enjoy the preponderant majority. In the event, seventy-seven members of the new Senate were Nationalists, compared with thirty in the old one.

Then, with the ground prepared for victory, Strijdom convened another joint sitting of both Houses in February 1956 and submitted to it a South Africa Act Amendment Bill which (a) removed the entrenchment of voting rights from the constitution; (b) debarred any court from inquiring into the validity of any law other than a law dealing with the only remaining entrenchment, namely, equality of language rights; and (c) validated the Separate Representation of Voters Act of 1951. With the overwhelming support of its cohorts in the new Senate, the Nationalist government won the day by 173 to 68 votes. In November 1956, the new Appellate Division ruled both the Appellate Division Quorum Act and the Senate Act valid by ten votes to one – and the Coloured voters were finally off the common roll, after a six-year struggle which had shaken the constitutional structure of South Africa to its foundations.

The form of representation now enjoyed by the Coloured people must be regarded as temporary. It corresponds with the representation granted to the African people in 1936 and is likely to prove of even less value and shorter duration. For it contradicts the basic Nationalist doctrine that the separate non-White groups should develop 'on their own lines', with their own representative institutions, preferably in their own 'homelands', and must not enjoy rights or representation in the White areas or the White parliament.

The disappearance of Havenga from the political scene made it possible for the Nationalists to proceed with the total disfranchisement of the African people. This took the form of the quaintly worded Promotion of Bantu Self-Government Bill, introduced in the 1959 parliamentary session, which linked the

E

abolition of African representation in Parliament with the concept of separate territorial development, or the establishment of 'Bantustans' as the new African tribal 'homelands' have come to be known. Theoretically, the abolition of all parliamentary representation for Africans was supposed to be balanced by the creation of 'self-governing' African territories, which would enjoy their own representative institutions or parliaments. All that need be said at this stage is that African representation was abolished before any 'self-governing' Bantustan had come into existence, and that for some years now Africans have been totally deprived of any voice at all in the councils of the nation.

A White Paper explaining the background and purpose of the Bill declared that all impediments to the development of the African areas had to be removed.

The greatest impediment is the representation of the Bantu in the highest institution of European government. . . . On the one hand it is the source of European fears of being swamped by the Bantu in the political sphere, and on the other hand it fails to stimulate the development by the Bantu of Bantu institutions because it fosters expectations of greater participation in European political institutions and promotes the desertion of trained human material from service within its own community. . . . Participation in the government of the guardian territory does not form part of the preparation of the subordinate units for the task of self-government. . . . (It) is in effect a signpost to the alternative direction which has been rejected. . . . Such representation is, therefore, now to be abolished.

During the debate in the Assembly, the Prime Minister said: 'One cannot confuse two systems and two directions.' He gave two reasons for the removal of the Native Representatives. 'The one is that they do not form part of the pattern we are now choosing, and the second is that they abuse their position as Members of Parliament by inciting the natives against the national policy in the Reserves, to which they only have access as such (Members).'

Opposition to this aspect of the Bill was widespread throughout the country. The Native Representatives had been by far the most consistent opponents of the government's apartheid policies. Doyen of the group was Mrs Margaret Ballinger, who had represented Africans in the Assembly ever since the first election following the passage of the original Act in 1936 and was regarded as an institution in her own right. Her colleagues had included members of the Liberal and Communist Parties, all of whom had made a significant contribution to the struggle against racial rule.

Perhaps the most forceful parliamentary opposition to the Bill was provided by J. D. du P. Basson, a member of the Nationalist Party, who was expelled from his party caucus over the issue. He said:

Parliamentary democracy is never exposed to greater and more actual danger than when a political party which is in power at a specific moment and which has been given a limited mandate for a period of five years, uses the parliamentary machine to change the constitution of Parliament in a way which, deliberately or otherwise, strengthens its own political position.

Basson also revealed that the Promotion of Bantu Self-Government Bill, with all its profound implications, had never been discussed within the Nationalist Party before it was introduced in Parliament.

This radical change which has been introduced into the party's policy . . . has taken place without any of the senior governing bodies . . being consulted on the matter in advance – neither the Federal Council, nor the Head Committee of the party . . . and not even the caucus of our parliamentary party; not to mention the voters.

The whole procedure was typical of the methods pursued by the new Prime Minister, Dr Verwoerd, who had been elected by the Nationalist caucus after Strijdom died in August 1958. Verwoerd believes – or pretends he believes – that he derives his authority from God, and that nothing he thinks or does can ever be wrong. In his first broadcast to the nation after becoming Prime Minister, he declared: 'The grief which plunged the whole country into mourning was His will. But the life of the nation goes on. In accordance with His will, it was determined who should assume the leadership of the government in this new period of the life of the people of South Africa.'

In his cartoons of Verwoerd for some time after this speech, David Marais, of the *Cape Times*, included a telephone with the cord leading straight up out of the frame of the picture – presumably linking the Prime Minister with Heaven. Judging by a remark he made on one occasion, Verwoerd was not amused!

Yet he has only himself to blame. A reporter on a Nationalist newspaper once asked Verwoerd whether his work did not tax or strain him, whether he never got ill under the burden of so much responsibility.

'No,' said Dr Verwoerd. 'I do not have the nagging doubt of ever wondering whether, perhaps, I am wrong.'

The Prime Minister does not argue with his opponents, he lectures them. His followers, if Basson's testimony is accurate, he apparently believes he can ignore. He, Verwoerd, will think for them.

Slowly, by consolidating the supremacy of the Nationalist Party among the White electorate, and eliminating any chance of challenge to that supremacy by the extension of the franchise to the non-Whites, the Nationalist Party increased its strength in the House of Assembly. In the 1953 general election it won ninety-four seats, to fifty-seven for the United Party and five for Labour. In the 1958 election the Nationalist Party gained 103 seats and the United Party fifty-three. Labour, whose seats had been won by agreement with the United Party, was eliminated because by 1958 the United Party considered the Labour Party an embarrassment and refused to renew the electoral alliance. In the 1961 elections (held eighteen months early because Verwoerd wanted the decks cleared for action in case non-Whites tried to put into effect their slogan of 'Freedom in 1963') the Nationalist Party advanced still further to 105, while the United Party obtained forty-nine seats, the National Union Party (led by J. D. du P. Basson and ex-Chief Justice Fagan in alliance with the United Party) one seat, and the Progressive Party one seat. The National Union later merged with the United Party. It had been formed with the idea of providing a bridge to the United Party for moderate Nationalists who were unhappy with Verwoerd's leadership, but had dismally failed.

The extent of the successive Nationalist victories is exaggerated, however, by the South African electoral system. The Nationalist Party came to power in 1948 although it had polled 140,000 votes fewer than its opponents. In 1953 it gained sixty-one per cent of the seats and only forty-five per cent of the votes. In the 1958 election the Nationalist Party polled 642,069 votes, to 503,639 for the United Party and a combined total of 6,096 votes for Labour, Liberals, and one anti-Nationalist Independent. But there were twenty-four seats for which United Party candidates were returned unopposed, and it is probable that if elections had been held in these seats, the United Party would once again have netted the largest number of votes.

The main reason for this paradox lies in the South Africa Act itself, which establishes five criteria for the delimitation of constituencies – community or diversity of interest, means of communication, physical features, existing electoral boundaries, and sparsity or density of population. Constituencies can be loaded by fifteen per cent above or below the basic quota, so that the difference in the number of voters between any two constituencies can be as high as thirty per cent.

A memorandum submitted to the tenth delimitation commission in 1952 by Advocate Arthur Suzman on behalf of the Torch Commando pointed out that over the years there had been 'a general though not entirely consistent tendency to weight a rural vote considerably more than an urban one.' The memorandum stressed that loading and unloading had increased substantially over the years. In 1923, for example, only four per cent of the seats had been loaded or unloaded between ten and fifteen per cent, whereas twenty years later the figure had jumped to fifty-nine per cent. The memorandum claimed that in consequence of loading and unloading under the 1948 delimitation, rural constituencies had gained six seats at the expense of urban ones which had meant in effect a difference of twelve seats, and that this was the way in which a minority of the electorate had been enabled to return a majority to Parliament.

Most rural seats were held by the Nationalist Party at that time; today all of them are. A further factor weakening opposition strength is the concentration of opposition voters in the urban constituencies, where their voting power is wasted because the seats are usually uncontested, whereas rural seats are often won by the Nationalists with very small majorities. Had seats been allocated according to votes, the Nationalists in the 1953 elections would have received seventy-one instead of ninety-four, and the opposition eighty-five instead of sixty-two.

Nevertheless, even allowing for these factors, the Nationalist position has steadily improved. In the republican referendum of 1960 it was possible for the first time to judge the relative strength of the parties in terms of actual votes cast. Those voting for a republic totalled 850,458; those against, 775,878. There were 7,436 spoilt papers and the average percentage poll was 90·75. Assuming that Nationalist Party members voted for a republic and that other parties opposed it (which is broadly what the position must have been), and assuming too that seats were allocated proportionately to votes, the Nationalist Party would have had 52·3 per cent of the total, or eighty-two members in the Assembly instead of the 102 it possessed at the time.

It is tempting to consider what the fate of South Africa might have been had the country enjoyed proportional representation, and had the United Party been sufficiently enlightened by the voting trend of 1948 to progressively extend the franchise. But facts have to be faced as they are, and the fact is that the United Party has sold the pass, failed to oppose Nationalist policies on basic principle, and by its tactics paved the way for successive Nationalist victories, with the gradual strengthening of the Nationalist grip on the South African body politic.

To some extent the United Party has been the prisoner of the country's steadily restricted franchise. Unable to strengthen itself from the ranks of voteless non-Whites, it has sought by a policy of appeasement to win over to its side the so-called 'moderate' Nationalists and has therefore always refused to adopt progressive policies which might alienate potential recruits. It has never been able to formulate a clear-cut alternative to apartheid. In fact, it accepts the basic doctrine of 'White supremacy', which it prefers to call 'White leadership', and differs from the Nationalist Party only over the details by which this is to be secured.

On 20 June 1957, the Prime Minister, J. G. Strijdom, proclaimed: 'If the white man is to retain the effective political control in his hands by means of legislation, then it means that the white man must remain the master. . . . We say that the white man must retain his supremacy.'

The leader of the United Party, Sir de Villiers Graaff, had said only the day before: 'When we get into power again there will also be discrimination.'

D. Mitchell, U.P. front-bencher from overwhelmingly English Natal, did not disagree: 'The United Party would never allow the effective political control of the country to pass into the hands of the non-Europeans.'

Nor did Senator Swart, U.P. leader in the Free State: 'Under our policy the white man will remain the master.'

These tactics, designed to assure the electorate that White supremacy will be safe under United Party rule, have convinced neither the U.P.'s friends nor its foes, and over the years since 1948 the party has shed support both to the right and to the left. We have already seen how the long-drawn-out dispute over the Coloured vote resulted in the breakaway of several U.P. members, most of whom subsequently joined the Nationalists. But there has also been a significant drift in the other direction. After the U.P. defeat in the 1953 election the Liberal Party was formed, at first advocating a limited franchise but then adopting a policy of universal adult suffrage in the hope of attracting non-White support. Similarly the U.P. defeat in 1958 was followed by the formation in 1959 of the Progressive Party, which stands for Cecil Rhodes's old policy of 'equal rights for all civilized men' irrespective of race. Showing more interest in parliamentary politics than the Liberal Party, which was by now concentrating more and more on the extra-parliamentary sphere, the Progressives were even able to win back some Liberals to the fold. Their impact on the electorate as a whole, however, has been limited, despite the courageous fight put up in parliament by their lone representative, Mrs Helen Suzman.

It is safe to say that so long as the future of South African politics is to be decided at the polls, so long will the Nationalist Party continue to dominate the scene – provided no overwhelming crisis, internal or external, supervenes, in which case some parties, and the alternatives to Nationalist rule submitted by the United and Progressive Parties, and even by the Liberal Party, are irrelevant because none of them will consider the mechanics of achieving power. The franchise cage itself, in which these parties are trapped, must be destroyed before politics can become free again in South Africa. That is why the real challenge to Nationalist rule is not presented by the parliamentary opposition, which has been reduced to a position of petulant impotence, nor by the Liberal Party, which still adheres to a policy of non-violent constitutionalism, but by the non-White peoples themselves who, denied the vote, are increasingly compelled to seek other and ever-more drastic channels of political expression.

*

While taking pains to strengthen their position in Parliament, and always being careful (once in power) to emphasize their respect for parliamentary democracy, the Nationalists have been equally assiduous in building up their battalions in the army and police force, the public service, the railways, and the courts. The same Broederbond-directed strategy which had won them the conquest of key positions *inside* the front of Nationalist Afrikanerdom was applied after the 1948 election to one sphere of public life after another. 'Smuts men' were chased out of office; Broederbond nominees took their places.

In the army, police force, railways, and public service, men who had lost promotion during the war because they had opposed the war effort were not only restored to the positions they would otherwise have reached but in several instances were given seniority over those who had loyally served their country. Grievances' commissions were appointed, and those who considered that they had been victimized because of their political affiliations during the war were given the opportunity of staking their claims to advancement.

In the railways, for example, the grievances' commission appointed by the Minister of Transport, Paul Sauer, received applications from 3,000 railway workers, and the grievances of 300 senior officials were upheld. The cost of the commission to the taxpayer was £52,000. To make way for their own nominee,

W. Heckroodt, the government forced the retirement of Marshall Clark as general manager of railways, at a cost to the country in compensation of £72,000.

An even more drastic purge was pursued in the army, and several experienced senior officers, with distinguished peacetime and war service, were relieved of command or forced to resign soon after the Nationalist government came to power.

Major-General W. H. Evered Poole, war-time General Officer Commanding the Sixth South African Armoured Division, was relieved of his appointment as Deputy-Chief of the General Staff three months after Erasmus became Minister of Defence. General Poole had been appointed to his position by the previous Minister of Defence, General Smuts himself, and in the normal course of events would have succeeded General Sir Pierre van Ryneveld as Chief of General Staff. Instead he lost his job, his post was abolished, and he was sent to Germany as head of the Union's military mission to the occupying powers. Later he was appointed to a diplomatic post as Union Minister to Greece, Italy, and Egypt. For political reasons, his military usefulness to the nation had been terminated.

When the Chief of Staff, General Sir Pierre van Ryneveld, retired, Erasmus recalled to service Major-General Len Beyers, who was appointed Chief of Staff for a two-year period with the rank of Lieutenant-General. But after completing only half of his two-year appointment, General Beyers resigned, stating:

My resignation was in fact tendered as far back as November 1949, in protest against the unconstitutional and unwarranted interference in the functions of the Chief of General Staff who, in fact and in law, is the Commander-in-Chief of the Forces in South Africa. The facts are that the Minister sought to change the strategic dispositions of units and to appoint, promote, and transfer both officers and other ranks, without sufficient knowledge of their qualifications and without reference to the General Staff, of which I was the head. Without reference to me, he created posts for the absorption of persons in whom, irrespective of their unsuitability or otherwise, he personally reposed political confidence. Political ambitions ... should not be allowed to intrude into the responsibility of command and functions of military organizations.

The Nationalist government's own nominee for the post of C.G.S. had found the methods of political indoctrination too much for him!

In 1952 a third senior officer, Brigadier J. T. Durrant, Director-General of the South African Air Force (South Africa's most experienced air officer, who had commanded a R.A.F. group in the war), resigned from the Union Defence Force. He stated that despite Ministerial assurances that there were no politics in the U.D.F., a senior officer on his own staff had said to the Chief of the General Staff (at that time Lieut.-General C. L. de Wet du Toit) in his presence: 'I want you to understand that I am 100 per cent Nationalist, and that anything I am reputed to have said or done has been in the interests of my Minister.'

When Brigadier Durrant had objected to this statement, the Chief of the General Staff ruled that such a declaration of politics could be made if so desired.

Commenting on affairs in the armed forces, Lieutenant-General George E. Brink, war-time General Officer Commanding the First South African Infantry Division, now retired, stated: 'A once magnificent defence organization has become a political toy, seething with discontent and frustration. . . . Men without war service are being appointed to command Active Citizen Force units . . . while we have witnessed the supersession, dismissal, and degradation of men who played prominent and distinguished roles as leaders in the field.' (*The Star*, 12 March 1952.)

Erasmus himself admitted in the House of Assembly that of 146 officers appointed to command *skietkommandos*, sixty-eight had had no military experience, while the previous experience of a further thirty-one was limited to school cadets. The chairman of a Nationalist Party branch wrote in a letter which was read out in the House: 'I know of a commandant who was appointed from outside the province concerned, and who at the first attempt missed all the shots at the target. He has had no military training, but wears the uniform and insignia of a commandant.'

Similar purges were conducted of the police, the public service, and every sphere in which the Nationalist government had power or influence. When the time came to appoint a Secretary for Native Affairs, the Nationalist government ignored the recommendation of the Public Service Commission and appointed Dr W. W. M. Eiselen, a Stellenbosch academic and apostle of apartheid, to the post. Even the courts were not immune. The composition of the Appeal Court was changed, of course, to suit the purposes of the Nationalist government in the struggle over the Coloured vote. But the day to day appointments of puisne judges were often politically motivated as well. Senator Leslie Rubin commented in an article 'Contempt of Court' (*Africa South*, January–March 1960):

Appointments to the Bench during the last few years have been puzzling and disquieting, for lawyer and layman alike. On the one hand members of the Bar, of impeccable character, ability, and experience, in some cases outstanding members of the profession, have been overlooked; on the other hand, lawyers of junior status and with limited experience have been appointed. To an extent not known before in the history of South Africa's courts, many cases are argued today by counsel before a judge who was several years his junior at the Bar. . . .

The Hon. Mr Justice Botha was appointed Judge-President of the Orange Free State Provincial Division twenty-two months after he had been appointed to the Bench, and at a time when he was junior to most of his colleagues on the Bench and to twenty-eight other puisne judges in the country. Among recent appointments to the Appellate Division, one is junior to fifteen, another to sixteen, and a third to twenty-three puisne judges in the country. The present Chief Justice, the Hon. Mr Justice Steyn, who had been law adviser to various government departments, was appointed to the Bench in the Transvaal (in the face of vigorous protests by the Transvaal Bar) in 1951, and to the Appellate Division in 1955. He is junior to two Judges of Appeal, and in judicial experience to seventeen of the fifty-nine judges in South Africa. His appointment as Chief Justice overlooked Appeal Judges Schreiner (seventeen years at the Bar, appointed to the Bench in 1937 and to the Appellate Division in 1945, who acted as Chief Justice) and Hoexter (called to the Bar in 1918, appointed to the Bench in 1938, and to the Appellate Division in 1949). The Hon. Mr Justice Beyers was appointed to the Bench of the Cape Provincial Division in 1955, and to the Appellate Division in 1958. In 1959 he returned to the Cape Provincial Division as Judge-President of a court which includes three judges senior to him in judicial experience.

While the courts are still nominally independent, there is little doubt that as a result of Nationalist manipulation the judiciary has swung sharply to the right. No outspoken Liberal, no matter how eminent in the profession, has any hope of an appointment to the bench today. On the other hand, men of more modest attainments may confidently look forward to preferment if they can satisfy the government that on race questions they are above suspicion.

The influence of the English-speaking section in the public service was reduced by the strict application of tests for bilingualism. At the time of Union the public service was largely English-speaking (nearly eighty-five per cent in 1912), so that the advancement of the Afrikaner tended to bring the service more into line with the proportions in the population as a whole. Even after the Nationalist government came to power there were inequalities. According to Sauer when he was still Minister of Railways, eighty per cent of railway personnel were Afrikaans-speaking, but sixty-seven per cent of those in the £1,000 a year and over income group were English. In 1951, however, the railway administration decided to group administrative posts in three categories based on the degree of bilingualism. One man was even refused promotion because he could not name the bones of the hand in Afrikaans!

In December 1953 the Deputy Postmaster-General gave figures indicating that while sixty-eight per cent of the total personnel in the Post Office were Afrikaans-speaking, only forty per cent of the senior posts were held by Afrikaners. No doubt a similar position existed in other branches of the service. In all, the requirements of bilingualism were more and more stressed with a view to redressing the balance, but often the results were unfortunate. In 1951 the Transvaal Provincial Administration lost a number of highly trained nurses, specially recruited in England, because they were unable to obtain promotion without passing bilingual tests. Similarly, the Air Force between 1947 and 1949 brought to the Union 284 specially selected R.A.F.

technicians, but more than 100 of them resigned by 1951 because of 'language difficulties'.

The net result of all this government intervention is that the Nationalists are today possessed of an army, a police force, and a public service overwhelmingly Afrikaner in complexion, and with all the key posts occupied by men acceptable to the Broederbond. The Nationalist stranglehold on Parliament is paralleled by complete domination of the bureaucracy. The apparatus of the State, in fact, has been effectively 'Nationalized'.

9. South Africa's Nuremberg Laws

> A people that fails to preserve the purity of its racial blood thereby destroys the unity of the soul of the nation in all its manifestations.
>
> HITLER in *Mein Kampf*

Nationalist legislation has been aimed, on the one hand, at preventing all forms of integration which might lead to the establishment of a united South African nation with a common citizenship and loyalty irrespective of race; and, on the other hand, at promoting the 'separate development' of the various races and ethnic groups 'in their own areas'. There are sixteen million South Africans, but the Nationalist government does not envisage that they will ever constitute one nation. On the contrary, it plans to unmix what has already been mixed, to separate one section from another, to enforce isolation and difference, to establish a rigid caste system backed with all the force of law. If the Nationalists have their way, South Africa will, economically, take the form of a pyramid, with the Whites at the apex, the Coloureds and Asians in the middle, and the Africans at the bottom. Politically and socially, however, the various groups will never meet, being separated from one another by impenetrable legal barriers as well as physical distance and the imponderable force of custom. (The Nationalist claim that under 'parallel development' the Blacks will be able to rise to the top in 'their own areas' shows few signs so far of being substantiated in practice.)

Here is a brief list of the laws, set down in the years of their passing, by means of which the Nationalists hope to have laid a secure foundation for the apartheid state.

1948 SESSION

Asiatic Laws Amendment Act. Withdrew Indian representation in Parliament (see page 124).

Electoral Laws Amendment Act. Made more stringent the conditions for registering Coloured voters (see page 124).

1949 SESSION

Citizenship Act. Lengthened the period of residence to five years for British subjects and six for aliens before South African citizenship could be obtained. The Act also provided for the withdrawal of acquired citizenship by the Minister of the Interior under certain circumstances.

Prohibition of Mixed Marriages Act. Made marriages between Whites and non-Whites illegal and placed the onus of deciding the race of any person on the marriage officer himself. If a person domiciled in South Africa entered into a mixed marriage outside the country, the marriage was to be void in South Africa.

Asiatic Land Tenure Amendment Act. Strengthened existing measures against 'penetration' by Indians of urban areas in Natal and the Transvaal, and prevented Indian 'penetration' of the Cape. (By law no Indians at all are permitted into the Free State or South-West Africa.)

Unemployment Insurance Amendment Act. Excluded from the benefits available under the Act all those whose earnings did not exceed £182 a year (the majority of African workers) and all migratory workers irrespective of their earnings.

Native Laws Amendment Act. Created special labour bureaux for Africans. These bureaux are designed, not primarily for the benefit of the workers, but to restrict the flow of African workers to the towns so that an abundant supply of labour is always available for the mines and the farms.

South-West Africa Affairs Amendment Act. Provided for the representation of South-West Africa's White citizens in the South African Parliament (see page 122).

1950 SESSION

The Population Registration Act. Established a racial register of the population to be compiled as soon as possible after the 1951 census. The population was to be classified into three main groups – Europeans, Coloured people, and Africans – with the Coloured people and Africans classified as well according to their ethnological section. Ultimately everyone would have to carry an identity card on which his race would be indelibly stamped once and for all. The crossing of racial boundaries by the so-called 'play-Whites' would become impossible.

The racial group of an individual was to be determined by his appearance and by general acceptance and repute. But in practice classification procedures have sometimes been crude in the extreme. A pencil shoved into the hair of a person under interrogation has been taken to demonstrate racial origin – if it remains fixed, he is African; if it falls out, Coloured, because the hair is smoother.

In a country where racial origin is the passport to success or failure, this Act has brought disaster into thousands of homes. White families have been declared Coloured at the stroke of a bureaucratic pen, with all the tragic consequences. At the beginning of February 1963 it became compulsory for every South African to be in possession of an identity card, yet there were still 20,000 Coloured-White 'borderline' cases to be settled. The Act, of course, has created at least as many problems as it has solved. Nature cannot be trifled with so easily. There are dark-looking people who have been classified as White, and light-skinned people who have become officially non-White. As a means of keeping the White community White, the Act must inevitably fail.

Suppression of Communism Act. Outlawed the Communist Party and much else as well (see page 165).

Immorality Amendment Act. Prohibited illicit carnal intercourse between White and non-White (the original 1927 Act prohibited intercourse only between White and African). No Act has done more to injure the reputation of South Africa in the eyes of the world, for thousands of people, ranging from visiting seamen to Dutch Reformed Church nominees and the private secretary to a Prime Minister have fallen foul of its provisions and been sent to jail. A total of 3,890 people were convicted under this Act between 1950 and 1960, according to figures given by the Minister of Justice in Parliament. By the very nature of the offence, the means of securing evidence is always distasteful, based on snooping and informing, the flashing of torches into motor-cars at night, the bursting into of private homes. No reasonable system of morality, furthermore, can tolerate the ethics of the Immorality Act, which condones immorality between people of the same race, but converts it into a criminal offence from the moment that the race groups are different.

Group Areas Act. Provided for the establishment of racial ghettoes in which ownership and occupation of land would be restricted to a specified population group. This immensely complicated Act, which cuts across all property rights, has been amended on innumerable occasions and is still in the process of enforcement, with many areas of the country not yet demarcated for the ownership or occupation of any group. Although in the 1962 session of Parliament the Minister of the Interior refused to supply any figures, trends so far indicate that the vast bulk of the country will be reserved for White ownership and occupation. To achieve the racial separation which is contemplated by this Act, hundreds of thousands of people will have to give up their homes and move to other areas; and as might have been expected, the majority of sacrifices will be made by non-Whites.

In Cape Town and the adjoining areas, the total numbers of people affected by Group Areas proclamations up to March 1961 were: White, 7,731; Coloured, 94,148; and Asian, 4,658. In Durban, according to a statement by the Minister of the Interior on 5 August 1958, a total of 1,000 Whites, 75,000 Indians, and 8,500 Coloured people will eventually have to be moved, together perhaps with 81,000 Africans. And if the central working areas and Clairwood should – as seems likely – also be zoned as White, an additional 54,000 Indians, 6,000 Coloured, and 44,000 Africans will be affected. In terms of proclamations made up to 1958, Indians would lose property with a rateable value of £5,548,620, while Coloureds and Africans would have to give up property worth £55,480 and £20,340 respectively. Indians maintain that the present market value of their affected properties is nearer £20 million.

Durban and Cape Town are the most racially mixed areas in South Africa, but a similar pattern results from Group Areas proclamations in other centres. Perhaps the most vicious application of the Act, indeed, has been in some of the country areas, where local authorities have put forward plans which would result in the dumping of the Indian population on bare veld some miles from the centre of the town and the site of their previous businesses. Such moves would result in the total ruination of the Indian communities concerned.

There have already been several cases of suicide by non-Whites whose homes and savings have been threatened by the application of the Act.

Privy Council Appeals Act. Abolished the right of appeal to the Privy Council from the South African courts.

1951 SESSION

Separate Representation of Voters Act. Provided for the removal of Coloured voters from the common roll (see page 126).

Bantu Authorities Act. Provided for the establishment of tribal, regional, and territorial Bantu Authorities in the reserves and abolished the Natives' Representative Council set up under the 1936 Representation of Natives Act. Bantu Authorities are not popularly elected but are appointed – and dismissed – by the Minister of Bantu Administration and Development.

Native Building Workers' Act. Permitted the training and registration of Africans as skilled building workers, but for work in African areas alone. Under this law, Africans are prohibited from working as odd-jobbers in urban areas, while Whites are prohibited from placing any contract with an African builder (see page 265.)

Prevention of Illegal Squatting Act. Prohibited anyone from entering upon any land or building, or any African location or village, without permission. Under this law, countless so-called illegal squatters have been ordered to remove themselves, and the structures or buildings erected by them have been destroyed.

1952 SESSION

Criminal Sentences Amendment Act. Provided that persons under fifty years of age convicted of certain offences, including robbery and house-breaking with intent to commit an offence, should be sentenced to a whipping not exceeding ten strokes, with or without imprisonment, though courts were empowered to suspend the sentence in whole or in part. The effect of this Act has been staggering. In the twenty years between 1942 and 1962, about 1,000,000 strokes have been administered to 180,000 offenders; *and 850,000 of these strokes have been administered since the 1952 Act was passed.* Latest figures show that more than 17,000 offenders receive more than 80,000 strokes each year, compared with 2,000 offenders and 12,000 strokes in 1942. But although the number of whippings has increased eight-fold in the last two decades, it has had no effect whatsoever on the incidence of crime, which has continued to mount at a greater rate than the increase of population.

High Court of Parliament Act. Passed to assist in the removal of Coloured voters from the common roll (see page 127).

Natives (Abolition of Passes and Coordination of Documents) Act. Provided, despite its fanciful name, for the consolidation of passes into a single document to be known as a reference book and issued to all Africans over the age of sixteen. Pasted in front is the identity card issued under the Population Registration scheme; and there are pages for entries relating to labour bureaux and influx control, the signatures of employers, poll tax receipts, any taxes imposed by Bantu Authorities, and other particulars. As the books are issued, finger-prints are taken and recorded in a central bureau.

Unlike the identity card of other races, which must be produced within seven days of demand, the reference book must always be carried on the person of the holder and produced on demand, failing which the offender may be arrested on the spot.

Under this Act African women have been subjected to the pass laws for the first time.

Native Laws Amendment Act. Provided that no African would be permitted to remain in an urban area for longer than seventy-two hours without a permit unless he had been born and was permanently resident there. Exceptions were to be made only in the case of those who had worked in one area continuously for one employer for not less than ten years, and for more than one employer for not less than fifteen years. The use of labour bureaux was made compulsory, so that no man might seek work without the permission of the local authority.

147

It is under this law that tens of thousands of Africans have been 'endorsed out' or summarily evicted from urban areas because their presence has been considered undesirable. Husbands have been separated from wives, parents from children, in order to ensure that the White-dominated economy gets its labour when, where, and how it wants it.

Linked with the pass laws has been the scheme – operated jointly by government departments, the police, and private farmers – whereby Africans who could not get work in the Johannesburg area, and those convicted of petty technical offences, have been contracted out to farmers, often against their will and without knowing that they had the option of appearing in court. A series of court cases in 1959, which exposed the whole scandal to the public, led the African National Congress to launch a potato boycott (the worst excesses were committed on the potato farms of the Eastern Transvaal), and eventually the government was forced to appoint a commission. But despite the exposure, and the extraordinary success of the boycott, which spread like wildfire through the country, the practice seems to be continuing, although on a smaller scale.

On many farms, labourers are forced to wear sacks as a working uniform, and are locked up at night in filthy, vermin-infested quarters; their bedding consists of sacks on bare concrete, and sanitation is of the primitive bucket type. Labourers are forced to work from sunrise to sunset on a diet consisting almost exclusively of mealie meal; and brutal assaults by 'boss boys' and farmers are an everyday occurrence.

Farmers do not attract labour in the ordinary way, because they refuse to pay an adequate wage and provide decent living and working conditions. They accordingly fall back on forced and convict labour as their main source of supply, for convict labour can be obtained at the rate of 9d a day from the numerous farm jails in South Africa.

Convictions for offences under influx control regulations and 'laws and regulations known as the pass laws' were:

1955	337,604
1956	356,812
1957	565,911

1958	396,836
1959	413,639
1960	340,958

The Native Services Levy Act. Laid down that urban employers of male Africans aged eighteen years and over should pay to the local authority a levy of 2s. 6d. a week for the provision and maintenance of water, sanitation, lighting, or road services outside an African township. In certain circumstances, the levy may also be used for subsidizing African transport services or for making loans and grants towards the provision and maintenance of services within an African township.

1953 SESSION

Bantu Education Act. Transferred Bantu Education from the provinces to the Department of Native Affairs (see page 205).

Immigration Regulation Amendment Act. Provided that the wives and minor children of Indian men permanently resident in South Africa should no longer be permitted to come from India to join them, except by special permission.

Reservation of Separate Amenities Act. Permitted any person in charge of any public premises or public vehicle to reserve such premises or vehicle for the exclusive use of any race or class. Such action was not to be ruled invalid (as had been done by the courts) on the ground that provision was not made for all races, or that the separate facilities provided for the various races were not substantially equal.

In other words, the doctrine of 'separate but unequal' was enshrined in South African law.

Native Labour (Settlement of Disputes) Act. Outlawed strikes by African workers and established a complicated machinery for the settlement of industrial disputes involving Africans (see page 265).

Criminal Law Amendment Act. Prescribed very severe penalties for the breaking of any law as a political protest (see page 170).

Public Safety Act. Provided for rule by decree in an emergency (see page 170).

1954 SESSION

Natives Resettlement Act. Provided for the establishment of a

Resettlement Board to undertake the forcible removal of 57,000 Africans from Sophiatown, Martindale, Newclare, and Pageview, the so-called 'black spots' in the western areas of central Johannesburg, to Meadowlands and Diepkloof, over ten miles south-west of the city. Sophiatown was one of the few remaining areas in South Africa where Africans enjoyed freehold land ownership rights. Such rights would not exist in the new townships, and furthermore all Africans were to be segregated there along tribal patterns. The population of the western areas was overwhelmingly opposed to the move, which had to be undertaken on military lines at gun-point.

Native Trust and Land Amendment Act. Removed the obligation on the government to find alternative land for displaced squatters. It was estimated that at least one million squatting labour tenants and other squatters would be affected if the Act were rigidly enforced.

Riotous Assemblies and Suppression of Communism Amendment Act. Removed the onus on the Minister to give a hearing to any person he proposed to ban, and rendered all 'named' Communists ineligible for election to Parliament or the Provincial Councils (see page 170).

South-West Africa Native Affairs Administration Act. Transferred the administration of African affairs in South-West Africa from the Administrator of the territory to the South African Minister of Native Affairs.

1955 SESSION

Departure from the Union Regulation Act. Laid down that no South African over the age of sixteen years should leave the Union unless in possession of a valid passport or permit, and empowered the Minister of the Interior to withdraw a passport at any time. This Act has been used as a weapon of widespread political intimidation. Not only is it exceedingly difficult for a non-White, particularly an African, to get a passport, but even prominent White opponents of the government such as Mrs Jessie MacPherson, Chairman of the Labour Party, and Alan Paton, author and Liberal Party leader – not to mention all those to the left of them – have had their passports withdrawn because they dared to criticize aspects of government policy.

Appellate Division Quorum Act. Enlarged the Appeal Court and qualified its right to pronounce on the validity of Acts of Parliament (see page 129).

Senate Act. Enlarged the Senate to facilitate the passage of the Separate Representation of Voters Bill (see page 129).

Criminal Procedure and Evidence Amendment Act. Empowered the police to enter and search premises without a warrant. In the debate on this measure the Minister of Justice made it clear that the Bill was aimed at the extra-parliamentary political opposition.

Natives (Urban Areas) Amendment Act. Prohibited owners of buildings in an urban area from allowing more than five Africans to reside in any one building at any time except with special permission from the Minister of Native Affairs. The Act was aimed at the so-called 'locations in the sky' – the increasing number of domestic servants housed at the top of blocks of flats. It was estimated that up to 20,000 Africans in Johannesburg alone would have to move out of their quarters and be obliged to pay increased rent and transport costs.

Motor Carrier Transportation Amendment Act. Gave the National Transport Board or local boards the power to enforce apartheid on transport services. The general manager of Johannesburg's municipal transport department estimated that if the policy of apartheid were abandoned, Johannesburg could make a profit of £500,000 a year on its bus and tram services instead of running them at a loss.

Criminal Procedure Act. Extended the powers of the police to kill someone suspected of committing an offence who was fleeing or resisting arrest.

1956 SESSION

Industrial Conciliation Act. Provided for the splitting of the trade union movement on racial lines and for the reservation of jobs on a racial basis (see page 270).

Native Administration Amendment Act. Permitted banishment orders to be served without prior notice to the person concerned.

Natives (Prohibition of Interdicts) Act. Laid down that, when an African was in receipt of a removal or banishment order, no court might issue an interdict which would have the effect of suspending execution, or suspend the order until the outcome of review proceedings or an appeal. The African – even if he were the wrong man and had had a notice served on him by mistake – was to remove himself first and argue his case afterwards, even though irreparable damage might have been caused to him and his family in the meantime.

Natives (Urban Areas) Amendment Act. Empowered an urban local authority – if it considered the presence of any African under its jurisdiction to be detrimental to the maintenance of peace and order – to instruct such an African to leave the area within a specified period and not return except with the local authority's permission. The Act was specifically aimed at so-called 'political agitators'.

South Africa Act Amendment Act. Revalidated the Separate Representation of Voters Act of 1951 (see page 129).

1957 SESSION

Native Laws Amendment Act. Contained *inter alia* the notorious 'church clause', in terms of which the Minister of Native Affairs was empowered to direct that the attendance of Africans at any church service in a White area should cease. Involving as it did the freedom of worship, this clause aroused widespread opposition, and the Christian Council of South Africa issued a statement declaring: 'If this clause ... becomes law, we shall be forced to disregard the law and to stand whole-heartedly by the members of our churches who are affected by it, and, if necessary, to suffer with them as our brethren in Christ.' With typical obstinacy the Nationalist government insisted on placing the clause on the statute book, but it was so impressed by the opposition that it has not invoked its powers against the churches yet.

In addition to placing further limitations on the right of Africans to enter and remain in an urban area, the Act made it an offence for any non-resident to enter or remain in an African location, village, or hostel without the permission of the managing official.

Group Areas Amendment Act. Prohibited members of a disqualified racial group from attending a public cinema, or partaking of refreshments in a licensed restaurant or refreshment room or tea room or eating house, or visiting any club, in a particular group or controlled area except under permit.

Native Laws Further Amendment Act. Gave the Minister power to deport so-called 'foreign natives', whose presence in South Africa was considered by the Minister not to be in the public interest.

Nursing Act. Provided for the introduction of apartheid into the nursing profession. Separate registers and rolls were to be kept of White, Coloured and African nurses, while the Nursing Council in control of the profession was to consist of White persons only.

Immorality Act. Increased the maximum penalty for illicit carnal intercourse between Whites and non-Whites to seven years imprisonment, while making it an offence not only for a White and a non-White together to commit an indecent or immoral act, but also to solicit one another to the commitment of any such act.

1958 SESSION

Criminal Procedure Amendment Act. Empowered the Supreme Court to apply the death penalty in cases of robbery or attempted robbery where the accused was proved to have inflicted or threatened to inflict grievous bodily harm, as well as in cases of house-breaking where the accused was proved to have carried a dangerous weapon, or to have committed or threatened assault.

As with other Nationalist legislation that has increased penalties for specified crimes, this Act has had no effect on the incidence of serious crime, which has continued to mount at a greater rate than the increase of population.

Electoral Laws Amendment Act. Extended the franchise to White persons over eighteen years of age (see page 123).

Natives Taxation and Development Act. Provided that every male African of eighteen years and over should pay basic general tax at the rate of £1 15s. a year instead of £1 as previously. Men earning over £180 a year would pay increased amounts on a sliding scale, while African women were made liable to pay general tax for the first time.

1959 SESSION

Bantu Investment Corporation Act. Established a corporate body known as the Bantu Investment Corporation of S.A. Ltd to promote and encourage the economic development of Bantu persons in the Bantu areas, by the provision of money, technical, or other assistance, and expert advice. The affairs of the corporation were to be managed by a board of directors appointed by the Minister and consisting of Whites alone.

Africans (mainly Bantu Authorities) had invested £224,000 with the corporation by May 1962, while the bulk of development initiated by the corporation so far has been the establishment of general dealers' businesses, butcheries, cafés, etc. and is negligible in relation to the economic needs of the Reserves as a whole. Meanwhile, the development of an African middle class in the urban areas has been discouraged, with Africans told that they must look to the Reserves for their economic expansion.

Criminal Laws Amendment Act. Provided for 'week-end' periodical imprisonment and laid down minimum sentences for certain categories of offence.

Prisons Act. Made it an offence to sketch or photograph or publish a sketch or photograph of a prison or prisoner, or to publish false information about a prisoner or ex-prisoner or the administration of any prison, with the onus placed on the publisher to prove that he had taken reasonable steps to ascertain the veracity of his story. The effect of this Act has been to discourage the Press from exposing jail atrocities.

Extension of University Education Act. Provided for the exclusion of non-White students from the hitherto open universities and the establishment of segregated colleges on ethnic lines for the various non-White races (see page 216).

University College of Fort Hare Transfer Act. Transferred control of the college to the Minister of Bantu Education, to change an open university of high academic standards into a tribal college of low ones, with a staff carefully purged of all liberal elements (see page 216).

Industrial Conciliation Amendment Act. Gave the Minister of Labour power to outlaw strikes in the canning industry.

Motor Carrier Transportation Amendment Act. Enabled Transportation Boards to enforce apartheid in taxi services throughout the Cape and Natal. In the other two provinces such discrimination already existed.

Promotion of Bantu Self-Government Act. Abolished African representation in Parliament and outlined procedures for the establishment of so-called 'self-government' in the Reserves (see page 129).

1960 SESSION

Factories, Machinery, and Building Work Amendment Act. Empowered the government to order the provision in factories of separate entrances, clocking-in devices, pay offices, first-aid rooms, protective clothing, crockery, cutlery, and work-rooms for the various races. The government already possessed such powers in relation to the provision of separate sanitary conveniences, washrooms, changing rooms, rest rooms, dining-rooms and work places where the employees of different races worked in the same room.

Referendum Act. Provided for the holding of a referendum on the establishment of a republic (see page 134).

Reservation of Separate Amenities Amendment Act. Provided for the enforcement of apartheid on beaches.

Senate Act. Reduced the size of the Senate, which had been enlarged in 1955 to facilitate the passage of the Separate Representation of Voters Bill, from eighty-six to fifty-four members. In the new Senate the government has thirty-nine representatives and the opposition, fifteen.

Unlawful Organizations Act. Empowered the Governor-General to ban the African National Congress and the Pan-Africanist Congress (see page 176).

1961 SESSION

Defence Amendment Act. Empowered the Minister of Defence to order any person or class of persons to evacuate or assemble in any particular building or premises or area in time of war or during operations for the prevention or suppression of internal disorder. To avoid the suspicion that he was aiming at the establishment of concentration camps, the Minister limited the period for which such an order can remain in force to four days, though the order itself may then be renewed.

Defence Further Amendment Act. Extended the period of military training for White youths selected by ballot.

Police Amendment Act. Provided for the recruitment of a White police reserve.

General Law Amendment Act. Provided for detention without bail for up to twelve days (see page 180).

Indemnity Act. Laid down that no proceedings, whether civil or criminal, arising from acts committed during the 1960 state of emergency, could be brought in any court of law against the government and its officers. It had been announced in the Press that in consequence of the disturbances at Sharpeville, 244 claims had been instituted against members of the government for a total of £450,000 – made up of approximately £250,000 for compensation on account of the death of breadwinners, £150,000 for personal injury, and £50,000 for alleged unlawful arrest. As a result of the Act, none of these claims could be pursued.

Liquor Amendment Act. Removed all restrictions on the purchase of alcohol by Coloured people and Asians for off-consumption, and empowered holders of off-consumption licences to sell liquor to any African aged eighteen and over.

Republic of South Africa Constitution Act. Established the Republic, headed by the State President, and outside the Commonwealth since the Prime Ministers' Conference of March 1961.

Urban Bantu Councils Act. Permitted an urban local authority to establish an urban Bantu Council for any African residential area under its jurisdiction, such council to consist of elected and selected members, with the number of selected members not exceeding the number elected. Urban Bantu Councils were to be vested with civil and criminal jurisdiction and with a limited control of finances. Designed to replace the advisory board system, the councils are intended as a substitute for the direct representation of Africans on the urban local authorities themselves, a practice contrary to government policy. By March 1963, no urban Bantu Councils had yet been established.

1962 SESSION

Coloured Development Corporation Act. Established a Coloured Development Corporation to encourage and promote the economic development of the Coloured people in 'their own areas'. The Board of the Corporation is to consist only of Whites.

General Law Amendment Act. The so-called 'Sabotage Act' laid down a minimum penalty of five years and a maximum of death for sabotage, and provided for the placing of government opponents under house arrest (see page 183).

General Law Further Amendment Act. Provided that anyone who painted slogans on walls should be liable to imprisonment for a period not exceeding six months in lieu of or in addition to any other penalty which might be imposed under another law. This was the government's answer to a political slogan painting campaign which had flourished in many centres during 1961 and 1962.

National Education Advisory Council Act. Provided for the establishment of a National Education Advisory Council, to consist of not less than fifteen members appointed by the Minister of Education. This measure is regarded as a further step towards centralized government control of education, at present under the control of the provinces (see page 204).

1963 SESSION

Defence Amendment Act. Enabled members of the Citizen Force and Commandos to be called out in support of the police to suppress internal disorder.

Better Administration of Designated Areas Act. Provided, *inter alia*, for the mass removal of population and the elimination of freehold land ownership rights for Africans in Alexandra Township, near Johannesburg.

General Law Amendment Act. Provided for the detention of persons without trial for the purpose of interrogation (see page 189).

Bantu Laws Amendment Act. Eliminated Africans' rights to residence in the urban areas (see page 312).

Transkei Constitution Act. Provided for so-called 'self-government' in the Transkei (see page 307).

Coloured Persons Education Act. Surrendered the control of education for Coloured persons to the Department of Coloured Affairs (see page 214).

Publications and Entertainments Act. Provided for the censorship of newspapers, books, films, stage shows, and art exhibitions (see page 241).

Have all these laws produced peace and contentment in South Africa?

In 1912, one out of every twenty-two persons was brought before the courts. *By 1960 the figure was one in eight.* More startling still, ONE IN EIGHT OF THE AFRICAN POPULATION ALONE WAS CONVICTED. In 1920, serious crime constituted 6·8 per cent of all crime. *In 1960 it was 10·16 per cent.* In 1913, 0·9 per 1,000 of the White population were convicted of serious crimes, and 3·6 per 1,000, of the non-Whites. In *1960 the figures were 4 per 1,000 of the White population and six per 1,000 of the non-Whites.*

A decade after Union, in 1920, the average number of persons convicted each year for murder was eighty-five. In 1960 *it was 403.* Convictions for murder have gone up five times, while South Africa's population only just doubled in the same period.

A total of 276 people were executed in South Africa between 1 July 1957, and 30 June 1961. During the same period, 475 people were sentenced to death, but the sentences were not carried out because of appeals, retrials, or commutation to imprisonment.

In 1920, one person in 10,000 lost his life through violence. *In 1960 the figure was three times as high.* ELEVEN PEOPLE EVERY DAY DIED VIOLENT DEATHS (excluding suicides or car accidents).

And still the crime rate increases. Now the jails are filled with political prisoners. Trials and convictions for sabotage are on the increase.

According to statistics released by the Commissioner of Prisons, Verster, in June 1963, more than 10,000 people were awaiting trial in South African prisons at the end of April, 1963. The Commissioner himself described the total number of people in prison at that time – 67,636, or roughly one in every 236 South Africans – as an 'all-time record'.

Apartheid breeds poverty, crime, and insecurity among all sections of the population. The law has become so involved, complex, and confusing that it no longer corresponds with morality. It is the perpetually changing instrument of a ruling group which is prepared to go to any lengths to maintain itself in power.

. .

10. Eliminating All Opposition

> Democracy is the breeding ground in which the bacilli of the Marxist world pest can grow and spread.
>
> HITLER in *Mein Kampf*

From the very inception of their rule in 1948, the Nationalists have held it as a faith that those who are not with them are against them AND MUST BE TREATED AS DEADLY ENEMIES. The basis of their power has always been far too narrow for them to practise tolerance towards their opponents. And the nature of their objective has made it impossible for them ever to make concessions to those who differed from them without endangering their whole apartheid programme. The result has been the adoption of the rigid and uncompromising 'granite wall' approach which their critics have found to be one of the most objectionable features of their régime.

The *Cape Times* on 18 November 1948, reported a speech by J. G. Strijdom:

Before the Nationalist Party could reach its ultimate goal – a republic – it would have to solve the colour problem. Anybody who purposely tried to upset the government's plans to put into operation its apartheid policy or who failed to do their duty towards the realization of that aim would be guilty of treason, just as those who refused to take up arms in defence of their country would be guilty of such a crime. The main principle of apartheid as he saw it was the continuation of European supremacy (*baasskap*).

Those who challenged White supremacy would be guilty of treason. And they have been legion. The implementation of apartheid has caused such manifest injustices, led to such brutality and suffering, that the years since 1948 have been years of mighty and swelling protest in which at one stage or another all sections of the population have joined except those directly under Nationalist influence. The growing frustration of parliamentary politics has driven one section of the people after another into extra-parliamentary political activity, some in the hope of strengthening the hand of the parliamentary opposition, others with a view to substituting for it the mass action of the voteless masses themselves. To all the Nationalists have turned a deaf ear. Criticism has been acceptable only from those who have shown themselves prepared to accept apartheid in the first place. All others have been ignored, unless their protest contained within it the seeds of rebellion, when they have been ruthlessly crushed.

Outstanding among the movements of protest have been the Torch Commando, formed in 1951 to defend the constitution against the threat of the Separate Representation of Voters Bill; the Black Sash, formed in 1955 to defend the constitution against the Senate Act; the Churches, especially the Anglican Church which has given the country outstanding figures like Bishop Reeves and Father Huddleston and which openly defied the State on the issue of the 'church clause'. These and other bodies have done valuable work in keeping alive the spirit of conscience, especially among the White section of the population. But their protest has been limited because they are not political parties and have therefore proposed no real alternative to apartheid, mapped out no programme for the achievement of political power. (The Torch Commando did, it is true, enter into a United Front alliance with the United Party and Labour before the 1953 election, but this move proved to be its undoing, and it did not survive electoral defeat.)

The main threat to Nationalist rule in the extra-parliamentary sphere has come from those who have consciously worked out an alternative to apartheid and who have organized the people to implement it. Where the Nationalists have preached apartheid, they have accepted integration; to discrimination they have opposed equality, to White supremacy, the doctrine of democratic rule. Ranging from the Communists on the left through the national organizations of the non-White people right up to the Progressive Party, these have constituted the real traitors to apartheid in Nationalist eyes. And the vials of Nationalist wrath have been poured upon their heads in increasingly massive doses.

F

Even the United Party has not been excluded from the list of undermining organizations in South Africa. In his maiden speech to Parliament on 19 August 1948, Dr Diederichs, now Minister of Economic Affairs, declared:

What is at issue (between the United and Nationalist Parties) is two outlooks on life, fundamentally so divergent that a compromise is entirely unthinkable. . . . On the one hand we have nationalism, which believes in the existence, in the necessary existence, of distinct peoples, distinct languages, nations, and cultures, and which regards the fact of the existence of these peoples and these cultures as the basis of its conduct. On the other hand we have liberalism, and the basis of its political struggle is the individual with his so-called rights and liberties . . . This doctrine of liberalism that stands for equal rights for all civilized human beings . . . is almost the same as the ideal of communism.

From the very outset the Nationalists have tended to lump all their opponents together, and to smear the one with the alleged crimes of the other.

The *Cape Argus* on 15 March 1952, reported a speech by Dr Malan: 'All six members of the Labour Party in the House of Assemby were "liberalistic". Some of them came very close to Communism. The Native Representatives wanted equal rights for Natives in all ways and they were also not far from Communism.'

It has been in the mounting tension of the last year or so, however, that the Nationalists have launched their most unbridled propaganda assault against the integrationists – even imposing administrative restrictions on some leading members of the Liberal Party.

In a speech reported in the newspaper *Dagbreek* on 18 November 1962, the Minister of Justice, B. J. Vorster, who on coming to office had fathered the memorable phrase 'rights are getting out of hand', stated: 'United Party policy held the same future for South Africa as that of Progressives and Liberals: total destruction of White leadership.'

The Minister of Posts and Telegraphs, Dr Albert Hertzog, in a speech reported in *Die Transvaler* on 3 November 1962, declared that the recent sabotage in the Republic had been the work of liberalist agitators. Liberalism, which was the precursor of Communism, constituted the greatest danger threatening South Africa, even more dangerous than Communism for its methods were much subtler.

White Liberals have been publicly accused of complicity in mass disturbances and murders during recent months, though to date no sort of evidence has been offered in any court.

The real case of the Nationalists against the Liberals was most succinctly voiced by the Cape Town Nationalist newspaper *Die Burger* in a series of editorials during February 1963, which defended the banning of Liberal Party leaders. 'The simple truth is,' proclaimed the paper, 'that the Liberal Party is the bearer of a policy (one man, one vote) the outcome of which, so far as we can judge, differs so little from Communism as to make precious little difference to the minority groups in South Africa. The party's whole line of thinking is subversive of civilization and order in South Africa.'

A similar and even more sinister attack was made on Mrs Helen Suzman, the lone Progressive Party Member of Parliament, after she had dared to criticize the inhumanity of the pass laws in the debate on the Bantu Administration vote in the House of Assembly on 29 May 1963. Nationalist back-benchers were stung to fury. Accusing her of being unpatriotic, of smearing South Africa and inciting the non-Whites, they predicted that her days in Parliament were numbered.

P. J. Coetzee, Nationalist M.P. for Langlaagte, said: 'She is a danger for us in the Assembly.' G. P. van den Berg, Nationalist M.P. for Wolmaransstad, addressed her directly: 'You are the greatest political enemy of this country.' Even the Minister himself, de Wet Nel, said Mrs Suzman was being advised by voices that were trying to destroy South Africa. She was not doing her fatherland a service.

So the United Party, Progressives, Liberals, Communists – all aimed at the destruction of White supremacy, all were the enemies of Afrikaner Nationalism. Yet, taking a leaf from Hitler's book, it was with the Communists that the Nationalists began – because the Communists were more vulnerable on account of the cold war, and because the Communist Party in 1948 was the only political party in South Africa, and had been for a generation, which stood for full and complete equality between all sections of the South African population and which made no distinction in its membership on grounds of race or colour.

While in opposition the Nationalists had long campaigned against Communism in South Africa. In 1937 the Cape Province Congress of the Nationalist Party had called for the combating of the Communist menace by (a) stricter immigration laws; (b) the penalizing of undesirable propaganda, through deportation and otherwise; and (c) stricter application of the Riotous Assemblies Act.

In 1943 Eric Louw had written a pamphlet on *The Communist Danger* which preferred as the main charge against Communism that it 'recognizes no distinction of colour or race. . . .

'At meetings of the Communist Party, White, Black, and Brown persons sit together. At socials they drink tea together and at dances the Black native whirls with his arms around the waist of the White girl, and what follows?'

Louw didn't lift the curtain, but he concluded: 'Joe Stalin becomes the comrade of Jan Smuts. . . . The effect of such (Communist) inflammatory propaganda was quickly visible in the impertinent and even challenging attitudes of natives towards Europeans.'

This was the essence of the Nationalist charge against Communism – that it undermined 'traditional' race attitudes in South Africa. As soon as the Nationalists themselves came to power, therefore, they appointed a departmental committee to 'investigate' Communism. On the eve of the 1949 provincial elections the Minister of Justice, C. R. Swart, told the House of Assembly that the committee's report disclosed 'a national danger' which made it imperative to combat 'the dangerous undermining' by the Communists of 'our national life, our democratic institutions, and our Western philosophy'.

Early in 1950 the Dutch Reformed Church urged the government to close the Soviet Consulate in Pretoria and to tighten the law punishing incitement of non-Whites against Whites. On 6 March its Church Congress called for State action against Communism, and the Nationalist government obliged by bringing before the 1950 session of Parliament an Unlawful Organizations

Bill which barely mentioned Communism and raised a storm of protest from the public because its terms of reference were so wide. The government had started with too much too soon and was forced to withdraw, but it returned before the same session with a Suppression of Communism Bill which eventually became law and has since formed the spearhead of the Nationalist attack on the civil liberties of all sections of the population, Communist and non-Communist alike.

Communism, according to the definitions clause of the Act:

means the doctrine of Marxian socialism as expounded by Lenin or Trotsky, the Third Communist International (the Comintern) or the Communist Information Bureau (the Cominform) or any related form of that doctrine expounded or advocated in the Union for the promotion of the fundamental principles of that doctrine and includes, in particular, any doctrine or scheme –

(a) which aims at the establishment of a despotic system of government based on the dictatorship of the proletariat under which one political organization only is recognized and all other political organizations are suppressed or eliminated; or

(b) which aims at bringing about any political, industrial, social, or economic change within the Union by the promotion of disturbance or disorder, by unlawful acts or omissions or by the threat of such acts or omissions or by means which include the promotion of disturbance or disorder, or such acts or omissions or threat; or

(c) which aims at bringing about any political, industrial, social, or economic change within the Union in accordance with the directions or under the guidance of or in cooperation with any foreign government or any foreign or international institution whose purpose or one of whose purposes (professed or otherwise) is to promote the establishment within the Union of any political, industrial, social, or economic system identical with or similar to any system in operation in any country which has adopted a system of government such as is described in paragraph (a); or

(d) which aims at the encouragement of feelings of hostility between the European and non-European races of the Union the consequences of which are calculated to further the achievement of any object referred to in paragraph (a) or (b).

The significance of these ludicrous definitions of Communism is that, although a severe maximum penalty of ten years' imprisonment is laid down for any infringement, nobody has yet

been *convicted* under the main definition or even under sections
(*a*), (*c*), or (*d*). There have been some convictions under section
(*b*) – that which aims at bringing about change by the promotion
of disturbance or unlawful acts – notably during the Defiance
Campaign of 1952, when the leaders in the Transvaal and
Eastern Cape were found guilty of what a judge called 'statutory
Communism'. But in the main the definitions have not been
employed in prosecutions.

The bringing of prosecutions in a court of law was not, however, the primary purpose of the Act, which equipped the
government with a formidable battery of administrative weapons
for striking down its political opponents. The Act declared the
Communist Party to be unlawful (the party had, in fact, anticipated this by dissolving itself a month before the Bill became
law) and gave the Governor-General the power to outlaw any
other organization which professed itself to be promoting the
spread of Communism or which engaged in activities calculated
to further the achievement of any of the objects of Communism
as set out in the definitions clause.

Furthermore, the Act provided for the appointment of a
liquidator who was authorized to compile a list of former members and supporters of the Communist Party. Once on the list, an
individual became subject to a number of restrictions, including
an order to resign from any organization or public body, even
Parliament.

The Governor General was empowered to ban any periodical
or other publication which promoted the spread of Communism
or 'serves mainly (later amended to "*inter alia*") as a means for
expressing views or conveying information, the publication of
which is calculated to further the achievements of any of the
objects of Communism'.

The penalties laid down under the Act were not confined to
listed Communists. Under section 9 of the Act, anybody,
whether listed or not, could be banned from attending gatherings; and under section 10, prohibited from being within
defined areas. The Minister was also given the power to ban
gatherings.

The Bill provoked a storm of opposition throughout the

country. The Johannesburg Bar, in a considered statement, declared:

The objects of Communism as defined in the Act are very wide indeed. They include many liberal and humanitarian objects which are advocated and cherished by persons who are very far from being Communists. These provisions have no legal bounds and, coupled with the denial of any right of access to the courts, are a complete negation of the liberty of the subject as guaranteed by the rule of law.

The United Party's approach to the Bill was typical of its methods of opposition. It proposed to make Communism a treasonable offence, punishable in certain circumstances by the death penalty; but opposed the provisions of the Act which by-passed the courts. In this way it was enabled to go through the motions of opposition while at the same time making it impossible for the government to charge it with lending aid and succour to the Communists.

The main opposition to the Bill came from outside Parliament. The African National Congress, the South African Indian Congress, the African People's Organization and the Communist Party entered into an alliance for the purpose of staging a one-day strike in protest against the Bill on 26 June 1950. After the dissolution of the Communist Party had been dramatically announced in Parliament by Communist M.P. Sam Kahn, preparations for the protest strike were carried forward by the other organizations, to culminate in the first of those mass demonstrations which were to be so prominent a feature of politics in the ensuing decade. From this year onwards 26 June became known as Freedom Day and was observed by all the people's organizations, later to be welded together in the Congress Alliance.

Along with the passage of restrictive legislation, the government expanded the scope of the Special Branch of the police. Not a public meeting was held by the Congress organizations without the presence of a battery of note-taking policemen. Telephones were tapped and correspondence tampered with, while the latest electronic devices used in detection were imported from the United States. One police chief announced that

167

the Special Branch no longer relied on informers because other means of obtaining information were now available to it.

All these measures, however, far from producing the result desired by the government, further excited opposition. Towards the end of 1951 a Joint Planning Council of the African National Congress and the South African Indian Congress was set up to organize a campaign for the repeal of discriminatory legislation. The African National Congress considered the proposals of this council in December 1951 and then sent a letter to the Prime Minister, reiterating the demand for direct representation of the Africans in Parliament and warning the government that if certain laws were not repealed by 29 February 1952, 'mass action' would be taken. The laws specifically objected to were the pass laws, the Group Areas Act, the Separate Representation of Voters Act, the Suppression of Communism Act, the Bantu Authorities Act, and the so-called 'rehabilitation scheme' in the Reserves.

Unlike Verwoerd, who boasts that he throws such letters into the waste-paper basket, Dr Malan had the courtesy to reply.

'While the government is not prepared to grant the Bantu political equality within the European community,' he said, 'it is only too willing to encourage Bantu initiative, Bantu services, and Bantu administration within the Bantu community.' He advised the Congress to reconsider its decision and warned that the government would use all its powers to deal with any infringements of the law.

On 11 February the Congress replied to the Prime Minister. Nothing contained in the Bantu Authorities Act was a substitute for direct representation in the Councils of State. As a defenceless and voteless people, the Africans had explored other channels without success and now had no alternative but to embark on a concerted defiance of unjust laws. Nelson Mandela was appointed National Volunteer-in-Chief and the recruiting of volunteers began. On 26 June, Freedom Day, the campaign was launched.

Within the first fortnight over 500 non-Whites, mainly Africans and Indians, had been arrested in the Eastern Province and another 100 on the Witwatersrand for such offences as contravening curfew regulations, ignoring apartheid notices at stations or post offices, and entering African townships without permits. The campaign spread rapidly to other centres and by 30 September the number of arrests totalled 5,000. The volunteers defended their cases in court but, when convicted, refused to pay fines and went to jail instead. It was the most impressive protest demonstration ever conducted by non-White organizations in South Africa. By the end of the campaign over 8,000 people, including a handful of Whites, had gone to jail.

The government's reply was to wield the big stick. Even before the campaign had got under way, the Minister of Justice began to issue notices under the Suppression of Communism Act. The liquidator had by this time placed between 500 and 600 names on his list of former members and supporters of the Communist Party. In May the Minister dispatched notices to a number of prominent trade unionists and leaders of the African and Indian Congresses – ordering them to resign from various organizations, prohibiting them from attending any gatherings other than church services or purely social and recreational functions, and, in some cases, confining them to the provinces in which they lived. Several of the leaders chose to disregard these orders as their own contribution to the Defiance Campaign, and were sentenced to between four and six months' imprisonment.

In May, too, the weekly newspaper, *Guardian*, was banned under the Suppression of Communism Act. One week later a paper called the *Clarion* (later named *Advance*) appeared with the same management and staff as the *Guardian*.

On 25 May the Minister of Justice notified Sam Kahn M.P. and Fred Carneson M.P.C. that, since they had been found by a Select Committee to be Communists, their membership of Parliament and the Provincial Council respectively was terminated.

Kahn's place in Parliament was taken by B. P. Bunting,[1] also a listed Communist, who in turn was ejected under the Suppression Act in 1953. The election to fill the vacancy was again won by a listed Communist, Ray Alexander, banned Secretary of the Food and Canning Workers' Union. In the meantime, however, the government had amended the law to make listed

[1] The Author.

Communists ineligible for election to Parliament or the Provincial Council, and Miss Alexander was forcibly prevented from taking her seat.

The 1953 session of Parliament saw the introduction of two further laws designed to prevent future campaigns of passive resistance, and to equip the government with sweeping powers to deal with any emergency which might arise. The Criminal Laws Amendment Act made it a serious offence, punishable by a fine of £300 and/or three years' imprisonment and/or ten lashes, to break any law by way of protest or as part of a campaign against any law. Furthermore, the leaders of any future defiance campaign, i.e. those who 'incited' or 'procured' others to commit an offence by way of protest or as part of a campaign against any law, could be punished with a fine of £500 and/or five years' imprisonment and/or fifteen lashes.

During the course of the debate, United Party member Dr Smit pointed out that under the Magistrate's Courts Act the maximum number of strokes which could be imposed was ten. The Minister of Justice, Mr C. R. Swart, replied: 'What are five strokes between friends? I accept the Hon. Member's amendment.'

The second measure was the Public Safety Act, which gave the government the power to proclaim a state of emergency for a period of up to twelve months and to rule by decree. At the end of any period of twelve months, the state of emergency could be extended if the government thought fit, and decrees could be issued on any subject except the Defence Act, the Industrial Conciliation Act, and the rights and duties of Parliament and its members.

The United Party decided to support both measures, fearing, if they did not, that they would be accused of supporting riot and insurrection, and that this would damage their chances in the general election due in less than two months' time. Only the handful of Labour members and the Native Representatives voted against the new tyrannical laws.

The pattern established by the Defiance Campaign has been repeated ever since. Each time that the non-White organizations have voiced their grievances or demonstrated their demands, the police have moved into action. Forms of public protest which are regarded as normal in other countries are subject in South Africa to massive police surveillance and intimidation with the ever-present threat of criminal sanctions. Loopholes in the law have been closed and new laws imposed to meet new situations. Steadily the extra-parliamentary struggle has been driven underground.

In December 1953, the African National Congress, at a meeting in Queenstown, declared that only a national convention representative of all racial groups could improve the deteriorating state of race relations. Then, in March 1954, the executives of the A.N.C., the S.A. Indian Congress, the S.A. Coloured People's Organization, and the S.A. Congress of Democrats met in Natal under the chairmanship of Chief A. J. Lutuli and decided to hold a Congress of the People at which a Freedom Charter would be adopted.

It was resolved that the people themselves should declare how they would like to be governed in a democratic South Africa. Hundreds of meetings were accordingly arranged in town and township, in factories, mines, shops, farms, and in the Reserves, while a network of local committees were formed through which the people transmitted their demands and grievances. Eventually the Congress itself was held at Kliptown, a small village near Johannesburg, on 25 and 26 June 1955, and three thousand delegates from all over the country adopted the Freedom Charter by acclaim.

The preamble to the Charter announced:

We, the people of South Africa, declare for all our country and the world to know: that South Africa belongs to all who live in it, Black and White, and that no government can justly claim authority unless it is based on the will of all the people; that our people have been robbed of their birthright to land, liberty, and peace by a form of government founded on injustice and inequality; that our country will never be prosperous or free until all our people live in brotherhood, enjoying equal rights and opportunities; that only a democratic state, based on the will of all the people, can secure to all their birthright without distinction of colour, race, sex, or belief; and therefore, we, the people of South Africa, Black and White together – equals, countrymen, and brothers – adopt this Freedom Charter. And we pledge ourselves to strive together, sparing nothing of our strength and courage, until the democratic changes here set out have been won.

The main demands would have been unnecessary in any civilized democratic state.

The People shall govern.
All National Groups shall have Equal Rights.
The People shall share in the Country's Wealth.
The Land shall be shared among those who work it.
All shall be Equal before the Law.
All shall enjoy Equal Human Rights.
There shall be Work and Security.
The Doors of Learning and Culture shall be Opened.
There shall be Houses, Security, and Comfort.
There shall be Peace and Friendship.

From the outset, however, the government of South Africa chose to regard the plan for a Congress of the People as treasonable. Preliminary meetings were raided by the police and documents confiscated, with the warrants used for the raids disclosing investigations into a charge of treason. The Congress itself was invaded by a large force of armed policemen who took down the names and addresses of all present and impounded a large quantity of literature.

Then, in September, the homes of over 400 people were raided and searched by the police, still investigating their allegation of treason. One year and three months later, on 6 December, the birthday of the Minister of Justice, C. R. Swart, the police swooped at dawn on 156 people in all corners of South Africa and brought them before court in Johannesburg on a charge of high treason.

In the dock were the principal leaders of the people's organizations and those cadres who had taken the most active part in the preparations for the Congress. It was undoubtedly the government's hope in one fell swoop to decapitate the resistance movement, either by securing a mass conviction or by immobilizing the accused for the duration of the trial. The details of the treason trial are by now too well known to require repetition. It is sufficient to say that after dragging through the courts for four years the case ignominiously collapsed and all the accused were acquitted.

Meanwhile government action under the Suppression of Communism Act was being intensified. Banning orders, which had at first been issued for two years, were now issued for five, while the restrictions imposed by the bans were more severe. Most people banned were also prohibited from playing any part in the affairs of a long list of organizations ranging from the Congresses themselves to Parent-Teacher Associations and the Civil Rights League; many of them were restricted to the city in which they lived. By 1957 the liquidator had placed a total of 608 names on his list of former members and supporters of the Communist Party (235 Whites, sixty-seven Coloureds, forty-seven Asians, and 259 Africans). Of seventy-six trade union officials named, no fewer than fifty-seven had been ordered to resign from their unions and forbidden to play any part in the organization of workers. The refusal of passport facilities to the more outspoken of the government's opponents had become an established practice and was enforced by special legislation.

Yet despite the ever-increasing repression, popular resistance was not in any way diminished. The issuing of reference books (pass books) to African women which started in 1956 led to widespread incidents of pass burning and a mass demonstration of 20,000 women at the Union Buildings in Pretoria where over 7,000 individually signed protest forms were deposited on the doorstep of the Prime Minister. The treason arrests themselves provoked such massive demonstrations of support for the accused in the streets of Johannesburg that the police were unable to control the situation and the case was later transferred to Pretoria. An increase of a penny in bus fares on certain routes in Johannesburg and Pretoria at the beginning of 1957 led to a bus boycott by the Africans in the townships which lasted for more than three months. Over 50,000 people walked to and from work every day – in some cases a distance of eighteen miles – because their wages were so low that they simply could not afford the increase. The government chose to treat the boycott as a challenge and attempted to smash it by force – thousands of Africans in the affected areas were arrested for technical offences – but such was the discipline and unity of the boycotters that they eventually won widespread support from commerce and industry, and the old fare was restored.

In the Zeerust and Sekhukhuneland Reserves of the Transvaal full-scale revolts broke out in 1958 over government attempts to impose passes on African women and the whole Bantu Authorities scheme. The government immediately unleashed a reign of terror in order to restore control. Behind a close-drawn curtain of secrecy (the Press was excluded from both Reserves) a special police squad went into action and did not hesitate to use the most extreme forms of violence to enforce submission. Hundreds of men, women, and children fled from the Zeerust area across the border into Bechuanaland in search of safety and lived in conditions of considerable want rather than return to the hell which had been their home. Those who did venture to return when the terror seemed to have abated were subjected to heavy penalties by the government-appointed chiefs.

Regulations were promulgated banning the African National Congress in both areas, forbidding entry without a permit, prohibiting any statement 'which has the intention ... of subverting or interfering with the authority of the State or any of its officials or of any chief or headman', and outlawing any propaganda for a boycott. Hundreds of tribesmen were arrested in both Reserves on charges ranging from public violence to murder, and in Sekhukhuneland a number of Africans were sentenced to death.

Similar disturbances occurred in other areas. In Natal, during August 1959, it was estimated that 600 African women were in jail as a result of unrest and rioting throughout the Province. Fines imposed were reported to have totalled £13,000 and alternative jail sentences 228 years. The Secretary for Bantu Administration who toured the area put the blame on A.N.C. agitators. But Chief Lutuli, A.N.C. President-General, who himself lives in Natal, listed the causes as: (1) mass removals and the demolition of homes; (2) influx control, passes for women, and the refusal of permits to seek work in the towns; (3) increases in rents and taxes; (4) forced labour by women without payment; (5) low wages in relation to the ever-increasing cost of living.

The clashes between the people and the authorities both in urban and rural areas reached a climax in 1960. On 21 March the Pan-Africanist Congress, an off-shoot of the A.N.C. opposed to the multi-racial character of the Congress Alliance, launched a non-violent anti-pass campaign at a number of points in the Union. The campaign was met with deliberate violence by the police, and the shootings at Sharpeville and Langa made an impact on the outside world which has not been obliterated to this day. Between 21 March and 9 April a total of eighty-three non-White civilians were killed and 365 injured by police bullets. Casualties among the police themselves totalled three Africans killed, and thirty-three Whites, one Coloured, and twenty-five Africans injured.

The killings roused the Africans to fury. In Cape Town the entire population of the African townships went on strike for a period of almost three weeks, while a one day stay-at-home called by the A.N.C. in mourning for the dead of Sharpeville and Langa was successful in all the main centres of the country and marked the start of a new pass-burning campaign. Using its powers under the Public Safety Act, the government declared a state of emergency and issued a set of regulations which gave it virtually limitless powers to deal with the situation. Some 2,000 leading figures in the Congress movement, Pan-Africanists, Liberal Party members, and others were detained without trial for up to five months. Almost 20,000 Africans were arrested under another section of the emergency regulations and thousands of them sent to prisons or work camps after conviction at secret trials held in the jails. In Cape Town, hardest hit by the strike, parties of police roamed the streets openly assaulting Africans and even Coloureds in an attempt to force them back to work. After house to house searches by the police in the townships, many Africans simply disappeared and were not seen by their families again for months. Allegations were also made that police removed valuables and money from several homes. Jails were overcrowded, and numbers of prisoners were reported to have died of 'pneumonia'.

Special legislation was passed by Parliament to outlaw the A.N.C. and the P.A.C., while the newspapers *New Age* and *Torch* were banned under the emergency regulations, reappearing only when the emergency ended on 31 August. The underground Communist Party publicly announced its existence for the first time, and both the A.N.C. and P.A.C. made preparations to continue their work outside the law.

The disruption caused by the emergency had a catastrophic effect on the economy of the country. The confidence of investors was shaken and large sums of capital fled South Africa. The property market slumped and new construction plans were abandoned. In his 1961 Budget speech, the Minister of Finance reported that in the previous year South Africa's gold and foreign exchange reserves had dropped by £61 million, compared with a rise of £40 million in 1959. There had been a capital outflow of £81 million. H. F. Oppenheimer, Chairman of Anglo-American Corporation, declared that the quoted holdings of his group had fallen by twenty-three per cent in 1960. The market value of the investments controlled by the General Mining and Finance Corporation declined by forty per cent in the eighteen-month period to June 1961. The government was forced to impose strict financial controls, and only the great economic resources of South Africa – especially her mounting gold production – prevented collapse.

The formal ending of the emergency on 31 August 1960 did not, however, end the state of crisis into which the government's policies had plunged the country. Barely three months later emergency rule had to be imposed in the Transkei following a series of disturbances in the five eastern districts of the territory. Once again the background was widespread popular opposition to the government-run Bantu Authorities and rehabilitation schemes. One of the most serious incidents took place on 6 June, when the police attacked a tribal gathering at Ngqusa Hill leaving eleven Africans dead and thirteen wounded behind them.

Later a mass meeting of 6,000 tribesmen near Bizana, in Pondoland, decided to pay no more taxes as a protest against Bantu Authorities, and to boycott stores run by Whites in

Bizana. Rule in the area began to pass into the hands of a revolutionary organization known as 'the Congo', the leadership of which was known as 'the Hill', and which declared that it was working for a programme of democratic reform.

The government's emergency proclamation provided for detention without trial, and massive forces of police and soldiers arrived to restore 'law and order'. Hundreds of tribesmen were arrested for offences ranging from murder to tax and pass offences. Government chiefs and headmen were provided with strong bodyguards and their opponents jailed or deported. But despite the continuing presence of special units of troops and police, the emergency proclamations are still in force throughout the area, while detentions and deportations without trial continue to this day.

Deportation, or banishment, has proved to be one of the most vicious weapons in the government arsenal. The Nationalists were not, of course, the first to use it – ruthlessness is seldom without precedent in South Africa – but they have resorted to it on a scale far beyond that of any previous régime. Between 1948 and 1962, 120 Africans were banished, mainly from the Reserves. And among the number were three children – one only twelve years old. Of what possible crime could a child of twelve be guilty, to warrant such a punishment? His name is Tlou Matlala, the son of Mokoena Matlala, and he was banished from Matlala's Reserve to Kingwilliamstown in 1954. Police, armed with a banishment order, pulled him out of school and sent him into exile. He was regarded by the tribe as heir to the chieftainship, and the government had other plans. Twenty men and three women were banished from the Reserve between 1952 and 1954. The son and daughter of Maphuti Seopa, aged fifteen and fourteen respectively, were also amongst the exiled.

Five of the Matlala people have already died in banishment; only two have ever returned to the Matlala Reserve – to die within a few weeks. Sixteen were still in banishment in 1962, after eight years.

Banishment without trial is permitted by the Native Administration Act of 1927, which empowers the Governor-General (today the State President), whenever he deems it expedient in

G

the general public interest, to order any tribe, portion of a tribe, or single African to withdraw from one district to any other district and not to return to the district from which he came or move to any other district without the written permission of the Secretary for Native Affairs.

Of the 120 banished between 1948 and 1962, forty-four were still in banishment at the end of that period; nothing whatever was known of seven others; eleven had died in banishment; and twelve had fled to other countries. Only forty-six had ever gone home, little more than one third of the total, and of these fourteen were still living under the threat of the withdrawal of their permits to return.

The government has cleverly avoided the stigma of classic concentration camps, complete with guards, searchlights, barbed-wire fences, and tracker dogs on the Nazi model. The camps are there – at Frenchdale, and Driefontein – but they are open to the wide world, pathetic clusters of huts in the most desolate parts of the country.

This is one spot, described in a pamphlet issued by the Human Rights Welfare Committee:

Semi-desert, on the edge of the Kalahari, scrub country, dry, barren, and scorchingly hot in summer. There is no shade except that given by the overhang of the roof of the huts – the men sit close up to the wall. The nearest inhabitants are about half a mile away, the nearest store thirteen to fifteen miles away, the nearest bus stop thirty miles away, and the nearest town sixty miles off. There is no school, no post office, no medical facilities, no opportunity for work.

Here is another:

Twelve round stone huts with thatched roofs, 104 miles from the nearest town. The men are dumped here and told to stay. The huts are empty. There is no furniture, no utensils. They must acquire these out of the £2 allowance which is sometimes offered (by the government), not always, and not always taken, or out of wages amounting to about £2 to £4 a month. Three of the occupants here give their ages as 63, 65 and 72.

One exile wrote: 'My experience of banishment is that you

are taken to an empty room and nobody seems to care for you. In other words you are like a person who is buried alive.'

Families of the exiles are left destitute. A teenage daughter, whose mother died while her father was in exile, wrote: 'Tell me in the name of God who it was who banished my father and sentenced me to a living death.'

With the increase of disturbances in the Reserves, such is the fate that has overcome the most militant opponents of the government's policies – chiefs, headmen, people of consequence in their community. Some have been rotting in exile for ten years and more. Some who are old men will never see their homes again. But it is the children who suffer most. One of the fathers wrote: 'The case of my children is a very pathetic one indeed because I hear that they are scattered all over the country like a bird's chickens. The boy is in . . . as far as my information goes, and what he wants there, young as he is, I cannot tell, except assuming that it must be hunger and poverty that must be moving him about. He has no one to finance his education. This is the heaviest blow that the deportation has meant to me.'

In 1961 the people's organizations prepared for the next assault on the citadel of White supremacy. Over 1,000 delegates attended the All-in African People's Conference held at Pietermaritzburg on 25 and 26 March and heard an inspiring address by Nelson Mandela, whose ban from attending gatherings had only recently expired. The conference called for a national convention of elected representatives of all adult men and women, without regard to race, creed or colour, to be held not later than 31 May – the day on which the new Republic was to be proclaimed – to draw up a new constitution for South Africa. If the government ignored this demand, the people would be called upon to organize mass demonstrations on the eve of the declaration of the Republic. All Africans should refuse to cooperate with the Republic or any other form of government 'which rests on force to perpetuate the tyranny of a minority', while Indians, Coloureds, and democratic Whites should join with the Africans in opposition to 'a régime which is bringing South Africa to disaster'.

The call for a national convention was a reasonable, democratic demand which found support among wide sections of the people, White as well as non-White. But the government's re-action to it was typically instransigent. A special General Law Amendment Act was propelled through the 1961 session of Parliament empowering an Attorney-General, if he considered it necessary in the interests of public safety or the maintenance of public order, to direct that an arrested person be detained in jail for up to twelve days without bail. The Act also tightened up the provisions of the law relating to 'intimidation' and the banning of meetings, and on 19 May all gatherings were banned until 26 June.

Homes and offices were raided by the Special Branch of the police, and all the leaders who could be found were held under the twelve-day no-bail law. Then, between 3 May and the end of the month, thousands of police conducted large-scale raids all over the country to round up Africans suspected of 'vagrancy', contraventions of the pass laws, tax offences, and the like. Ten thousand or more of what the police referred to as 'the tsotsi element' were arrested. During the last ten days of May all police leave was cancelled and army units were 'brought to a state of preparedness for service'. The State, railways, several local authorities, and a number of private employers warned their African workers that they would be penalized if they took part in the three-day stay-at-home, from 29 to 31 May, which had been called by the Action Council of the Pietermaritzburg Conference. Distressingly, the Pan-Africanist Congress, by word of mouth and leaflets, assisted the authorities in their attempts to break the strike.

Because of the massive campaign which had been launched to meet it, the three-day stay-at-home, though it constituted the greatest national general strike ever held in the country, with hundreds of thousands staying away from work in the main centres, was acknowledged by Nelson Mandela, Secretary of the National Action Council, to have failed to reach the anticipated proportions. Yet it made an overwhelming impact on the country. The Republican celebrations were completely over-shadowed. The people's power had been demonstrated by the very exertions necessary to contain it.

As it turned out, the 29 May campaign proved a watershed in South Africa's political development. During the fifties the entire resistance movement had been based on non-violence, as the treason trial judges themselves acknowledged when they acquitted the accused at the end of the case. The campaigns of 1960 and 1961 had also been non-violent both in conception and execution. Yet more and more popular non-violence had been met with violence. The brutality displayed during the 1960 emergency and the 1961 stay-at-home campaign left its mark on the popular movements of opposition. There was more and more talk, particularly among the youth, of the need for 'new methods' of struggle. Every little demonstration, every poster parade, every meeting seemed to result only in more prosecutions and jailings. Was there any point in carrying on in the old way? The government would not be moved by reason or argument. The parliamentary opposition was powerless. Nowhere did the non-White people have a voice in the Councils of State. Was it not time for a change?

How far the national liberatory organizations were permeated with these ideas it is impossible to say. On 26 June, a statement from Nelson Mandela, spokesman for the National Action Council and leader of the May strike, declared that the next phase of the freedom struggle would be a full-scale campaign of non-cooperation, and that he, Mandela, would work 'underground' to lead it.

Mandela, wanted on a charge of incitement, announced that he would not give himself up, but would separate himself from his wife and children, close his business, and abandon his profession as an attorney, to 'live as an outlaw in the land of my birth' and fight the government side by side with his people, 'inch by inch and mile by mile, until victory is won'.

Calling upon the people to join in the fight for freedom, Mandela said: 'I have made my choice. I will not leave South Africa nor will I surrender. Only through hardship, sacrifices, and militant action will freedom be won.'

Mandela eluded the police for over a year before he was captured in Natal and sentenced to three years' imprisonment for his part in the 29 May strike and to a further two years – the maximum sentence – for having left the country (briefly, for consultation with African leaders abroad) without a passport. Rumours that Mandela had been 'given away' by Communists can be discounted as pure mischief and were vigorously refuted by Mandela himself in his speech from the dock.

On the night of 16 December 1961 – a public holiday formerly called Dingaan's Day and now known as the Day of the Covenant, celebrating an Afrikaner victory over the Zulu Chief at the Battle of Blood River – ten explosions, five in Johannesburg and five in Port Elizabeth, marked the birth of a new organization, Umkhonto we Sizwe (the Spear of the Nation). During the day Verwoerd had made a speech appealing for 'national unity between the two White races'. A poster distributed by Umkhonto we Sizwe proclaimed:

> This is a new, independent body formed by Africans. It includes in its ranks South Africans of all races. . . . Umkhonto we Sizwe will carry on the struggle for freedom and democracy by new methods which are necessary to complement the actions of the established national liberation organizations. . . .
>
> We hope that we will bring the government and its supporters to its senses before it is too late, so that both the government and its policies can be changed before matters reach the desperate stage of civil war. We believe our actions to be a blow against Nationalist preparations for civil war and military rule. In these actions we are working in the best interests of all the people of this country, Black, Brown, and White, whose future happiness and well-being cannot be attained without the overthrow of the Nationalists. . . .
>
> The people's patience is not endless. The time comes in the life of any nation when there remain only two choices – submit or fight. That time has now come to South Africa.

South Africa was again face to face with organized sabotage as an instrument of political policy, but this time from a very different source. The 'granite' policy of the Nationalist government was provoking the inevitable response. At the beginning the sabotage attempts were made largely with home-made bombs, and in the first attack one of the saboteurs was killed and another injured when a bomb went off prematurely. But the organization quickly improved and, despite prosecutions and jailings, the number of attacks steadily increased. Questioned in the House of Assembly, the Minister of Justice during the 1962 session of Parliament refused to give the number of sabotage attacks which had occurred, declaring that it was not in the public interest to do so. But since December 1961 nearly 100 instances have been reported in the Press. Attacks have for the most part been confined to government installations, particularly those connected with the policy of apartheid and race discrimination, such as pass offices.

The reply of the Minister of Justice was the General Law Amendment Act of 1962, commonly called the Sabotage Act. Of the twenty-two clauses in the new law, only one is concerned with sabotage as such. The remainder equip the Minister with sweeping powers to administer action against his political opponents.

The sabotage clause is in two parts. The first makes it an offence for anyone to commit any wrongful or wilful act whereby he obstructs, injures, tampers with, or destroys: (a) the health or safety of the public; the maintenance of law and order; (b) the supply of water, light, power, fuel, or foodstuffs, sanitary, medical, or fire extinguishing services; postal, telephone, telegraph, or radio services, or the free movement of traffic; (c) any property; or if he attempts to commit such offence; or if, in contravention of any law, he possesses any explosives, firearm or weapon, or *enters or is upon any land or building*.

In other words, a person who is guilty of as little as trespass may be successfully prosecuted for sabotage under this Act. Once the trespass alone is proved, he becomes liable to penalties ranging from a minimum of five years' imprisonment to the death sentence, unless he can prove that his offence was not committed with intent: (a) to cause or promote general dislocation, disturbance, or disorder; (b) to cripple any industry or the production and distribution of commodities; (c) to seriously injure or endanger the safety of any person or to cause substantial financial loss to any person or to the State; (d) to further the achievement of any political aim, including the bringing about of any social or economic change in the Republic; (e) to cause or encourage feelings of hostility between different sections of the population; (f) to cause forcible resistance to the government or to embarrass the administration of the affairs of the State.

The only safeguard possessed by an accused is that his trial must be ordered by the Attorney General and not by an ordinary prosecutor. But once prosecuted an accused is virtually doomed, for to *prove* innocence of the conditions listed from (a) to (f) is intimidatingly difficult, no matter how able the defence.

The adminstrative restrictions which may be imposed under the Sabotage Act include the following: (a) anybody who in the opinion of the Minister is furthering the objects of Communism may be subjected to house arrest or prohibited from performing any act; (b) listed and banned persons and former members of banned organizations may be prohibited from belonging to any organization or class of organization; (c) listed or banned persons may be required to report daily to the police and must notify any change of address or occupation to the police; (d) any new newspaper which applies for registration may be required to deposit £10,000 with the Minister of the Interior, and if the newspaper is subsequently banned, the deposit will be forfeit to the State; (e) publication in any form of statements by banned persons is prohibited.

The penalties for breach of these restrictions range from a minimum of one year to a maximum of ten years' imprisonment. Opposition to the Sabotage Act was widespread, and public meetings and demonstrations were held in many centres. The International Commission of Jurists declared that the Bill reduced the liberty of the citizen to a degree not surpassed in the most extreme dictatorship of the Left or Right. The measure was a culmination of determined and ruthless attempts to enforce the doctrine of apartheid, and was not worthy of a civilized jurisprudence. The Christian Council of South Africa stated that it viewed the harsh and extreme terms of the Bill with 'consternation and dismay'.

Introducing the second reading of the Bill, the Minister proclaimed that the country was calm and peaceful despite the 'artificial agitation made outside'. He wanted to keep it that way. It was not the government's intention to restrict freedom of speech as a whole. The Bill was designed purely and simply to render subversive elements and Communists harmless and to punish saboteurs.

It is not generally realized that the Sabotage Act consists largely of amendments to the Suppression of Communism Act and that to some extent Vorster won acceptance for it with his argument that it was only the Communists who would get hit. The wide powers granted under the Act, however, have been used by the Minister indiscriminately against Communists and non-Communists alike. The first person to be placed under house arrest, Mrs Helen Joseph, is not and has never been a Communist; indeed, she made this so clear in her evidence during the treason trial that the accusation was not even levelled against her by the prosecution. Of the twenty persons placed under house arrest up to 15 February 1963, thirteen were listed Communists, but seven were not. The overwhelming majority of people banned from attending gatherings were not listed Communists. Of the 154 persons banned up to the end of March 1963, sixty-seven were listed Communists, but eighty-seven were not, and amongst these last have been Liberal Party members as avowedly anti-Communist as the Minister of Justice himself.

The penalty of house arrest has in all instances been imposed for a period of five years, during which the victims are forbidden to leave their homes except for the hours specified in the Minister's notice, and may not receive any visitors at home except for a lawyer or a doctor – provided that neither is listed or banned. Some of the twenty people house-arrested by 15 February 1963 were prohibited from leaving their homes for twenty-four hours a day, on the assumption that they had 'private means' and so had no cause to leave their homes. The Minister announced, however, that if they found 'bona fide' jobs, their orders would be varied so as to enable them to take up employment, and those under twenty-four hour house arrest have generally been allowed three hours a day in which to seek work. If allowed out to work at all, anyone under house arrest must report daily to a police station.

Banning notices have also been greatly tightened up since the passing of the Sabotage Act. Those banned are prohibited from attending not only all political gatherings, but also any gathering where people have social intercourse with one another, are forbidden to enter any non-White area, location, or hostel, are forbidden to enter the premises of any factory, are forbidden to communicate in any manner whatsoever with any other named or banned person, are confined to a single magisterial district or sometimes even a single township, and are ordered to report once a week to a specified police station.

Action has also been taken against the Press. In November 1962 the newspaper *New Age* (successor to the banned *Advance,* itself successor to the banned *Guardian*) was banned. The staff of the paper, anticipating the ban, had registered another newspaper *Spark,* before the Sabotage Act became law and thus avoided the need to pay the £10,000 deposit which would undoubtedly have been demanded of them had they attempted to register a new paper. *Spark* came out weekly after *New Age* was banned, but the Minister, in response, then resorted to other of his new powers under the Sabotage Act. On 22 February 1963, a notice was gazetted prohibiting any named or banned person or anyone formerly a member of a banned organization from belonging to any organization 'which in any manner prepares, compiles, prints, publishes, or disseminates any publication'. Finally, individual notices were served on the editor and other leading staff members of *Spark* forbidding them from being in any place 'which constitutes the premises on which any publication . . . is prepared, compiled, printed, or published' and in addition prohibiting them from 'preparing, compiling, printing, publishing, or disseminating in any manner whatsoever any publication' or preparing any matter for publication. Men and women who had spent a lifetime in journalism were prohibited by a stroke of the ministerial pen from continuing with their profession, even as free-lance journalists for local or overseas papers. Deprived of its existing, and any potential, new staff, *Spark* published its last issue on 28 March 1963. A weekly paper which had been published for over twenty-five years without ever having fallen foul of the law was done to death by a government which never dared to challenge it in a court of law.

In February 1963 the government also banned the monthly magazine *Fighting Talk*, which had had an equally blameless career but which had been an equally staunch opponent of apartheid. The Minister might claim that both *Spark* and *Fighting Talk* were edited by listed Communists, but in demanding a deposit of £5,000 from the magazine, *The New African*, a mildly liberal, somewhat academic monthly which had applied for registration, he was taking a free swing at those who had never betrayed any love for Communism and showing again that behind the screen of anti-Communism the government would attack the liberties of all who opposed its policies.

A further administrative punishment meted out by the government under the Sabotage Act was a notice gazetted on 28 December 1962, prohibiting any named or banned person or anyone formerly a member of a banned organization from taking part in the affairs of 'any organization which in any manner propagates, defends, attacks, criticizes or discusses any form of State or any principle or policy of the government of a State, or which in any manner undermines the authority of the government of a State.' In other words, no person falling under any of the three categories listed could belong to any organization which ever at any time discussed politics. Registered trade unions or employers' organizations were exempted from the ban, but the unregistered South African Congress of Trade Unions and other unions lost their leading personnel as a result.

Despite the torrent of repression, peace, for some strange reason, refused to return to South Africa. The most daring and spectacular acts of sabotage were committed after the Act came into force, including the dynamiting of electricity pylons and sub-stations, of the Pretoria office of a Cabinet Minister, and of the offices of a Nationalist newspaper in Durban. The police have made every effort, including the offer of large rewards, to bring the saboteurs to book, but have admitted that so far they have been unable to 'break their security'.[1] Saboteurs trained in

1 On 11 July 1963, armed police surrounded and raided the home of Arthur Goldreich, well-known artist at Rivonia, near Johannesburg. They captured and arrested Walter Sisulu, former secretary general of the banned African National Congress, who had been living in hiding after being sentenced to six years' imprisonment for incitement to strike and furthering the aims of a banned organization.

various African states and even as far afield as Cuba are reported to have slipped back into the country and reinforced the ranks of Umkhonto we Sizwe.

The close of 1962 also witnessed the emergence of a new menace to White South Africa – the organization known as Poqo, believed to be an outcrop of the banned Pan-Africanist Congress. According to its acting chief P. K. Leballo in a statement issued from Basutoland in March 1963, Poqo consisted of an army of 150,000 men throughout South Africa which was preparing for a final assault on white supremacy during 1963. South African police hold it responsible for the murder of three policemen in Langa location, Cape Town, eight murders of African and Coloured 'informers' in Paarl, the murder of a headman in the Transkei, the attempted murder of the government stooge chief Kaiser Matanzima in the Transkei, and, worst of all, a series of attacks on Whites.

On the night of 21 November 1962, a body of Africans marched out of the township of Mbekweni near Paarl and, after an unsuccessful attack on the police station, went on the rampage in the neighbourhood, sacking and looting shops, attacking private homes, and murdering a young man and a young woman who had been roused from their beds. Other Whites were hacked with pangas. Five Africans were reported killed in the riot, and afterwards several hundred were arrested on a charge of murder.

On the night of 2 February 1963, about fifty Africans descended on a road camp near Bashee River Bridge in the Transkei and, using petrol bombs and firearms, murdered five Whites who were sleeping in caravans.

On the night of 8 February 1963, a White businessman making his weekly debt collections in Langa location was set upon at night and murdered.

Also arrested were seventeen other men, both White and non-White, including a number of known leaders of the Congress movement, some of whom had also been in hiding after being placed under house arrest. On 9 October 1963 Sisulu and six others who had been arrested with him and detained in solitary confinement for eighty-eight days under the no-trial law (see page 190) were brought to trial on a charge of sabotage together with Nelson Mandela and three other detainees. If convicted the eleven accused face a minimum sentence of five years' imprisonment and a possible death penalty.

All these crimes and a number of others have been placed at the door of Poqo and have sent a shiver of fear through White South Africa. The police themselves have pointed out that whereas the banned A.N.C. (acknowledged by its leaders abroad to be responsible for the birth of Umkhonto we Sizwe) goes in for finely-planned acts of sabotage in which the object is not the taking of lives, Poqo has directed its attack against the White community as a whole. In an interim report the judge who was appointed to investigate the Paarl riot recommended that new legislation be placed on the statute book to deal with the 'Poqo menace', and the Minister of Justice hastened to oblige.

Barely a year after the passage of the Sabotage Act, another General Law Amendment Bill was presented to Parliament and inevitably passed, to become the most drastic law ever placed on the statute book by the Nationalist government. Here are its main provisions:

(a) Any person serving a sentence under the Suppression of Communism Act, the Public Safety Act, the Criminal Law Amendment Act of 1953, the Riotous Assemblies Act, or the Sabotage Act may be kept in jail after the expiry of his sentence if the Minister is satisfied that he is likely to advocate, advise, defend, or encourage the achievement of any of the objects of Communism. The Minister admitted that this clause was specifically aimed in the first place at the continued detention of Robert Sobukwe, P.A.C. leader, who was due to be released from prison after the expiry of a three-year sentence for incitement arising from the P.A.C. campaign in 1960. Nelson Mandela and other political leaders would also be affected.

(b) A minimum of five years imprisonment and a maximum of death shall be imposed on: (i) any person who since July 1950 has advocated, advised, defended, or encouraged the achievement by violent or forcible means of any object directed at bringing about any political, industrial, social, or economic change in the Republic with the cooperation or assistance of any foreign government or body; (ii) any person who since July 1950 has

undergone any training outside the Republic or obtained any information from a source outside the Republic which could be of use in furthering the achievement of any of the objects of Communism or of any body or organization which has been declared to be an unlawful organization ... and who fails to prove beyond a reasonable doubt that he did not undergo any such training or obtain any such information for the purpose of using it or causing it to be used in furthering the achievement of any such object.

It is to be noted that under this clause the death penalty can be imposed for crimes which were not crimes at the time that they were committed. A law passed in 1963 has been made retrospective to July 1950, the month in which the Suppression of Communism Act came into force.

(c) Accused persons my be tried summarily before a superior court without the benefit of a preparatory examination.

(d) Mail may be opened if suspected of having been sent to further the commission of an offence.

(e) The State President may by proclamation deem any organization which existed after 7 April 1960, to be the same as an unlawful organization. This provision was intended as authority to equate Poqo with the banned P.A.C., but could in fact be applied to any other organization, the members of which would immediately become subject to severe criminal penalities.

(f) Any commissioned police officer may without warrant arrest or cause to be arrested any person whom he suspects upon reasonable grounds of having committed or having intended to commit any offence under the Suppression of Communism Act, or the Unlawful Organizations Act (outlawing the A.N.C. and P.A.C.), or the offence of sabotage, and cause him to be detained for interrogation in any place for up to ninety days 'on any particular occasion when he is so arrested'. No person save a magistrate shall have access to such person and no court shall have jurisdiction to order his release.

(g) Entry to certain places or areas without a permit may be prohibited, and any unauthorized person who enters such place or area will be liable to imprisonment for fifteen years.

So disappeared the rule of law and *habeas corpus* from the South African scene. To its shame the United Party opposition voted for the second reading of the Bill, though it opposed certain of its provisions in the committee stage. Only the lone Progressive, Mrs Helen Suzman, voted against the Bill in all its stages. With her honourable exception, the parliamentary representatives of White South Africa presented a solid front against the 'Black peril'.

Mrs Suzman warned that the panic legislation which the government was rushing through the House at unprecedented speed would do nothing to end the South African emergency. For emergency it has now become. In the period between 1952 and 1963, some 500 people have been killed and more than 2,000 injured in clashes between the people and the police. Of this total, only nineteen of the dead and seventy of the injured were White.

Introducing his 1963 General Law Amendment Bill, the Minister of Justice announced on 24 April that there were 894 cases pending against 1,155 alleged Poqo members, and that recently a further 200 to 300 had been arrested. In twenty-six Poqo cases the accused had been indicted for murder; 124 accused had already been found guilty and seventy-seven had been committed for trial after preparatory examination. Since the enactment of the Sabotage Act, 2,994 persons had been prosecuted under its provisions. Up to the end of March 1963, three death sentences and eighty jail sentences totalling over 1,200 years had been passed for sabotage.

Further details of government reprisals were given by the Minister in a speech to Parliament on 13 June, 1963. Under the Sabotage Act, 126 people had been convicted, while 511 were still to appear. A total of 3,246 Poqo members had been arrested, with 124 found guilty of murder and seventy-seven still awaiting trial. More than 100 had appeared charged with attempted murder, and fifty-three had been detained for the Bashee River murder of five Whites. Action had been taken against 690 people for furthering the work of banned organizations, and cases against 1,357 were still pending.

Both the Minister and the Commissioner of Police boast that Poqo has been given a 'knock-out blow.' But these draconic laws, mass arrests, and savage sentences are the symptoms of social breakdown. After fifteen years of Nationalist rule, South

Africa is beginning to reap the whirlwind. In one form or another, the struggle continues and is being intensified. The people's resistance to tyranny is real and cannot be dispersed with words.

11. Indoctrinating the Young

> The struggle for the language was waged perhaps in its bitterest
> form around the school; because this was the nursery where the
> seeds had to be watered which were to spring up and form the
> future generation. The tactical objective of the fight was the
> winning over of the child, and it was to the child that the first
> rallying cry was addressed: 'German youth, do not forget
> that you are German' and 'Remember, little girl, that one day
> you must be a German mother'.   HITLER in *Mein Kampf*.

For the apartheid state to endure, the Nationalists must exercise
complete control over the minds of the young. The Afrikaner,
the Englishman, the White man and the Black man – each must
be brought up to understand the role which has been allotted to
him by the State. There must be unquestioning acceptance, by
the White man of his superiority, by the Afrikaner of his right
to leadership, by the non-White races of their duty to serve. To a
programme of education for all sections of the people the
Nationalists devoted the same intensive preparation as had gone
into the draft constitution issued during the war.

A congress for Christelik-Nasionale Onderwys (C.N.O.) or
Christian National Education was held by the F.A.K. (Federation of Afrikaans Cultural Organizations, a Broederbond off-
shoot) at Bloemfontein in July 1939, mainly to devise an answer
to the Hertzog government's dual medium education plans
which were regarded, in the words of Prof. van Rooy as 'a renewed attempt to anglicize our children'. The congress set up an
Institute (I.C.N.O.) to propagate the 'historic ideal' of C.N.O.,
and directors included some of the most prominent names in
Nationalist Afrikanerdom – Dr T. E. Dönges, present Minister
of Finance; Dr E. G. Jansen, later to be Governor-General of
South Africa; Advocate G. F. de Vos Hugo, later to be Chairman of the Group Areas Board and still later to be elevated to the
Bench; J. H. Greijbe, former President of the Transvaal
Afrikaans Teachers' Association; Dr C. Coetzee, Rector of the
University of Potchefstroom; Dr J. G. Meiring, later Superintendent-General of Education in the Cape and now Principal of
the apartheid university college for Coloured students; Rev.

D. P. Laurie, Prof. H. P. Wolmarans, Dr E. Greyling, and Rev. G. D. Worst.

Ten years later, in February 1948, the I.C.N.O. issued a pamphlet containing its recommendations. Prof. van Rooy, Chairman of the Broederbond and of the F.A.K., wrote a preface in which he explained that various drafts of policy had been considered by all the directing bodies of the F.A.K. and all the organizations on which the F.A.K. and the I.C.N.O. were represented, 'and that means by all Afrikaans bodies and organizations that have any interest in education. Therefore, the policy in its present form has been approved by the whole of Afrikanerdom in so far as it is represented by the F.A.K.'

This declaration should be carefully noted in the light of later half-hearted attempts by some Nationalist leaders to disavow the I.C.N.O. programme when it became politically embarrassing to them.

Prof. van Rooy congratulated the I.C.N.O. on formulating this policy as a guide in 'our cultural struggle, which is now also a school struggle'. He added:

There is too much at stake for us to relax in the struggle. With the use of our language as medium, we have not yet got everything. On the contrary, we have got very little. Afrikaans as a medium of instruction in a school atmosphere that is culturally foreign to our nation is like sounding brass and a tinkling cymbal. The true cultural stuff is not yet there. Our culture must be carried into the school and that cannot be done merely by having our language as medium. More is needed. Our Afrikaans schools must not merely be mother-tongue schools; they must be places where our children will be saturated with the Christian and National spiritual cultural stuff of our nation. The dual medium struggle has opened our eyes, and there is going to be a struggle about the realization of these ideals. We want no mixing of languages, no mixing of cultures, no mixing of religions, and no mixing of races. We are winning the medium struggle. The struggle for the Christian and National school still lies before us.

The programme enunciated in the I.C.N.O. pamphlet is fundamentalist and totalitarian. It is based on outmoded scientific and educational precepts, and envisages rigid centralized control of all educational establishments. It takes no account of the multi-racial character of South African society and proposes to enforce the views of a minority on the whole population.

Here are a few extracts from the pamphlet:

ARTICLE (1): *Basis*

All white children should be educated according to the view of life of their parents. This means that Afrikaans-speaking children should have a Christian-Nationalist education, for the Christian and Nationalist spirit of the Afrikaner nation must be preserved and developed.

By Christian, in this context, we mean according to the creeds of the three Afrikaner churches; by Nationalist we mean imbued with the love of one's own, especially one's own language, history, and culture. Nationalism must be rooted in Christianity.

ARTICLE (2): *Christian Education*

The key subject in school should be religion (the study of the Bible and the three Afrikaner creeds); and the religious spirit should permeate all subjects and the entire school.

ARTICLE (3): *Nationalist Education*

Teaching should also be nationalist, the child to become an heir to and worthy carrier of the national culture.

ARTICLE (6): *Content of Education*

(i) *Introduction.* In order to achieve the above aim, all God's creation and man's works must be studied. But the spirit of all teaching must be Christian-Nationalist; in no subject may anti-Christian or non-Christian or anti-Nationalist or non-Nationalist propaganda be made.

(ii) *Religious Teaching.* This includes Bible study and the study of the Christian doctrine. Religious teaching (key subject and permeating influence) must accord with the religious convictions of the parents as expressed in their church creeds. The recognized Church song of the Afrikaans Churches must be used in Schools.

(iii) *Mother-tongue.* This should be the most important secular subject, and the only medium of instruction except in teaching other modern languages. Bilingualism cannot be the aim of education, and the second official language should not be taught until the child has a thorough knowledge of his mother-tongue.

(v) *Geography*. Every nation is rooted in a country (Landsbodem) allotted to it by God. Geography should aim at giving the pupil a thorough knowledge of his own country and the natural objects pertaining to it, in such a way that he will love his own country, also when compared and contrasted with others, and be ready to defend it, preserve it from poverty, and improve it for posterity.

(vi) *History*. History should be seen as the fulfilment of God's plan for humanity. The turning-point of history is Jesus Christ – history teaching must therefore include such facts as the Creation, the Fall, the Incarnation, Life and Death of Christ, the Second Coming, and the End of the World; and history must be seen as the struggle between the Kingdom of God and the Empire of Darkness. Also, God has enjoined on each nation its individual task in the fulfilment of His purpose. Young people can only undertake the national task fruitfully if they acquire a true vision of the origin of the nation and of the direction of the national heritage. Next to the mother-tongue the history of the Fatherland is the best channel for cultivating love of one's own, which is nationalism.

ARTICLE (8): *Control of Education*

(i) *No Mixed Schools*. There should be at least two kinds of primary and secondary schools; one for the children of Afrikaans-speaking parents, with only Afrikaans as a medium, and the other for children of English-speaking parents, with only English as a medium. In each there should be the right relationship between home, school, Church, and State.

(iv) *The Church*. The Church must exercise the necessary discipline over the doctrine and lives of the teachers. The vigilance must be exercised through the parents. The Church must also stimulate all parents and give financial aid to needy ones to perform their educational task.

(v) *The State*. The State must ensure a proper scientific and moral standard in education, and therefore law and right in school life. It may not, however, determine the directing spirit of education providing that, as judged by God's law, it is not harmful to the State. Where the child's natural guardians, the parents, neglect their educational duties, the State, as paramount guardian, should step in and establish schools until such time as the parents desire to exercise their own rights.

(vii) *Organization of Education*. . . . Our ideal is the Christian-

Nationalist school; but for the time being we must be content to leaven the existing public schools.

ARTICLE (9): *The Teacher*

(ii) ... Training College personnel should also be Christian and Nationalist.

ARTICLE (11): *Higher Education*

(i) The basis for this should be the same as for schools.

(ii) The content should be scientific, but founded on the Christian Faith. The Christian doctrine and philosophy should be taught and practised. But we desire still more: the secular sciences should be taught according to the Christian and Nationalist view of life. University teaching should be thetic rather than anti-thetic, never purely eclectic and never reconciliatory. Science should be expounded in a positively Christian light, and contrasted with non-Christian science. Universities should never give unintegrated instruction, merely choosing here and choosing there; there should be no attempt to reconcile or abolish the fundamental oppositions; for Creator and created, man and beast, individual and community, authority and freedom remain in principle insoluble in each other. Especially in the universities do we need the right personnel; for professors and lecturers make the institution and determine its guiding spirit. It is all-important therefore that the teaching staff should be convinced Christian-Nationalist scientists.

ARTICLE (14): *Coloured Education*

The education of Coloureds should be seen as a subordinate part of the Afrikaner's task of Christianizing the non-White races of our fatherland. It is the Afrikaner's sacred duty to see that the Coloureds are brought up Christian-Nationalist. Only when he is Christianized can the Coloured be truly happy; and he will then be proof against foreign ideologies which give him an illusion of happiness but leave him in the long run unsatisfied and unhappy.

He must also be a nationalist. The welfare and happiness of the Coloured lies in his understanding that he belongs to a separate racial group (hence apartheid is necessary in education), and in his being proud of it.

Coloured education must not be financed at the expense of White education.

ARTICLE (15): *Native Education*

The White South African's duty to the native is to Christianize him and help him on culturally.

Native education should be based on the principles of trusteeship, non-equality, and segregation; its aim should be to inculcate the White man's view of life, especially that of the Boer nation, which is the senior trustee.

The mother-tongue should be the basis of native education but the two official languages should be learned as keys to the cultures from which the native will have to borrow in order to progress. Owing to the cultural infancy of the native, the State, in cooperation with the Protestant Churches, should at present provide native education. But the native should be fitted to undertake his own education as soon as possible, under control and guidance of the State. Native education should lead to the development of an independent, self-supporting Christian-Nationalist native community.

Native education should not be financed at the expense of White.

The assumptions implicit in this programme are: that C.N.O. is valid not only for the Afrikaner but also for the English-speaking South African; that the outlook of the Afrikaner is to be dominant in South African education; that the views of the White man are to be imposed on the non-Whites through the medium of education; that the aim of education is the indoctrination of the child with Christian-Nationalism. In other words the outlook of the Broederbond is to be imposed on the rest of the population by means of education, whether they like it or not.

Quite understandably, many educationists and parents became gravely concerned when the Nationalists came to power so soon after the publication of this pamphlet and members of the I.C.N.O. took up leading positions in the new government. There was an outburst of opposition and an Education League was established with the aim of exposing C.N.O. to the public at large. Nationalist spokesmen back-pedalled hurriedly, proclaiming that the pamphlet was entirely unofficial and did not represent government policy, but behind the scenes the government itself proceeded with the implementation of the C.N.O. programme almost to the letter.

APARTHEID BETWEEN ENGLISH AND AFRIKANER

Just as Hertzog, in the period following the Boer War, saw the salvation of the Afrikaner in isolation, so the C.N.O. supporter believed that his programme could only be implemented if the Afrikaans child was separated from the English. In parallel or dual medium schools, Afrikaans culture would be submerged. Only when the Afrikaans child was isolated from all foreign contracts could he be 'saturated with the Christian and National spiritual cultural stuff of our nation'.

In justification of his standpoint, the Nationalist invoked the historical precedent of the C.N.O. schools established by the Dutch Reformed Churches after the Boer War to resist Milner's avowed policy of anglicization. Milner flooded the State schools with teachers imported from England and made English the sole medium of instruction. The Afrikaner accordingly sought refuge in his own C.N.O. schools, of which several hundred were set up and maintained until financial pressure and the grant of self-government to the former Boer republics by the Liberal administration in England induced the Boer leaders to consider merging their schools with the State ones.

The significant fact about the C.N.O. schools of those days, however, is that they did not incorporate the principle of mother-tongue education which the Nationalists now hold to be sacred. Afrikaans itself was not taught in the C.N.O. schools – it was only recognized as an official language in 1925 – but Dutch, which was one of the two official languages. Nor were the C.N.O. schools single medium. Both English and Dutch constituted the media of instruction up to standard 3, while from standard 4 to matriculation English became the medium. Thus the Afrikaans child of those days was in reality educated through the medium of two foreign languages, while his mother tongue was ignored.

Now, however, Nationalist Afrikanerdom can only survive if its children are prevented from mixing with the children of other sections in the schools. Not only must there be apartheid between Black and White, but there must be apartheid between English and Afrikaner. Why? Are there different facts to be taught to the two sections?

Yes, there are. 'You can't,' declared Dr Stoker, a C.N.O. apologist, at a public lecture in Johannesburg, 'you can't have mixed schools because you can't teach Afrikaans-speaking children about their own heroes of the Boer War if there are English-speaking children in the same class-room.' For the purposes of Afrikaner Nationalism, the divisions of the past must be perpetuated. There must be no attempt to form a single nation, with a single outlook and a single loyalty. There must be different nations, even amongst the Whites.

Nationalist leaders may have been chary of acknowledging C.N.O. (with the exception of the egregious de Wet Nel, today Minister of Bantu Administration and Development, who when Minister of Education said, 'Christian-National Education should be the basis of all planning and the object should not merely be academical education'). But they have promoted C.N.O. in other ways.

In 1955 Dr W. Nicol, Administrator of the Transvaal, condemned dualism in the family, religion, or love, adding that in education 'it is cruelty to a child's mind and spirit comparable to a child's being horse-whipped by its parents'.

Harm Oost, Nationalist Member of Parliament for Pretoria District, declared during a language debate in 1952 that the bilingual child was not a problem child, but a bad Afrikaner, because he was 'neither fish nor flesh and had no national backbone'.

And Dr Verwoerd himself proclaimed in March 1953, while still Minister of Native Affairs: 'The fundamental thing about education is not the wish of the parents, often a selfish wish, but the interest of the child.'

As soon as they gained power over the provincial councils which control White education, therefore, the Nationalists introduced their policy of separatism. In the Transvaal from 1945 to 1949, when the United Party was in power, mother-tongue instruction was given as a rule – but with the final choice yielded to the parent – for primary education, and dual-medium education thereafter. After 1949, when the Nationalists acquired a majority in the provincial council, mother-tongue education was made compulsory up to standard 8 or the leaving age of sixteen, and parental choice eliminated, with inspectors and school principals empowered to decide the home language of a child. The same policy was extended to the Cape in 1953. Today the only province retaining parental choice is Natal, where the Nationalists are in the minority; and even there the Nationalist-appointed Administrator has made a bid to influence the course of events by promoting a well-known C.N.O. supporter to the position of Deputy-Director of Education, despite his unanimous rejection by the Natal Executive Committee of the Provincial Council.

In Nationalist-controlled provinces, many dual and parallel-medium schools have been disestablished, irrespective of the wishes of the parents concerned, while Afrikaans children have been prevented from attending English-medium schools and forced to attend 'their own' schools instead. The system of school board elections has been altered so that only parents of children actually at school may vote. This has worked in favour of the Nationalists because of the higher proportion of Afrikaners among the school-going population, and school board elections have often turned into political demonstrations with no holds barred on either side.

In all three Nationalist-dominated provinces, Nationalist propaganda is being assiduously disseminated through school textbooks. History is presented through the eyes of the Afrikaner, and racial prejudice against the non-Whites is commonplace. In the Transvaal, school reading has been controlled through the introduction of a book guide, and teachers are forbidden to allow on school premises any book which does not appear in the guide. In these circumstances, the opportunity of the teacher to promote independent reading or thinking by his pupils is reduced to a minimum.

Examples of Nationalist propaganda in textbooks published for the Transvaal schools are innumerable. English is branded as the 'language of the conqueror', and support is lent to the bulk of apartheid legislation. Here are some further titbits:

Although our forefathers since the time of Jan van Riebeeck had been in daily contact with the non-White inhabitants, there was virtually no inter-marrying.

(A ludicrous lie.)

Our forefathers believed, and we still believe today, that God Himself made the diversity of peoples on earth. It is therefore bad for White and non-Whites to inter-marry. . . .

It has become the traditional standpoint that although White and non-White share a common fatherland, there should be no mixing of races, and that there should be no eating, drinking, and visiting together. This viewpoint is also set down in various laws. Inter-racial residence and inter-marriage are not only a disgrace, but are also forbidden by law.

It is, however, not only the skin of the White South African that differs from that of the non-White. The White stands on a much higher plane of civilization and is more developed. Whites must so live, learn, and work that we shall not sink to the cultural level of the non-Whites. Only thus can the government of our country remain in the hands of the Whites.

In these trade unions which had Whites and non-Whites, social mixing at their meetings was common. They ate and drank together. Sometimes they had parties together. The Industrial Conciliation Act of 1956 put an end to many of these wrong things.

The *Special Branch* of the South African Police is responsible for the *internal security* of the country. Although these men receive no publicity, they have the most difficult task of all the police. It is *common knowledge* that *spies* from other countries are even at this moment trying to obtain *vital information* about South Africa. Every hour of the day *secret transmitters* transmit *messages in code* to various parts of the world.

In an era of *phone tapping* and *hidden microphones*, of *riots* and *sabotage*, the security forces have to *combat espionage* tactfully and efficiently without causing *international incidents*. This extremely difficult task is further complicated by the fact that *unscrupulou* *agents use embassies* of their country and *abuse the immunity accorded t* *diplomats in foreign countries.*

It is fortunate that the *average citizen* is unaware of the *plots* and *counterplots* that are hatched daily. . . .

Oral Composition: c(i) You are head of the Security Branch of the S.A. Police. In a secret interview with the Minister of Justice, tell him why you are so alarmed.

In reply to a resolution of protest by the National Union of South African Students against such indoctrination, the Transvaal Director of Education replied: '. . . As far as the Transvaal Education Department is concerned, we are convinced that the books in use are suitable.'

Suitable for brainwashing, yes. Suitable for the indoctrination of youth who are expected to defend themselves against a horde of enemies inside and outside the country. But quite unsuitable for teaching children how to discover the truth, to test, to criticize, to perform their functions as citizens in a free democratic society.

Article 9 (*i*) of the C.N.O. programme proclaims: 'Being a substitute for the parent, the teacher does the parent's work as the parent himself would do it were he able. Unless, therefore, he is a Christian, he is a deadly danger to us.' Since coming to power the Nationalists have accordingly exercised themselves to eliminate the 'conscience clause' incorporated in the statutes of all the universities. This clause reads:

No test of religious belief shall be imposed on any person as a condition of his becoming or continuing to be a professor, lecturer, teacher, or student of a university college, or of holding any office or receiving any emolument, or exercising any privilege therein, nor shall any preference be given to or advantage be withheld from any person on the ground of his religious belief.

In 1949 Potschefstroom sought parliamentary sanction to assume the status of a full university and in so doing sought, and achieved, an amendment to the conscience clause. The prohibition against a religious test for students was retained, but the clause concerning staff was amended to read: 'The Council shall ensure that the Christian historical character of the university shall be maintained: provided that no denominational test shall be applied.' Denominational was defined as 'the requirement of membership of any Church'.

Later the University of the Orange Free State attempted to eliminate the conscience clause from its statutes, but was unsuccessful. The Bill proposing the amendment was dropped from the parliamentary order paper after Bloemfontein doctors threatened to boycott the proposed medical faculty if the conscience clause was eliminated.

But the fight against the conscience clause continues. In October 1962 the Minister of Education, Senator Jan de Klerk, told the congress of the Society for Christian Higher Education in Bloemfontein that he fully backed its efforts. According to the Nationalist newspaper *Die Volksblad*, he expressed support for the Society's aims, 'which included the elimination of the conscience clause'.

None of the tribal colleges set up under the Extension of University Education Act was allowed to incorporate the conscience clause in its statutes. The Prime Minister, Dr Verwoerd, explained: 'Inasmuch as all Bantu education arose from religious instruction and is still and should be coupled with it, there will be no insertion of a conscience clause in their statutes.'

Direct State interference with school education is foreshadowed by the passage of the National Education Advisory Council Act of 1962. In terms of this Act, an Advisory Council of twenty-nine members (eighteen Afrikaans-speaking and eleven English-speaking) has been established to advise the Minister on the policy to be applied towards education. The aims of the Council as set down in the Act are to determine the broad, fundamental principles of sound education for the country as a whole and to coordinate educational policy to suit the needs of the country.

Since all the members are appointed by the Minister of Education, it may be assumed that the composition of the Council is designed to ensure the implementation of the policy he himself desires to promote. True, the Council is advisory, but non-Nationalists see its very establishment as one step further towards authoritarianism and a threat to local freedom and initiative in education.

APARTHEID BETWEEN BLACK AND WHITE

In 1949 the Nationalist government appointed a commission headed by Dr W. W. M. Eiselen to report on education for Africans 'as an independent race' and to devise 'syllabuses . . . to prepare natives more effectively for their future occupations'.

The very framing of the commission's terms of reference indicated the government's intention to implement the C.N.O. programme for African education.

The commission concluded that African education should be framed so as to fit the African child into the society to which he would eventually belong, and that this would not be the general South African society, but a separate African one for which a special type of education was required. The commission recognized that 'the Bantu child comes to school with a basic physical and psychological endowment which differs so far as your Commissioners have been able to determine from the evidence, so slightly, if at all, from that of the European child that no special provision has to be made in educational theory or basic aims'. Nevertheless, because the African occupied a different place in society from that of the White, his education should be entrusted to a separate department and should be linked with a programme for the development of the African people as a whole.

A Bantu Education Act withdrawing Bantu education from provincial control and transferring it, not to the Union Department of Education, but to the Department of Native Affairs, was passed in 1953. The Act itself contained no details of the type of education to be purveyed, but during the debate on the Bill the Minister of Native Affairs, Dr Verwoerd, stated:

When I have control of native education I will reform it so that natives will be taught from childhood to realize that equality with Europeans is not for them. . . . People who believe in equality are not desirable teachers for natives. . . . When my Department controls native education, it will know for what class of higher education a native is fitted, and whether he will have a chance in life to use his knowledge.

The Act gave the Minister unrestricted powers to decide what schools should exist, together with what the conditions of service for teachers and the content of African education should be. Once the Bill became Law, nobody might conduct any form of class for Africans without the Minister's permission.

Just how far the Minister was preparing to go was revealed by him in a statement to the Senate in June 1954. 'The general aims of the Bantu Education Act', he said, 'are to transform education *for* natives into *Bantu* education. . . . A Bantu pupil must obtain knowledge, skills, and attitudes which will be useful and advantageous to him and at the same time beneficial to his community. . . . The school must equip him to meet the demands which the economic life of South Africa will impose on him. . . .'

Verwoerd stressed that the principle of mother-tongue education would be applied to the Bantu, for any other system of education failed to prepare the child for life within a Bantu community and only served to create a class of educated and semi-educated persons which learnt to believe that 'its spiritual, economic, and political home is among the civilized community of South Africa'.

He continued:

There is no place for him (the Bantu) in the European community above the level of certain forms of labour. . . . For that reason it is of no avail for him to receive a training which has as its aim absorption in the European community. . . . Until now he has been subject to a school system which drew him away from his own community and misled him by showing him the green pastures of European society in which he is not allowed to graze.

Verwoerd maintained that the present system of education led to the creation of a class of 'imitation Europeans' for whom there were no openings in life and who as a result were frustrated and discontented.

What is the use of teaching a Bantu child mathematics when it cannot use it in practice? . . . That is absurd. Education is not after all something that hangs in the air. Education must train and teach people in accordance with their opportunities in life. . . . It is therefore necessary that native education should be controlled in such a way that it should be in accordance with the policy of the State.

The whole emphasis of education had to be changed. Instead of providing a comparatively expensive and intensive education for a small number of children, the aim of the government would be to give as many African children as possible such 'fundamental' educational facilities as could be provided with available funds. Effort would be concentrated on 'education in sub-standards A and B, and probably up to standard 2, including reading writing, and arithmetic through mother-tongue instruction, as well as a knowledge of English and Afrikaans, and the cardinal principles of the Christian religion'. The present 'standard 6 mentality' of the teachers would have to be abandoned.

Verwoerd took the opportunity of issuing a word of warning to the teachers. For those who were not faithful to the government's programme there was no room in Bantu education, he said.

The Bantu teacher must be integrated as an active agent in the process of development of the Bantu community. He must learn not to feel above his community with a consequent desire to become integrated into the life of the European community. He becomes frustrated and rebellious when this does not take place, and he tries to make his community dissatisfied because of such misdirected ambitions which are alien to his people.

One of the means by which Verwoerd proposed to bring about the desired frame of mind in the African teacher was the lowering of his salary scale. 'The Bantu teacher serves the Bantu community, and his salary must be fixed accordingly.' Not only were present salaries sufficient and any demands for increases quite unrealistic, but

in the new conditions of service for teachers which will be published soon, there will appear new salary scales for newly-appointed teachers, and these scales will be possibly less favourable than the existing scales. In future those who wish to choose the teaching profession are, therefore, warned in time, so that they should take this into consideration. The salaries which European teachers enjoy are in no way a fit or permissible criterion for the salaries of Bantu teachers.

The existing scales were low enough. Unqualified teachers (there were about 3,000 of them) earned £6 10s. a month including cost of living allowance. Trained teachers earned from £6 10s. to £12 10s. (with cost of living allowance) or from £9 to £19 10s. according to qualifications. University graduates could earn from £16 10s. a month to £29 (excluding cost of living allowance) after thirteen years. Women earned less; and there were no pensions for African teachers.

Improved salary scales were not introduced until 1963, when the key scale became £48 × 9 – £156 × 12 – £192 × 18 – £300 × 24 – £540 × 30 – £900 × 36. . . . The new scales provide for consolidation of the existing cost of living allowances up to the maximum rate of £320 a year for married male teachers. Needless to say these scales are far below those of European teachers, substantial increases for whom were also announced in 1963. The lowest starting salary for a European male teacher is £603 a year, and for a European female teacher £510.

The government has adhered strictly to the principle that the development of African education should not take place at the expense of Whites. Before the Bantu Education Act came into force, all the funds required for African education had been drawn direct from the Consolidated Revenue Fund, with the estimates placed on the votes of the Union Department of Education, Arts, and Science. In other words, it had been accepted by the United Party government that African education should be a charge on the community as a whole. Between 1945, when the United Party government had adopted its formula, and 1954, when the Nationalist formula was substituted for it, expenditure on African education had risen from £2,248,529 to £8,016,247, and the number of pupils from 587,586 to 938,211. The *per capita* cost had increased from £3·83 in 1945 to £8·54 in 1954.

After 1954 the formula was completely changed. The contribution from the Consolidated Revenue Account was permanently pegged at £6½ million, and to this sum was added four fifths of the revenue derived from the direct general tax levied on the African people. The government made it plain that if there was to be any expansion in African educational services, it would have to be financed by the Africans themselves. Not a penny more would be given by the central government. The estimated revenue of the Bantu Educational Account for 1962–3 was:

Fixed statutory appropriation	£6,500,000
Four fifths of African general revenue	£3,200,000
Miscellaneous receipts (boarding fees, etc.)	£300,000
	£10,000,000[1]

1 The Minister of Finance, Dr Dönges, announced in his 1963 budget speech that an additional sum of £1·7 million would be transferred to the Bantu Education Account for higher education, to cover the period 1962–4. He also stated that in future the full amount of the Bantu general tax and not four fifths as at present would in future accrue to Bantu Education.

This expenditure covered a school population of approximately 1,600,000 African children. (The last figure supplied was 1,562,843 for the year ended 31 March 1962, excluding a total of 121,583 children in Church and private schools.)

The Nationalists freely boast that they have more African children at school than ever before, and that more money is spent on African education in South Africa than in any other territory on the continent. But the facts require careful examination to show exactly what is happening.

The last year for which figures are available of the comparative amounts spent on the education of the various racial groups was 1953, when the position was:

	Per pupil	Per head of population
Whites	£63 18 5	£13 9 5
Coloured and Asians	20 4 3	3 19 7
Africans	8 19 11	17 10

Since then the *per capita* figure for Africans has steadily declined.

Year	Expenditure on each African pupil
1953–4	£8·54
1955	7·84
1956	7·94
1957	7·89
1958	7·14
1959	7·05
1960	6·90
1961	6·90
1962	6·15

Thus the Nationalist government is spending less per head on African pupils than at any time since it came to power in 1948, and the trend is still downwards. How then has the increase in school population been achieved?

Double sessions have been introduced in the sub-standards,

H

with two shifts of three hours each per day. 'It is wrong to utilize expensive teaching staff to supervise large classes of bored pupils while thousands of children are kept out of school,' said Dr Verwoerd in the Senate in 1954. Asked what the children would do for the rest of the day, he replied: 'It is not the function of the school to keep children off the streets or the veld by using well-paid teachers to supervise them.'

As far as possible women teachers have been appointed for the primary grades at lower rates of pay. Dr Verwoerd declared in 1954: 'Today about seventy per cent of the teaching force is male; it would be preferable had we that percentage of female teachers. This measure in the course of time will bring about a considerable saving of funds.' And he promised another change: 'The Department (will) do away entirely with the European teacher in Bantu primary schools.'

Farm schools have been graded into junior and senior schools with a corresponding saving on salaries, and school feeding funds have been devoted to the expansion of educational facilities. As a result of this last innovation, many children attend school in a condition of semi-starvation, which makes it impossible for them to benefit from their instruction.

Far less equipment is supplied to African schools than was formerly the case, and very small allowances are made for libraries. The schools themselves have to find the money needed for replacements of furniture and repairs to buildings, while the pupils have to supply their own writing materials. The only textbooks provided are readers in three languages issued to primary schools annually on the basis of one quarter of the enrolment.

Even the money for financing the erection of school buildings is squeezed from the African community. Rents in some municipal housing schemes have been increased by levies of up to 2s. a month to pay for the erection of lower primary schools, while school boards are expected to collect money for building higher primary and secondary schools and then to apply to the Department for grants on a £ for £ basis. It has often happened, however, that school boards have completed their own part of the bargain, at tremendous sacrifice to the community, only to find that the Department has no more funds at its disposal.

According to an estimate made by the Minister of Bantu Education himself, African parents, who constitute the lowest paid section of the population and live mostly below the bread-line, have to pay an average of £35 for each child between standard 1 and Junior Certificate (standard 8). The newspaper the *Natal Mercury* has estimated that African parents pay three times as much in direct costs as do Whites.

The purpose of Bantu Education, of course, as its exponents have stressed, is to equip the African child for his place as servant and labourer in South African society. A certain proportion of children may be allowed to filter through the screen to 'serve their own community' as doctors, teachers, lawyers, and the like, but the main emphasis remains upon teaching the child the three R's, so that he may be made capable of following simple instructions in both official languages – and no more. Thus in 1961 the distribution of pupils was 72·2 per cent in the lower primary classes, 24·9 per cent in the higher primary ones, and only 2·9 per cent in post-primary classes. There is automatic promotion up to standard 2, when the first weeding out takes place, and then again till the second weeding out at the end of standard 6. Only the chosen few – chosen for character and reliability as well as academic attainment – are allowed to proceed any further.

The emphasis is on quantity, not on quality. At the time of the transfer to Bantu Education in 1953–4, of the 5,819 schools then in existence, 4,827 were aided private schools (mostly mission schools) and only 992 government schools. The type of education given was in general the same as that offered by the European schools. Then, in August 1954, all church bodies controlling subsidized schools were given a choice between relinquishing control over their schools or accepting a gradual reduction in their subsidy. Of forty denominations, only the Roman Catholic Church chose to retain its schools, and since 1958 it has ceased to receive any subsidy from the government. By 1960 the number of government and government-aided schools had reached 6,750 of which seventy per cent were graded as 'community schools' under school board control.

There were only 720 unaided Church schools (mostly Roman Catholic) with about 90,000 pupils.

Neither the number of schools nor the number and quality of the teachers has kept pace with the increase in the number of pupils. In 1961 only 686 out of 13,101 male teachers employed by the Bantu Education Department had passed a university degree course; only a further 614 had passed standard 10. The corresponding figures for female teachers were 210 with degrees and 291 matriculants out of a total 15,002. Classes of fifty and sixty children are common, and conditions in some schools have to be seen to be believed, with children squatting on the floor and writing on their knees or jammed four to six into a desk intended for two. Many of the buildings are very dilapidated and not even weatherproof.

Perhaps the factor which has caused most distress to the Africans themselves has been the enforced introduction of education in the vernacular, with the allocation of equal time to both official languages. Previously, education had been started in the vernacular, but after the first couple of standards had been pursued in English (most of the schools were English mission schools). Today all teaching is done through the medium of the vernacular up to and including standard 6, and the aim is to continue the process all the way to matriculation. The intention behind this policy, of course, is to link the school with the system of tribal authorities and effectively to separate 'Bantu Education' from all other education through the use of the vernacular. When matriculation is taken in the vernacular, the African matriculant automatically loses eligibility for entrance into any non-African university. His 'Bantu matric' will qualify him for entrance into his appropriate tribal university – and nowhere else. He will not even be able to leave the country and, on the basis of his educational qualifications, proceed with his university studies elsewhere. His education will lead in one direction only – that mapped out for him by Dr Verwoerd.

Vernacular instruction itself has led to a startling drop in educational standards. There are seven vernacular languages, with the result that there is a lack of suitable textbooks, and for the most part the children have to rely on the instruction of the teacher. Then, after education through the vernacular in the primary school, there is at present a sudden switch to the two official languages as media of instruction in the secondary schools. Children have found the whole pattern extremely unsettling, and the standard of English in particular has dropped disastrously.

The effects of all these changes were evident in the appalling decline in matriculation passes from the time that Bantu Education was introduced. Whereas in 1947 and 1948 the percentage of passes had been 54·8 and 52·8 respectively, by 1958 the percentage had dropped to 37·6, by 1959 to 19, and by 1960 to 17·9 per cent, with only 128 out of 716 entrants passing. In the next two years there was an improvement, with 215 out of 828, or twenty-six per cent, passing in 1961, and 364 out of 894, or forty per cent, in 1962. But the shock of the bad years profoundly affected all sections of the African people, and there has been a widespread demand for the reintroduction of English as the medium of instruction in Bantu Education schools – a demand supported by none other than Chief Kaiser Matanzima, Chairman of the Transkei Territorial Authority and a well-known government supporter. The government has appointed a commission to inquire into the medium of instruction in Bantu Education schools, but at the time of writing it had not completed its report.

Africans are deeply disturbed about the course that Bantu Education is taking. They appreciate that education is the key to their future and they have everywhere shown themselves willing to make enormous sacrifices in order to ensure that their children get the chance of a good education. They are now faced with a terrible dilemma, for they either accept Bantu Education or get no education for their children at all. Their attitude was expressed by Mrs Lilian Ngoyi, Chairman of the South African Federation of Women, who said: 'The Bantu Education Act will make African mothers like fowls who lay eggs for other people to take away and make what they like with them.'

'Native education,' announced the C.N.O. pamphlet in 1948, 'should be based on the principles of trusteeship, non-equality, and segregation; its aim should be to inculcate the White man's

213

view of life, especially that of the Boer nation, which is the senior trustee.'

The White teacher has been practically eliminated from the Bantu government school, and great play is made of the fact that the majority of government schools are run by the various African communities themselves. Cabinet Ministers boast that South Africa has more educated Africans than all the other African countries put together – 2,000 university graduates, 15,200 matriculants, 75,000 with the Junior Certificate, and 295,600 who have passed standard 6. Yet Bantu Education remains a system of indoctrination run by Whites for Blacks. Of the 143 higher administrative and professional posts with a maximum salary exceeding £1,250 in the Bantu Education Department, NOT ONE is occupied by an African. The reins are being tightly kept in the hands of the 'senior trustee'.

Now what has been done to African education is to be extended to Coloured and Indian education as well. In February 1962 the Minister of Indian Affairs announced that in due course Indian education would be transferred to his Department. In 1961 Coloured vocational and technical education was transferred to the Coloured Affairs Department, and in 1963 the Coloured Persons Education Act transferred Coloured primary and secondary education as well.

Coloured education today is much the same as African education was in 1953. In 1961 there were 1,491 schools for Coloured and Asian children in the Cape, and of these 1,247 were aided mission schools. Doubtless the mission influence will be excluded, as it has been excluded from African education, and the State will assume absolute control. What will happen then has been made clear in a speech by the Minister of Coloured Affairs, P. W. Botha, on 31 October 1962. 'There are basic faults in Coloured education,' he said. 'We shall give no inferior education, but shall most certainly give Coloured people differentiated education. It would not help to give them only academic education and then throw them on to the market as frustrated people.' It all has a depressingly familiar ring.

As for Botha's promise that 'we shall give no inferior education', the parliamentary opposition put it to the test during the committee stage on the Bill, with an amendment to insert a clause that would guarantee Coloured children the same standard of education as Whites. Botha refused to accept the clause, explaining that 'many Coloured people could not cope with the education Whites received; many teachers had only reached standard 8'.

Myburgh Streicher, United Party M.P. for Port Elizabeth West, commented that he had never heard such rubbish. But there it is. Coloured education will no doubt be framed to equip the Coloured child for his station in life – a little above the African, but well below the White. Not surprisingly, all Coloured teachers' associations opposed the transfer, and even the stooge Union Council of Coloured Affairs only accepted it on certain conditions – to which the government did not agree.

UNIVERSITY APARTHEID

There has always been a considerable degree of apartheid at the South African universities. All the Afrikaans-medium ones – Potchefstroom, Pretoria, Orange Free State, and Stellenbosch – have, of course, from the outset restricted admission to Whites, while of English-medium universities, Rhodes in the Eastern Cape admitted only White students, though it had an arrangement with Fort Hare whereby the latter's students graduated with Rhodes degrees. Fort Hare was an open university and enrolled White students from time to time, but its 1957 enrolment of 378 was typical, with its break-down into 283 Africans, forty-eight Coloureds, and forty-seven Indians. Natal University admitted non-Whites but ran parallel classes for them, so that no mixing with White students might be risked. Its enrolment of non-White students in 1957 broke down into twenty-four Coloureds, 350 Asians, and 181 Africans.

Only the universities of Cape Town and the Witwatersrand were 'open' universities in the sense that members of all races were freely admitted, but even then it was only an academic integration, and a strict colour bar was applied in social and sporting events. In 1957 Cape Town had 306 Coloured, 121 Asian, and twenty-nine African students, while the University of the Witwatersrand in Johannesburg had twenty Coloureds,

135 Asians, and fifty-nine Africans. In all, at the three universities of Natal, Cape Town, and the Witwatersrand there was a total of 1,225 non-White students enrolled, compared with a total of 24,237 White students registered at all the South African universities (the correspondence classes of the University of South Africa are excluded).

Yet to the Nationalist government this tiny number of non-White students represented a deadly danger. As *Die Transvaler* had said on 27 February 1957, in relation to the controversy over the Church clause:

It is not so much the overwhelming numbers of non-Europeans but the destruction of the feeling of difference and otherness which is the great danger for the preservation of the European and his civilization in this multi-racial land. As long as liberalistic bishops and canons, professors, students, and politicians can freely attend church and hold meetings and socials together, apartheid will be infringed in its marrow.

After much propaganda and several preliminary attempts, the Nationalist government finally passed in 1959 two Acts which sounded the death knell for higher education in South Africa – the so-called Extension of University Education Act and the University College of Fort Hare Transfer Act. In terms of the former, it became a criminal offence for any non-White student to register at any of the hitherto open universities without the written consent of the Minister. Instead, the Act provided for the establishment of special university colleges for non-White students, who were to be separated on racial and ethnic lines.

The University College of the Western Cape, to serve the Coloured, Malay, and Griqua groups, was officially established on 1 November 1959, with classes started in an old school until such time as permanent buildings could be constructed. The Rector is Dr J. G. Meiring, former Superintendent-General of Education in the Cape and one of the members of the Institute for Christian-National Education which produced the C.N.O. programme of 1948. The language medium of the college is Afrikaans, and the enrolment at the beginning of the 1962 academic year was 351.

Two new colleges for Africans were officially opened on 1 August 1959. The University College of the North, to serve the Sotho group, is at Turfloop, about eighteen miles east of Pietersburg in the north-eastern Transvaal. The University College of Zululand, to serve the Zulu group, is at Ngoya, in the Mtunzini district of Natal. Dr Verwoerd declared in 1954:

An increase in the number of institutions for higher education located in urban areas is not desired. Steps will be taken deliberately to keep institutions for higher education, to an increasing extent, away from urban areas, and to establish them as far as possible in the Native Reserves. My Department's policy is that education should stand with both feet in the Reserves and have its roots in the spirit and being of Bantu society.

He is keeping his word.

New buildings have been erected for these colleges, and to preserve their tribal flavour they have been equipped, not with common rooms for the students, but with circular *lapas* – roofless areas with built-in seats and in some cases central fireplaces. Where the students are supposed to congregate when it rains has not yet been stated.

The enrolment at Turfloop in 1962 was 197, of whom ninety-seven had not matriculated; and at Ngoya ninety-four of whom thirty-two were not matriculants.

A university college for Indians was opened during 1961 in buildings formerly used by the Navy on Salisbury Island in Durban Bay. The administration of the college is still in the hands of the Minister of Education, Arts, and Science, but is ultimately destined for the Department of Indian Affairs. The enrolment in 1961 was 120, and in 1962, 440.

Meanwhile, in terms of the Fort Hare Transfer Act, the government has moved to convert Fort Hare from an open university to a Xhosa tribal college. Fort Hare had been incorporated as an institution for higher learning under the Education Act of 1923 and was affiliated to Rhodes University for examination and degree purposes in 1951. Under the University Act of 1955 it ranked as a university, and would in time have qualified for its own charter; by the end of 1958 it had awarded 1,132 degrees and 771 diplomas and certificates. The staff was multi-racial, consisting in 1959 of twenty-eight Whites, ten Africans, and one Coloured, while of the 430 students, only thirty-eight per cent were of Xhosa origin, thirty-four per cent came from other African groups, fourteen per cent were Coloured, and fourteen per cent Indian. At earlier periods in its history there had been White students at the university, and indeed one of the first four students to matriculate there in 1918 had been White.

But in the eyes of the Minister, Fort Hare was nothing but an English university for non-Whites, as he complained in the debate on the Transfer Bill. What the Xhosa needed was an institution of their own, expressing their own culture and rooted in their own community. He would even like to see Fort Hare moved into the heart of the Transkei, he declared, so that it could be in touch with the real feelings of the Xhosa.

Everything has changed since the transfer – but the Xhosa still have not got their own university. The Council of Fort Hare – as the councils of all the tribal colleges – is all White, under the chairmanship of Professor S. Pauw, Principal of the University of South Africa. Prof. H. Burrows was not reappointed as Principal and was replaced by Prof. J. J. Ross from the University of the Orange Free State. The Vice-Principal, Prof. Z. K. Matthews, was told that he would be reappointed as a State employee if he resigned from the African National Congress. He refused to do so.

During September 1959 seven English-speaking White members of staff were informed that their appointments would be terminated at the end of the year. They were the heads of the departments of Law, English, Philosophy and Politics, and Geography, the Registrar, a lecturer, and the Librarian. The Minister of Bantu Education explained: 'I disposed of their services because I will not permit a penny of any funds over which I have control to be paid to any persons who are known to be destroying the government's policy of apartheid.' One of the victims, Sir Fulque Agnew, declared that he regarded his dismissal as 'a certificate of decency'. The sacking of these men was followed by the resignation of several leading staff members, including Dr D. Mtimkulu, Prof. C. L. Nyembezi, Dr M. Webb,

S. B. Ngcobo, and A. M. Phahle. They were paid gratuities but forfeited their pension rights.

The tribal colleges today are staffed largely by Whites, most of them Afrikaners, who are known to be firm supporters of apartheid. At Fort Hare, Turfloop, and Ngoya there were in 1962 only two African professors and twenty-one African lecturers as against twenty-eight White professors and eighty-one White lecturers. The staff is divided into two clearly marked categories according to race. White members of staff are Council employees, but African members are civil servants and subject to oppressive restrictions. There are substantial differences in pay between White and Black. The maximum salary for an African male professor at Fort Hare is less than the minimum salary for a White female professor. The African professor's scale is £1,400 – £50 – £1,600. The scale for a White female professor starts at £1,730 and rises by £60 stages to £2,030. A White male professor starts at £1,950 and reaches £2,250. If he is married he gets an additional £225, which gives a total of £2,475, or £875 a year more than an African professor. Similar discrimination is applied to the lecturing staff. In all categories the salaries paid to the White personnel are much higher than those received by their non-White colleagues.

When the debate took place in Parliament on the university apartheid Bills, the Minister indicated that non-White students would still be allowed to enter the White universities for courses which were not yet offered at the tribal colleges, or to complete courses which they had already begun. During the 1960 session the Minister of Education announced that 127 Coloureds and 526 Asians had applied for permission to enter one or other of the White universities. He had granted all the applications from Asians because no college had yet been established for them, but had refused permission to forty-eight Coloureds because alternative facilities existed. The Minister of Bantu Education, however, was much less accommodating. He reported that he had received 190 applications from Africans to enrol at the White universities, but had approved only four. The rest had been rejected because alternative facilities existed at the tribal colleges or by correspondence through the University of South

Africa. And seven applicants who wished to study engineering at the University of the Witwatersrand had been refused permission because, in the Minister's opinion, there were as yet 'no prospects of employment for qualified Bantu engineers'. For them there were no alternative facilities. They were simply informed that they might not study engineering.

It is clear that the tribal colleges, like the Bantu Education schools, are not universities in the true sense of the word and never will be, no matter how much money is spent on their development. They are not intended to be centres of learning, culture, and education, where the student may acquire access to the treasure-house of world knowledge, but forcing houses for apartheid. 'Surely,' stated Prof. Matthews in an article for *Africa South* (July–September 1957), 'if the policy of apartheid or separate development is all that it is claimed to be, it ought to mean that within their separate university institutions the non-Whites will have all the freedoms normally associated with university life in other societies, instead of being expected to work in an atmosphere of compulsion.' But both students and African staff are subject to the most stringent and humiliating restrictions, restrictions which would not be tolerated for one moment at any White university. At the Bantu Education schools and the tribal colleges, discipline indeed is enforced literally at the point of a gun.

Both the Bantu Education schools and the tribal colleges have been racked with disturbances from the outset. The very inauguration of Bantu Education in the schools was met with a massive boycott, called by the African National Congress, which in several centres established cultural clubs as an alternative to the schools. Unfortunately, in terms of the law the cultural clubs could not teach, and the African parent wants his child to be educated. In the end there was no alternative but to send the children back to school.

Other disturbances have been produced by the very stringency of the regulations employed to control the students. A complaint about food here, a show of student initiative there, has been met with reprisals which have provoked the student body as a whole to strikes and demonstrations. The response of the authorities has generally taken the form of mass expulsions or suspensions and careful re-screening of applicants. There already exists a formidable blacklist of students who have been expelled and prohibited from ever again being admitted to any government school.

Other student protests have been directly political. When Prof. Ross and du Preez, the new Registrar, paid their first call on Fort Hare in October 1959, they were greeted by a large number of protesting students who wore black armbands, let down the tyres of their cars and threw tomatoes at them. On 29 May 1961, students at Fort Hare and a number of Bantu Education schools in the Eastern Cape and Natal stayed away from classes in support of the Pietermaritzburg Conference call for demonstrations in protest against the establishment of a Republic. When the Fort Hare students were sent home, Rhodes University students staged a two-day sympathy strike – the first time that White students have given such mass support to their non-White colleagues.

The authorities do not hesitate to call in the police at the slightest sign of disturbance. The Special Branch are frequently in attendance, while spies and informers operate in the schools and colleges. At St John's College in Umtata during 1961 there were at one time, out of a total 300, as many as 174 pupils in jail awaiting trial on a charge of public violence after the burning of a government lorry in the school grounds. The remaining students continued their classes under police surveillance. Armed police, night searches, Saracen armoured cars, and tracker dogs – the African students have been introduced to the whole paraphernalia of police state repression. The indoctrination continues – but so does the resistance.

In October 1959 the Fort Hare students, protesting at the proposed murder of their university, passed the following resolution:

Let it be noted, once and for all, that our stand as students at Fort Hare and as the future leaders of our country, upholding the principles of education as universally accepted, remains unchanged and uncompromising. Our outright condemnation of the university apartheid legislation remains steadfast. . . .

We wish to warn the architects of White domination, the whole country, and the world at large that we will not be held responsible for the disastrous repercussions of this apartheid policy, which in the foreseeable future will destroy the entire social, political, and economic structure of our country.

The students read the future correctly, and have shown in a thousand ways since then that they have remained true to their trust and to their people. C.N.O. will fail in the African schools. The Afrikaner Nationalist may educate his own children to believe that they are superior, but he cannot succeed in educating the children of others into a belief that they are inferior. The tribal schools and colleges nourish, despite every precaution, the struggle of the African people for their right to human dignity and equal treatment in the land of their birth.

12. The Control of Ideas

> This process of cleansing our 'Kultur' will have to be applied in practically all spheres. The stage, art, literature, the cinema, the Press, and advertisement posters, all must have the stains of pollution removed and be placed in the service of a national and cultural idea.
>
> HITLER in *Mein Kampf*.

'Everyone has the right to freedom of opinion and expression; this right includes freedom to hold opinions without interference and to seek, receive, and impart information and ideas through any media and regardless of frontiers.'

So reads Article 19 in the Universal Declaration of Human Rights as adopted by the General Assembly of the United Nations on 10 December 1948. For obvious reasons South Africa refused to sign the Declaration, and the Nationalist government feels under no obligation to honour it. The policy of apartheid is in its very essence a violation of the fundamental human rights of the majority of the population. How could the Nationalists be expected to respect the freedom of the Press when they were ruthlessly assaulting every other freedom?

In fact, the record of the Nationalists since they came to power is one of sustained attack upon the freedom of the Press, and the attack has mounted in intensity during recent years in direct proportion to the crisis which has overtaken the country. Control over the means of propaganda has become for them an absolute necessity, for without it they must fail in their bid to dominate the country.

For the Nationalist government remains basically weak. Taking the 1960 referendum figures as a guide, it speaks for fifty-two per cent of the White population, and by virtue of the very nationalism which constitutes its strength, it can never attract to its banner more than a small proportion of the remaining forty-eight per cent, for the English are unlikely to accept absorption by an alien culture, though by virtue of their minority position they may have no alternative but to concede its overlordship. As for the non-Whites, it can be assumed that the overwhelming majority are bitterly opposed to apartheid, and the savage laws which have been put on the statute book are testimony to the resistance which has more and more been forthcoming from their ranks.

To preserve themselves in power, therefore, the Nationalists have had to mobilize their resources on all fronts with the greatest care and skill. By careful husbandry they have succeeded in harvesting for themselves a majority of votes. But votes are not everything. The one sphere where they have felt a permanent weakness is that of ideas, the written and spoken word, the Press, books, cinema, and stage. Day after day insidious, undermining ideas have been circulated in South Africa, liberal, unnational ideas, infiltrating the population in its millions, weakening the resolve of the faithful, producing in the very citadel of Afrikanerdom itself a succession of minor if unsuccessful revolts. It has taken all the ingenuity and cunning of the Nationalist leaders – with the frequent display of force – to combat this intellectual erosion. But they have dedicated themselves to the struggle against freedom of opinion and expression with all the determination of ultimate despair. The white supremacist is playing for high stakes. He must either win or die. There is no room for compromise in the battle of ideas.

Unhappily for the Nationalists, this is a battlefront on which they do not enjoy a superiority in weapons. Ask for guns, armoured cars, baton charges, detention without trial, hangings, lashes, and all the other trappings of physical intimidation and they can prove their advantages. But ask them for an idea which can stand the moral scrutiny of the world, and their deficiencies are immediately exposed. Apartheid is built on too much suffering to be allowed to survive.

The very weakness of their position has made the Nationalists all the more determined to ensure that they obtain absolute control over the instruments of expression. Nothing must be said in South Africa which undermines their authority; nothing sent out of the country which stimulates antagonism. The only answer is – censorship. And the Nationalists have had this in mind ever since they came to power.

The difficulties that the Nationalists have had to contend

with are best revealed by a comparison of the following figures,
which cover the circulations of the Nationalist and non-Nationalist daily and weekly newspapers:

DAILY NEWSPAPERS

	Circulation in 1962
Nationalist	
Die Burger, Cape Town	47,000
Die Vaderland, Johannesburg, evening	54,000
Die Transvaler, Johannesburg, morning	39,000
Die Volksblad, Bloemfontein	26,000
	166,000
Non-Nationalist	
Cape Times, Cape Town, morning	66,000
Cape Argus, Cape Town, evening	97,000
Daily Dispatch, East London	21,000
Eastern Province Herald, Port Elizabeth, morning	26,000
Evening Post, Port Elizabeth, evening	24,000
Diamond Fields Advertiser, Kimberley	6,000
Rand Daily Mail, Johannesburg, morning	111,000
Star, Johannesburg, evening	162,000
Pretoria News	18,000
Friend, Bloemfontein	9,000
Daily News, Durban, evening	68,000
Natal Mercury, Durban, morning	58,000
Natal Witness, Maritzburg	11,000
World, Johannesburg	23,000
Daily Representative, Queenstown	2,000
	702,000

WEEKLY NEWSPAPERS
Nationalist

Die Burger, week-end edition	63,000
Oosterlig, Port Elizabeth, tri-weekly	30,000
Die Vaderland, week-end edition	41,000
Dagbreek en Sondagnuus, Johannesburg	150,000
Die Volksblad, week-end edition	31,000
	315,000

Non-Nationalist

Cape Times, week-end edition	105,000
Cape Argus, week-end edition	147,000
Weekblad, Cape Town	18,000
Landstem, Cape Town	165,000
Suid-Afrikaanse Stem, Johannesburg	94,000
Evening Post, week-end edition	46,000
Sunday Times, Johannesburg	348,000
Star, week-end edition	124,000
Sunday Express, Johannesburg	165,000
Sunday Tribune, Durban	116,000
World, week-end edition	22,000
Post, Johannesburg	75,000
	1,431,000

The list of daily papers quoted above is complete. The list of weeklies, however, does not include communal and religious publications. If it did, the non-Nationalist total would be even larger.

From these figures it can be seen that in the world of the Press the Nationalist government is at a hopeless disadvantage. The figures show that not all Nationalists read the Nationalist Press, and that many Nationalists read the non-Nationalist Press.

So long as this position is permitted to persist, it will be impossible for the Nationalists to eliminate all foreign political and cultural influences. The man who daily reads the newspapers of his political opponents is bound in the long run to be influenced by what he finds there. Whether he is conscious of it or not, he will be exposing himself daily to non-Nationalist ideologies, perhaps even to humanism and liberalism. Some of the ideas that he encounters may sooner or later win acceptance from him.

Two courses were open to the Nationalists to combat this danger. They could found rival papers in competition with the English Press, or they could force the English Press to conform. The first alternative was out of the question. The English Press, linked as it is with the great mining and financial houses, has financial resources which are beyond the reach of Nationalist competition. The English papers are bigger and brighter and contain far more news and features than the Nationalist papers, which concentrate largely on propaganda. Not surprisingly, a Johannesburg survey has shown that whereas only one to four per cent of English-speaking South Africans read an Afrikaans daily, between twenty and forty per cent of Afrikaners read an English daily newspaper. And this trend is unlikely to be reversed in the foreseeable future.

The alternative was control, and on this front the Nationalists after more than a decade of agitation and pressure, have been able to achieve a great measure of success.

The Nationalist government was not the first to try and control the Press or to introduce censorship. In the 1830s Lord Charles Somerset suppressed the newspaper of Thomas Pringle and James Fairbairn, *The South African Commercial Advertiser*, and deported George Greig, the editor and printer. Pringle and Fairbairn are names now known to every schoolboy because of the fight they undertook in defence of the freedom of the Press. They rallied support both in the Cape and in London and after a bitter three-year battle managed to get the autocratic Governor's order reversed. Pringle wrote of the atmosphere in the Cape at the time:

It was difficult to conjecture to what lengths the violence of arbitrary power would at this dismal period proceed. Fear is the most cruel of all passions, and infuriated by fear or exposure, the Colonial government seemed determined to strike down every man who should dare even to look or think disapprobation of the deeds. A frightful system of espionage pervaded every circle of society, and rendered perilous even the confidence of the domestic hearth . . . Informers and false witnesses abounded, and rumours of plots and disloyal combinations against the Governor were assiduously kept afloat, for purposes as obvious as they were mischievous.

There seems to have been very little change since those days! When the *South African Commercial Advertiser* reappeared, a special ordinance was passed providing that henceforth the Press would be under the protection of the law and immune from arbitrary suppression. In the days of the Transvaal Republic, President Kruger took a crack at *The Star*, but the paper appealed to the courts and its rights were fully restored. It was not until the time of the fusion government under General Hertzog that a serious attempt was again made to introduce censorship. The government's cause for complaint against the Press was that certain newspapers had insulted the heads of the Nazi and Fascist states in Europe, in consequence of which a complaint had been lodged with the South African government by representatives of the German Reich. Instead of brushing these complaints aside, Hertzog, by this time inclining ever more strongly to National Socialism, decided to take action against the Press. Dr A. J. R. van Rhyn, Nationalist M.P., told the House of Assembly in January 1950:

In 1937, General Hertzog called the editors together in his office and talked very seriously to them. He said that he was not satisfied with the attitude of the Press, and that he intended to introduce a strong Bill, in order to introduce a certain measure of control, if the situation did not improve.

The Press did not improve, and Hertzog circulated a draft censorship Bill which he intended to propose. The newspaper editors hastily got together in July 1939 and recommended the adoption of a code of discipline which they would apply themselves if Hertzog would agree to drop his Bill. The Prime Minister refused to budge, and announced his intention of proceeding with his Bill at the next session of Parliament. But then the war intervened, and Hertzog together with his Bill was swept into limbo.

The idea of Press censorship continued, however, to simmer in the Nationalist mind. Provision for it was made, as we have seen, in the draft constitution drawn up during the war. And soon after the Nationalist government came to power, in January 1950, Dr van Rhyn, a former editor of the Nationalist daily *Die Volksblad*, moved in Parliament:

That whereas this House is of the opinion that a free Press is essential to a free democratic country, and whereas it is convinced that a self-disciplined freedom ultimately constitutes the best safeguard for the maintenance of the freedom of the Press, and that all activities and tendencies to undermine or abuse such freedom which exist or are taking root in this country should therefore be combated, it accordingly requests the government to consider the advisability of appointing a commission. . . .

The government indicated during the debate that it looked upon this proposal with favour, and in October 1950 appointed its famous commission to inquire into the South African Press which has not completed its report to this day. The terms of reference were sweeping: (1) The measure of concentration of control, financial and technical, of the Press and its effect on editorial opinion; (2) accuracy in the presentation of news; (3) tendencies towards monopoly in the collection of news and the distribution of newspapers; (4) existing restraints on the establishment of new newspapers; (5) self-control and discipline by the Press; (6) sensationalism and triviality; (7) the extent to which any of the above factors militate for or against a free Press in South Africa and the formation of an informed public opinion.

Justice J. W. van Zyl, of the Cape Provincial Division of the Supreme Court, was appointed Chairman of the Press Commission, while the other members were Prof. L. I. Coertze, Dean of the Faculty of Law at Pretoria University and later Nationalist M.P. for Standerton; A. A. Frew, a former chief editor of the South African Press Association; Prof. P. W. Hoek, head of the Department of Accounting at Pretoria University; J. W. Lamb, a former President of the South African Stock Exchange and Vice-Chairman of the Board of Governors of the South African Broadcasting Corporation (S.A.B.C.); A. E. Trollip, M.P., later Administrator of Natal and now Minister of Labour; and Dr van Ryhn himself, later to be High Commissioner for South Africa in London.

The subsequent career of this commission constitutes one of the most extraordinary episodes in the history of the Nationalist régime. Its personnel has changed with bewildering rapidity. Where the British Royal Commission on the Press managed to complete its task (with a far wider field to survey) in a matter of two years, the South African Press Commission has already been busy for over twelve. Its report has been promised every year since 1953, but with magnificent consistency has year by year failed to appear, until at last in 1961 the *first* part of the report was published. The remaining sections of the report, according to a statement by the Minister of the Interior on 29 January 1963, were expected by the end of April, 1963 The total cost of the commission, up to 31 December 1962, was £152,000, and the final cost is expected to reach the neighbourhood of £175,000. The Minister indicated that Justice van Zyl and Dr Coertze were the only two original members of the commission involved in the final report. A portion of the report had been signed by Lamb and van Coller (who filled Trollip's place), but both of them had resigned and the State President had accepted their resignations.

What has the Press Commission been doing all these years? The journal of the South African Society of Journalists in September 1959 said:

It is understood that the commission is hopelessly behind its official schedule. Analysis and collation of material is likely to take from two to four years. The reasons given in informed political circles are that the work has been slowed down because of the complexity, bulk, and unwieldiness of the evidence; dissension among members of the commission; and the sweepingly broad terms of reference which give little guidance on what precisely is required. Not all the commissioners are believed to be active.

It has been a sorry tale indeed. Yet this commission has hung like a shadow over the whole South African Press ever since it was appointed. It has explored every aspect of newspaper management and control, grilled editors and journalists behind closed doors, confronted foreign correspondents with copies of their cables and demanded explanations. Nationalist politicians have on several occasions referred with confidence to the outcome of the commission's work, indicating that it would prove a bombshell for the English Press and pave the way for some kind of State control.

And yet, and yet. . . . The very thoroughness with which the commission went about its business reduced its ultimate value to the Nationalist government. Year after year passed by and there was no result, no report, not even an interim report on which to hang a Bill. When the commission's first report was finally issued in 1961, it proved something of a damp squib.

The commission dealt only with items 1 and 3 in its terms of reference – that is, the measure of concentration of control, financial and technical, of the Press of South Africa; and tendencies towards monopoly or the concentration of control relating to the collection of news and the distribution of newspapers and periodicals. From a welter of facts and figures presented by the commission, the following points emerged:

(a) That the South African Press Association, the only internal news agency, was dominated by the English-language newspapers, which controlled 87·4 per cent of the votes that could be cast at a general meeting. The Afrikaans Press accordingly performed no more than an advisory function on the S.A.P.A. Board. (b) That world news agencies could not compete for the dissemination of news about South Africa, because S.A.P.A. placed Reuters news agency in a position to beat its competitors in time. (c) That the three newspaper concentrations – the Argus Group, South African Associated Newspapers, and the Nasionale Pers – together dominated the South African Press. (d) That the Afrikaans and English dailies were so biased in the selection and presentation of news concerning racial and political affairs that it was impossible for Afrikaans or English unilingual readers to obtain an informed political opinion from newspapers. Afrikaans dailies all supported the Nationalist Party, while the English dailies split their support between the United Party and the Progressive Party. (e) That the Central News Agency enjoyed a monopoly of the distribution of newspapers and periodicals.

The commission recommended that S.A.P.A. curb its monopoly and cease its bias in favour of Reuters – failing which the Minister should revoke its licence – while voting safeguards should be introduced so as to provide the English and Afrikaans Press with an equal say. Finally, the commission suggested a Board of Trade investigation into the Central News Agency's monopoly of distribution.

Most of the facts which the commission had so laboriously and time-consumingly collected came as no surprise to the South African public, while even some sections of the Nationalist Press protested mildly at the attack on S.A.P.A., stressing that they did not suffer in any way by the present arrangement. The impact of the commission's report was also lessened by the fact that it was not made available to the public, which had to rely on the Press itself for all its information on the commission's findings. The commission's report earned headlines and editorials for a few days – and was then quietly dropped.

While the commission was busy with its explorations, the Nationalist government was compelled to carry on with the day-to-day business of administration and to face up as best it could to the challenge presented by a more or less informed public opinion. Alex Hepple in his invaluable pamphlet *Censorship and Press Control in South Africa*, published in 1960, enumerated thirteen laws and twenty-one provincial ordinances then in force which provided for censorship of one kind or another. Most of these were already on the statute book before the Nationalists came to power, but the new government applied them with an intensity which would probably have left the original legislators breathless.

Section 21 of the Customs Act, for example, prohibited the importation of 'goods which are indecent or obscene or on any ground whatsoever objectionable'. It was not the discovery of the Nationalists that this clause could be used to ban the importation of literature from abroad. Books had been banned by the United Party government before, though just how many cannot be established with certainty. It was not the practice prior to 1939 to report the names of banned publications in the Government Gazette. In 1956 the Nationalist government published a con-solidated list of bannings under the Customs Act since 1939, but gave no indication of the proportion of bannings for which it had itself been responsible. There were over 4,000 titles in that list, and by March 1962, a further 4,118 single publications and 198 series of publications had been banned from importation into the country, according to the evidence given by a J. L. Hattingh, Parliamentary Officer of the Department of Customs and Excise, to the Select Committee on the Undesirable Pub-lications Bill. Since the rate of bannings has been fairly even over the last decade, one may assume that most of the more than 8,000 books banned between 1939 and 1956 fell to the credit of the Nationalist government.

It is when one comes to examine the 8,000 titles that one realizes how the Nationalist government has used the Customs Act to impose a blatant political censorship on the South African people. A fair proportion of the banned titles consists of pure smut and pornography, and few would quarrel with its exclusion from the country. But amongst the banned are some of the most celebrated works of art, accepted as serious literature throughout the civilized world. Here are some of the works which have been banned, culled at random from the list:

Voltaire's *Candide* (following public outcry, it was later 'unbanned', and the Minister admitted that a 'mistake' had been made); Gorky's *Mother*; all the novels of James Alldridge; novels by Erskine Caldwell, James T. Farrell, Nadine Gordimer, Daphne Rooke, and others; *Sartre on Cuba*, by Jean-Paul Sartre; *Congo, my Country*, by Patrice Lumumba; all paperback editions of *I, Claudius* and *King Jesus* by Robert Graves; *Advertisements for Myself* by Norman Mailer; a book on Belafonte by Arnold Shaw; *Borstal Boy* by Brendan Behan; *I Speak of Freedom*, by Kwame Nkrumah; *Marilyn Monroe* by Maurice Zolotov; *South Africa – Yesterday and Tomorrow: The Challenge to Christians*, by Ambrose Reeves, the former Bishop of Johannesburg who was deported from South Africa by the Nationalist government; *African Profiles* by Ronald Segal; *In the Realm of Large Molecules*, by Soviet scientist R. Rozen; proceedings of a scientific session on the Physiological Teachings of Academician J. P. Pavlov, issued by the Academy of Medical Sciences of the U.S.S.R.; *Why I am not a Christian* by Bertrand Russell; *The Roots of Prejudice* by Arnold Rose (UNESCO pamphlet).

All works which violate the rigid moral code of the Calvinist Dutch Reformed Churches, all works which contradict the race theories of the Nationalist government, and all works without exception issued in any of the socialist countries or which are published under the auspices of any left-wing organization or individual in the West are automatically excluded from South Africa under the Customs Act as soon as they come to the knowledge of the censors. Anyone who imports or is found knowingly in possession of any banned publication is liable to a fine of £1,000 or imprisonment for five years or both.

Film censorship has in the past been effected under the provisions of the Entertainments (Censorship) Act of 1931 and has also been used as a weapon to keep from South Africans not merely smut and pornography but all concepts with which the Nationalists disagree. In the four-year period from 1958 to 1962, no fewer than 133 films were banned, mostly the products of famous motion picture companies abroad like United Artists, Metro-Goldwyn-Mayer, Columbia, and Rank. Among the films banned have been *Battleship Potemkin*, *I Passed for White*, *Taste of Honey*, *Lolita*, and *Boccacio 70*. In the case of the last-named there was an appeal to the Minister of the Interior, who overruled the decision of the Censorship Board and allowed the film to be shown – with appropriate cuts. (Perhaps the reason for the Minister's clemency is that the company circulating the film is an Afrikaans concern trying to make its way in competition with the non-Afrikaans companies already entrenched in the industry.) Many films passed for showing are so mutilated by the Censorship Board as to constitute an insult to any sophisticated cinema-goer. Some films are passed for adults, but not for children of various age groups. Some are passed for showing to Whites, Coloureds, and Asians but not to Africans, whose staple film diet – where they get the chance to see a film at all – is made up of Westerns.

One of the films banned in 1962 was *Men from Brazil*, produced by Moral Re-Armament. Asked in the House of Assembly why the film had been banned, the Minister of the Interior replied:

The film was prohibited in the light of the provisions of Section 5(2) (g) and (r) of the Entertainments (Censorship) Act which read as follows:

5(2) The Board shall not approve any film which in its opinion depicts in an offensive manner (g) scenes containing reference to controversial or international politics; (r) scenes of intermingling of Europeans and non-Europeans.

The Dutch Reformed Church, it should be explained, is strongly opposed to the activities of the Moral Re-armament movement because the latter acknowledges no colour bar.

Sometimes censorship exceeds the bounds of all sense. The

famous negro trumpeter Louis Armstrong was excised altogether from *The Glen Miller Story*, although advertisements containing his name appeared all over the country. The advertising posters of *The King and I* were designed to show Deborah Kerr embraced by a bare-chested Yul Brynner in the role of a Siamese King. Since Siamese are Asians, however, this could not be allowed, and the posters were altered to reveal Deborah Kerr in the arms of a raceless shadow. The poster for the film *Oceans 11* showed Sammy Davis Jr walking down the street side by side with Frank Sinatra and John Wayne. In the South African version, the two white stars are accompanied by a featureless black shape. Sammy Davis Jr has been eliminated, and White supremacy spared one more shock.

Yet despite the sweeping censorship powers which the Nationalists found ready to hand with their advent to government, and which they have utilized with almost Teutonic thoroughness, they still hankered after more – and used their political control to get them. The 1950 Suppression of Communism Act contained a section empowering the Governor-General to ban any publication which in his opinion professed to be a Communist publication, was published by or under the direction of a Communist organization, served mainly as a means for expressing views propagated by such an organization, or served 'mainly as a means for expressing views or conveying information, the publication of which is calculated to further the achievement of any of the objects of Communism'. By a later amendment, the word 'mainly' in the last part of that definition was replaced by '*inter alia*'. There was no appeal to the courts against such a ban unless it could be shown that the Governor-General had acted in bad faith – an impossible onus to discharge.

Using its considerable powers under this Act, the government banned the weekly newspaper *Guardian* in 1952, its successor *Advance* in 1954, and the succeeding *New Age* in 1962. The magazine *Fighting Talk* was banned under the Act in February 1963.

Further drastic powers to interfere with Press freedom were incorporated in the Criminal Laws Amendment Act and the

Public Safety Act of 1953. During the 1960 state of emergency the newspapers *New Age* and *Torch* were temporarily banned under the emergency regulations framed in terms of the Public Safety Act. The Liberal newspaper *Contact* was later convicted of 'subversion' as laid down in the emergency regulations and penalized by a heavy fine.

Not surprisingly, in January 1956 the International Press Institute, an organization of editors with headquarters in Zurich, found that in South Africa during the previous five years the encroachments of the government on the freedom of the Press had become increasingly serious. Citing the hostile attitude of the Nationalist government towards the opposition Press, the enactment of laws restricting Press freedom, and the suppression of *Guardian* and *Advance*, the Institute declared that the government's actions constituted a Sword of Damocles for the entire Press.

'There is, it is true, no censorship as such, nor do the government issue directives to the Press, but nevertheless they exert pressure by virtue of a body of laws, often laudable enough in intention, but which complicate the journalist's job, intimidate him, or even directly threaten him.'

The Institute recalled that the Editor of *The Star* in Johannesburg had written to the Institute in 1952 that 'editing a newspaper under these conditions is like walking blindfold through a minefield', and it went on to say that the restraints on publication in South Africa were so complex that in few countries in the world this side of the 'Iron Curtain' was a greater strain imposed on newspaper editors.

The Institute quoted figures to demonstrate how far the South African government was favouring Nationalist newspapers through copious official advertising.

In the Cape Province the *Cape Argus* carried advertising worth £820 and the *Cape Times* £854, while the *Burger*'s was worth £1,248. In the Transvaal the figures were £2,548 for the *Transvaler*, the main Nationalist daily, and £1,790 for *The Star*. In the Free State, £1,059 for the *Volksblad* and £514 for the *Friend*. These figures bore no relation to those for circulation and distribution.

Yet despite the menacing extent of its existing powers, the government was inevitably driven to seek even further control over the instruments of expression.

Desiring to extend to internal publications the powers that it possessed over imported ones under the Customs Act – and perhaps also despairing by now of ever getting a report in time from the Press Commission – the government in 1954 appointed a Commission of Inquiry into Undesirable Literature, under the Chairmanship of Prof. Geoffrey Cronje, of Pretoria University, one-time secretary of an appeal fund for Ossewa Brandwag members charged with high treason.

The commission's period of gestation was remarkably short, compared with the Press Commission, and in October 1957 its report was completed and published. Most of the commission's massive 285-page report was taken up with a discussion of the incidence of pornography in South African and imported publications, and means to control the evil; but the most serious sections dealt with political issues. Stating that evidence had been placed before it that 'the control of Communist publications is at present not as effective as it should be', the commission proposed that 'Communist' publications should fall under the draft Censorship Act included in its report, and that the Publications Board, the chief censoring authority, should be accorded legal recognition as the expert on what was 'Communistic' and what was not.

The commission produced no evidence that it had made any study of the nature of 'Communistic' literature in the Union. Not a single example was quoted of matter regarded as 'Communistic', and no newspapers, magazines, pamphlets, or leaflets were cited as evidence of the existence of Communism in the Union. From its own ludicrous definition of Communism it might be gathered that the commission was not very clear itself about just what Communism was.

What the commission did do was constantly emphasize that the White man should remain boss in South Africa, and that undesirable literature was that which was 'seriously undermining the European's position in this country. As the torchbearer in the vanguard of Western civilization in South Africa, the European

237

must be and *remain* the leader, the guiding light, in the spiritual and cultural field, otherwise he will inevitably *go* under.'

Elsewhere the commission remarked that the White man would be able to remain the boss only if he 'moves on a high moral and cultural plane and sets the non-European an example which is worthy of being followed'.

'The commission wishes to express its concern about the fact that magazines which frequently have highly objectionable covers are openly displayed in public and sold by non-Europeans – to a large extent to *European* women'.

The commission was very concerned with the effect of sexy magazine illustrations and advertisements on the standing of the European woman and even went to the extent of questioning several non-Europeans about their attitude towards it.

A certain non-European who occupies a responsible position declared that the European woman is held in high esteem and that she is in effect placed on a pedestal by non-Europeans. With reference to undesirable illustrations in which European women are portrayed and depicted in a reprehensible manner, he asserted that Europeans themselves are tumbling the European woman from her pedestal.

The report found that a conspicuous feature of weekly newspapers intended for non-Europeans was 'the high incidence of reports, articles, and other contributions which tend to engender ... friction or feelings of hostility between the European and non-European population groups of the Union'.

On the other hand the commission gave the Press as a whole a comparatively clean bill of health. 'The commission deems it necessary to record at the very outset that not much that is undesirable occurs in the reporting of newspapers in the Union. In fact, the occurrence of undesirability in this connexion must [be] regarded as trifling.' Since the commission's report was to pave the way for full-scale censorship, this finding is of more than ordinary significance.

The commission expressly approved the manner in which the Customs Act had been used to prevent the importation of undesirable literature into the Union. 'The commission was afforded the opportunity of perusing the contents of hundreds of banned titles and is convinced that a great service has been done to this country in prohibiting the publications concerned. This finding is given particular prominence and is especially emphasized.'

The commission's report gave the government the green light for which it had been waiting. In the 1960 session of Parliament, the Deputy Minister of the Interior introduced a Publications and Entertainments Bill providing for pre-publication censorship and referred it to a select committee for consideration after the first reading. The Bill shocked the country by its severity and led to an enormous public outcry, not least from the Afrikaans section of the community who would suffer most by censorship. The English writer, after all, if he fails to get his work published in South Africa, can always find a market overseas. But the Afrikaner must be read either in South Africa or not at all. There is no world market for his products.

Bowing to the storm, the government announced that it was not proceeding with the measure. But then came the counterblast. During the recess a deputation from the Dutch Reformed Church interviewed the Minister and pressed for some form of extended control over internal publications. The wishes of the Dutch Reformed Church were to be completely ignored in the matter of liquor legislation, but on the publication front the views of the Church happened to coincide with what the government itself intended.

Nineteen-sixty was the year of the Sharpeville massacre and the state of emergency, a year during which the fortunes of South Africa slumped and the reputation of the country was slashed in the overseas Press. Driven into a corner, the government hit back at its critics. Once again it held the English Press to blame. Opposition to apartheid was tantamount to treason. An obviously inspired and viciously sustained campaign of abuse was launched against the government's Press critics.

The Prime Minister, Dr Verwoerd, in a radio address on 7 October 1960, following the Nationalist victory in the republican referendum, proclaimed:

'A politically nonconformist Press will not be tolerated in the Republic.'

The Minister of Justice, Vorster, who after his appointment

had complained that 'rights were getting out of hand', on 10 August 1961, warned the Press that he would counter agitation with all the means at his disposal.

The Minister of Railways, Ben Schoeman, attacking what he called the licence of the Press during the 1961 session of Parliament, called *Sunday Times* columnist Stanley Uys, 'probably the most unscrupulous liar in South Africa and a self-confessed traitor'. Needless to say, he did not repeat his remarks outside of Parliament.

J. C. Greyling, Nationalist M.P. for Ventersdorp, speaking at Queenstown, announced that the time was approaching when the government would 'legislate to call the Press and its reporting to order'. Replying to an anti-Republican article in the Queenstown *Daily Representative*, Greyling said: 'I warn that the time for this type of newspaper is growing short. We can stand on our own feet, we can make our own rules, and damn the rest of the world.'

Eric Louw, Minister of Foreign Affairs, speaking at Brits on 12 August 1961, referred to a Press report that the managing director of an Athens newspaper and two of his assistants had been sent to jail for causing 'alarm and despondency'. 'I wonder if the time has not come,' he added, 'for us in this country to follow the example of the Greeks.'

Blaar Coetzee, M.P. for Vereeniging, in a speech during the week ending 2 September 1961, declared: 'On 18 October [date of the general election] a mandate will be sought to take the English Press by the throat.' The freedom of the Press was 'inviolable', but it could no longer be tolerated that lies should be told, as in some newspapers, that the good name of South Africa should be calumniated and the Black man incited against the White.

W. A. Maree, Minister of Bantu Education, said at the 1961 congress of the Nationalist Party in Natal that there were clearly serious objections to the role of the Press. Readers were being indoctrinated in favour of liberalism.

Dr C. de Wet, Nationalist M.P. for Vereeniging, who rose to fame when he complained in Parliament, before the full details of the Sharpeville shootings were known, that not enough

Africans had been killed, said at Johannesburg on 10 August 1961, that severe action should be taken against the 'English-language Press', which was guilty of 'crime and sabotage' against the Republic.

Against this background the Minister of the Interior introduced a new measure during the 1961 session of Parliament. Called the Undesirable Publications Bill, it was referred to a select committee after the first reading. Initially it seemed an improvement on the previous Bill, for the principle of pre-publication censorship had been dropped and the whole scope of the Bill had been narrowed. But the select committee, on which the Nationalists possessed an automatic majority, re-introduced pre-publication censorship and all in all fashioned an instrument which constitutes a deadly danger to freedom of expression and opinion in South Africa. The Bill in its revised form was then brought before the 1962 session of Parliament, but was not considered until the following year when, with minor modifications, it was put on the statute book as the Publications and Entertainments Act of 1963.

In terms of the Act, it is possible for the government (a) to prohibit the circulation of any newspaper which is not a member of the Newspaper Press Union (the reason for this exclusion will appear later); (b) to prohibit the circulation of any book, either imported or printed and published in South Africa; (c) to close down any stage or film show or art exhibition which is considered to be in any way undesirable; (d) to ban the work of any South African artist, novelist, poet, or sculptor; (e) to prohibit the importation of all publications produced by a specified publisher or which deal with a specified subject, except by special permit.

The Act also prohibits the importation of all paperback books costing less than five shillings without a special permit, on the theory that the major proportion of pornography is conveyed through the medium of the paperback.

The Publications Control Board set up by the Act is to consist of no less than nine members, 'of whom not less than six shall be persons having special knowledge of art, language, and literature or the administration of justice'. In terms of section 8 of the Act, the Board has the power to declare any 'publication or object' undesirable. In terms of section 5 of the Act, it then becomes an offence to 'distribute, display, exhibit, or sell, or offer or keep for sale' any publication or object which has been declared by the Board to be undesirable.

A 'publication or object' is defined as any newspaper not published by the Newspaper Press Union; any book, periodical, pamphlet, poster, or other printed matter; any writing or typescript which has in any manner been duplicated or made available to the public or any section of the public; any drawing, picture, illustration, painting, woodcut, or similar representation; any print, photograph, engraving, or lithograph; any figure, cast, carving, statue, or model; and any record or other contrivance or device in or on which sound has been recorded for reproduction.

A publication or object, declares the Act, shall be deemed undesirable if it or any part of it (a) is indecent or obscene or is offensive or harmful to public morals; (b) is blasphemous or is offensive to the religious convictions or feelings of any section of the inhabitants of the Republic; (c) brings any section of the inhabitants of the Republic into ridicule or contempt; (d) is harmful to the relations between any sections of the inhabitants of the Republic; (e) is prejudicial to the safety of the State, the general welfare, or the peace and good order; or (f) discloses indecent or obscene matter in relation to reports of judicial proceedings.

Some attempt is made to clarify what is meant by 'indecent or obscene or offensive or harmful to public morals', but no attempt at all is made to define what is meant by 'harmful to the relations between any sections of the inhabitants of the Republic'; 'prejudicial to the safety of the State, the general welfare, or the peace and good order'; or 'brings any sections of the inhabitants of the Republic into ridicule or contempt'. Theoretically there is an appeal from the decision of the Board to the courts, but considering the vagueness of these descriptions, it is doubtful whether this will constitute an effective safeguard.

The Board is also to be responsible for film censorship. In addition to the prohibitions mentioned above, it is forbidden to approve any films which propagate Communism as defined in the Suppression of Communism Act or which depict in an offensive manner the State President, the Republic's armed forces or any member thereof, death, human figures, love scenes, controversial or international politics, public characters, juvenile crime, criminality and the technique of crime, brutal fighting, drunkenness and brawling, addiction to drugs, scenes of violence involving White and non-White persons, intermingling of White and non-White persons, and violence towards or ill-treatment of women and children.

The Board is empowered to stop any suspected stage or art show, and the Act entitles any policeman to be admitted free to any show for the purpose of undertaking an inspection.

The penalties laid down for contravention of the Act are severe. For a first conviction, the penalty will be a fine of not less than £150 and not more than £250, or imprisonment for not more than six months, or both fine and imprisonment. For a second conviction the fine is to be not less than £500 and not more than £1,000 and/or imprisonment for not more than six months, while all subsequent convictions will entail fines of not less than £1,000 and/or imprisonment for not more than six months.

The Bill led to an outcry by South African artists, and particularly by Afrikaner intellectuals, who conducted a vigorous correspondence in the columns of the Nationalist newspaper *Die Burger* complaining that art, and in particular Afrikaans art, would be stifled by the proposed censorship provisions. After the Act had been passed, 172 of South Africa's foremost writers, painters, sculptors, and graphic artists, English and Afrikaans, signed a declaration of principles which was presented to the Minister of the Interior by a delegation consisting of Afrikaans authors W. A. de Klerk and Jan Rabie and best-selling English novelist Miss Mary Renault. While stating that circulation of obvious pornography should not be allowed, the signatories declared that the Act was 'in conflict with the most fundamental principle of art: that each work should be judged as a whole', and that 'the nature and intent of a literary work should be considered as a criterion of judgement'.

We are deeply alarmed for the future of creative effort in this country, since no frank discussion or honest inquiry or spiritual growth can be expected as long as the answer to such searchings may be silenced at the outset. Above all, writers who must publish inside the country are liable to be forced either into silence or superficiality, with fatal consequences – especially for Afrikaans literature.

The declaration made no mention of the dangerous political censorship empowered by the Act, which had already done irreparable damage even before becoming law.

Faced with the threat of censorship contained in the Bill, and wilting under the ceaseless Nationalist assault on the English Press, the members of the Newspaper Press Union had been persuaded to adopt a so-called 'code of conduct', in terms of which they agreed to censor themselves in return for exclusion from the provisions of the Publications and Entertainments Act. Voting on the code took place at a meeting of the N.P.U. on 13 March 1962, with seven newspaper managements voting against – the South African Associated Newspapers (*Rand Daily Mail, Sunday Times, Sunday Express*), the Bailey group (*Drum, Post*) and *Wings Magazine* – and 25 voting in favour – the whole of the Argus group (*Star, Cape Argus, Natal Daily News*, etc.), the whole Nationalist Press, and the *Cape Times*.

The board of directors of S.A. Associated Newspapers in February 1963 proclaimed its belief that political pressure had given rise to the adoption of the code, particularly as clause 3(*d*) had political implications. The board had decided, however, that it would not be in the interests of the company to dissociate itself from the code and that it would, therefore, accept it, together with the jurisdiction of the Board of Reference established to administer it, 'but under protest'.

The code itself consists of three clauses, each containing a number of sub-clauses, mostly setting out the principles of standard newspaper practice in general terms to which no one could reasonably have any objection. News should be truthful and accurate, and should not be distorted by omissions, while headlines should accurately reflect the contents of a story, and so on. But clause 3(*d*) reads: 'Comment should take due cognizance of the complex racial problems of South Africa and should take into account the general good and the safety of the country and its peoples.'

Strong objection to the whole code of conduct and in particular to clause 3(d) was voiced by the South African Society of Journalists, which protested that, as the only organization representing working journalists, it had never been consulted, while its representations on the matter had been ignored. Referring to clause 3(d) the Society declared: 'We say without hesitation that this clause requires the journalist and the editor to modify the expression of his honest opinion on political grounds. . . . we believe that the last clause of the code of conduct means plainly that criticism of present government policy must be toned down.'

In a memorandum submitted to the N.P.U. itself the Society stressed:

The Press should not relieve the government from the odium which will and should attach to political censorship of the Press. An evil is no less an evil because it is self-inflicted. . . . Censorship may be imposed upon the Press in this country, but not we hope until the Press has fought it to the last. No self-respecting journalist or newspaper can voluntarily submit to a so-called code of conduct which is political in its origins and intentions. We ask the Newspaper Press Union to join us in rejecting censorship and in refusing to act as the government's agent in imposing censorship on the South African Press. Our function as a Press is to resist any move to gag us – it is not our function to gag ourselves, in the hope that the process will in that way be made more comfortable.

The Society has advised its members to refuse to be associated in any way with the code.

The code is to be administered by a Board of Reference consisting of an ex-Judge and two employer representatives, one from the Afrikaans and one from the English Press. The members of the Board of Reference as first constituted were: Chairman, ex-Justice Heinrich de Villiers, former Judge President of the Eastern Cape Division of the Supreme Court; W. R. McCall, retired general manager of the Argus Printing and Publishing Co.; and H. R. Malan, retired managing director of the Nasionale Pers. This Board will have the power to reprimand any proprietor, editor, or journalist adjudged to have been guilty of an infringement of the code and force the offending newspaper to publish the reprimand 'in such manner as may be determined by the Board'.

One of the first decisions of the Board, announced on 22 April 1963, was to condemn the *Sunday Express* for publishing an article by Julius Lewin, Senior Lecturer in African Law and Administration at the University of the Witwatersrand, entitled 'So This Is Peace'. The complainant, B. Coetzee, a Nationalist M.P., alleged that the following statements from the article were untrue: (1) The government employ the political police (the so-called Special Branch) to restrain or silence almost every form of outspoken protest; and (2) This feeling is not expressed with more vigour because men are afraid of the personal consequences to themselves, or their businesses or jobs, if they speak their minds openly.

The *Sunday Express* replied that the complaint referred to a signed article and that the newspaper did not accept responsibility for the veracity of every statement in such an article. The Board rejected this explanation and found 'that the article complained of contains both overstatement and unfair comment and that the newspaper failed in its duty to avoid these violations of the code of conduct'.

This staggering rebuff to the freedom of expression was passed over practically in silence. The *Sunday Express* itself criticized the Board's decision, stating that Lewin had a right to his opinion and that the *Sunday Express* would 'strenuously defend his right to express his opinions in its columns. Any lesser stand would be an admission that this newspaper is prepared to accept voluntary censorship. And it is not willing to do that under any circumstances.'

But the rest of the Press preserved a discreet silence. Doubtless in future one will see fewer complaints about Special Branch intimidation published in the Press. At all events, it is doubtful if the Publications Board set up under the Publications and Entertainments Act could have served the government better in the way of recommending Press censorship. At least from the decisions of the Publications Board there is an appeal to the courts. From the Board of Reference established under the code of conduct there is no appeal at all. The Press must just grin and bear it – and try to reform.

The Press is the most important medium of propaganda, but it is not the only one. There are also the radio and television. The Nationalist government has decided not to introduce television to South Africa. The Minister of Posts and Telegraphs, Dr Albert Hertzog, has referred to television as nothing more than a 'little bioscope' in the home and cited its pernicious influence in other countries, particularly on the young. But it is widely suspected that the real reason for Nationalist hostility towards television is that it would be a medium of entertainment largely under foreign cultural influence. South Africa at the moment has not the resources to provide a full daily programme of television, especially in Afrikaans, and would depend largely on overseas programmes, particularly those emanating from Britain and America. Rather than permit an intrusion of foreign ideas in this way, the Nationalists would prefer to do without television altogether. Ghana, Egypt, and even neighbouring Rhodesia are among the African countries which already have television. South Africa, the most industrialized country on the continent, must do without. So sensitive is the government on this issue that even closed-circuit television displays at South African trade fairs are prohibited, in case too many people should get to know just how attractive is the entertainment of which they are being arbitrarily deprived.

The radio, on the other hand, is a government-controlled monopoly in South Africa and completely under Nationalist domination. Chairman of the South African Broadcasting Corporation is Dr P. J. Meyer who, according to a statement in the *Sunday Times* of 24 March 1963, is also Chairman of the Broederbond. In recent years the radio has become so blatant an instrument of Nationalist propaganda, indeed, that it has evoked widespread and bitter protests from non-Nationalist sections of the population. Though responsible for the appointment of the men who control the S.A.B.C., the government has made a habit of refusing to answer parliamentary questions about the corporation's activities, on the grounds that it is fully independent. The result, of course, is that the corporation has become a law unto itself, immune from criticism because it can afford to ignore it. The Nationalist attitude towards it was expressed by a front-bencher in 1962 when he said that criticism of the S.A.B.C. was a crime and that people who attacked the corporation should be dealt with in terms of the Sabotage Act.

In an attempt to voice the dissatisfaction of non-Nationalists, United Party member E. G. Malan in March 1963 moved a private member's motion condemning the government's refusal to supply Parliament with information on the activities of the S.A.B.C. and urgently requesting consideration of the advisability of appointing a commission to inquire into the policies of the corporation. On the question of political talks and news reports, he said that there were three criteria summed up in the questions: Are the news sources adequate? Are the criteria for selection correct? Is the presentation of news such as to avoid distortion?

'To each of these the answer is a qualified but definite "No",' he declared.

Seconding the motion, United Party member A. Gorshel complained that there was a consistent assault on the English culture by the S.A.B.C. and that any English-speaking person or organization would be able to produce evidence of this.

Using its majority, the Nationalist Party was able to defeat the motion and get Parliament to adopt an amendment approving the policy followed by the S.A.B.C. But the nature of the debate, and of the widespread public criticism which had preceded it, made it quite clear that the S.A.B.C. has now become a party political instrument in the hands of the Nationalists. It has altogether ceased to be an independent corporation serving the needs of the whole community and has been converted into an instrument for massive political indoctrination instead. Over 1,000,000 people pay wireless licence fees in South Africa, so that the Nationalists have been able to a substantial degree to make good by this means their shortfall in the sphere of Press circulation.

It is impossible to close this chapter without a reference to the South African Foundation, formed in 1959 to undertake 'the promotion of international understanding of the South African way of life, achievements, and aspirations' and 'positive campaigns which shall present to the world at large the true picture of South Africa'. The Foundation, in short, represents the alarm of South African big business as a whole, irrespective of party outlook, at the damage being done to the South African economy as a consequence of the unfavourable international reaction to apartheid. Chairman of the Foundation is Sir Francis de Guingand, Lord Montgomery's Chief of Staff from 1942 to 1945 and director of more than twenty South African companies. Vice-Chairmen elected at the first meeting were Dr H. J. van Eck, Chairman of the Industrial Development Corporation; Dr J. E. Holloway, former Union Secretary of Finance, Ambassador in Washington, and High Commissioner in London; Dr M. S. Louw, Chairman of Bonuskor and Federale Volksbeleggings, director of about thirty other companies and the recognized leader of Afrikaner business opinion; and C. W. Engelhard, an American financier who has acquired huge financial interests in South Africa. Other members of the Foundation include H. F. Oppenheimer, Chairman of De Beers and Anglo-American Corporation, Anton Rupert, the 'tobacco king', and leading figures in the business world, both English and Afrikaans-speaking, both Nationalist and anti-Nationalist, controlling over 400 industrial, finance, and mining companies.

The Foundation has strong links with the South African Press. Among the members are G. H. R. Edmunds, Chairman of South African Associated Newspapers, *Rand Daily Mail* Ltd, and the *Sunday Times* Syndicate; Adrian Berrill, Chairman of the Central News Agency, which has a virtual monopoly in the newspaper and periodical distribution trade; Clive Corder, director of the *Cape Times* Ltd; Colonel Eugene O'Connell Maggs, director of the Bantu Press Ltd, which publishes a string of papers directed to the African market; and Dr A. L. Geyer, a director of Nasionale Pers, owners of *Die Burger*. Dr M. S. Louw and Anton Rupert are both directors of the Nationalist weekly *Dagbreek*, while another member of the Foundation is Dr P. J. Meyer, Chairman of the South African Broadcasting Corporation.

The Foundation carries on propaganda activities both abroad and at home designed to reassure people with money that no matter what South African politics are like, the country is still a sound field of investment. Prominent business figures from abroad are taken on conducted tours of the country and shown the 'positive' side of apartheid, such as African housing in the locations. The cruder aspects of discrimination are glossed over or explained away. There is no doubt that the Foundation has had a pronounced impact on business circles abroad and has successfully used its influence to counteract the effects of the international boycott of South African goods. At home, meanwhile, the Foundation has also done a great deal to convince the English Press that in certain circumstances criticism of apartheid can be unpatriotic. South African newspapers today are reluctant to criticize the South African government's handling of foreign affairs – for example, its standpoint on the dispute over the status of South-West Africa. The government, through the Foundation and by other means, has largely succeeded in convincing the Press organs of White South Africa that it is in their own interests to present a united front to the outside world.

For, of course, the Foundation speaks only for White South Africa. It has no representation from non-White South Africa and has made no serious attempt to obtain any. In the first place, apart from the small Indian merchant class and a handful of Coloured and African businessmen, there is no non-White big business worth considering. Secondly, if non-Whites were brought into the Foundation on an equal footing with the Whites, the Nationalist members would promptly withdraw. So the Foundation stays White and acts White, reinforcing the impression that in the long run White supremacy is largely a matter of big business.

But what is true of the Foundation is true of the South African Press as a whole. It is overwhelmingly a White Press. Not a single African-owned newspaper exists in any shape or form anywhere in the country. The independent Coloured Press is represented by the tiny weekly, *Torch*. There are two or three Indian-owned weeklies in Natal. For the rest, the whole apparatus of propaganda resides in the hands of the Whites, to come, as we have seen in this chapter, increasingly under the control and influence of the Nationalist government. Even books are not freely accessible to non-Whites. The main libraries, with few exceptions, practise a rigid colour bar. The price of new books places them out of reach of the majority of the population, to whom even the cost of a paperback must be measured against the price of a loaf of bread. And on top of all this, there is now to be total internal and external censorship.

'Everyone,' states the Universal Declaration of Human Rights, 'has the right to freedom of opinion and expression; this right includes freedom to hold opinions without interference and to seek, receive and impart information and ideas through any media and regardless of frontiers.' In South Africa this right has long since ceased to exist.

13. Taming the Trade Unions

> The movement and the nation can derive advantage from a National Socialist trade union organization only if the latter be so thoroughly inspired by National Socialist ideas that it runs no danger of falling into step behind the Marxist movement . . . It must declare war against the Marxist Trades Union . . . It must declare itself hostile to the idea of class and class warfare and, in place of this, it must declare itself as the defender of the various occupational and professional interests of the German people.
> HITLER in *Mein Kampf*

'We know one person only to whom we owe an explanation, and that is the White worker in South Africa who has brought the National Party to the position it occupies today and who will keep it in that position in the future.'

So spoke B. J. Vorster, now Minister of Justice, in the House of Assembly in February 1956. And he spoke the truth. The Nationalist Party is a typical *bourgeois* nationalist party whose leading members have never shown any reluctance to enter commerce and industry and make profits just like their counterparts in other national groups. Nevertheless, it has always masqueraded, in the same way that the Nazi Movement did, as the party of the workers – though only the White workers, of course. And there is no doubt that it has won the support of many White workers by following policies which have buttressed their economic and social position, if at the expense of the rest of the community.

The trade union movement, as the main bastion of the rights and liberties of the working class, has been a target for Nationalist attack ever since the thirties, when the Broederbond decided that the volk as a whole should make a special effort to win over the workers. With the increasing urbanization of the Afrikaner people, tens of thousands of Afrikaners were being drawn into the ranks of the trade union movement, which had been founded and traditionally led in South Africa by non-Afrikaans, mainly English elements. It was intolerable to the Nationalist leadership that the Afrikaner worker should be subjected in this way to unnational and alien influences, exposed to the debilitating effects of English humanism and liberalism, embroiled in the class struggle. Unless a strenuous effort were made to win him back to the fold, he would be lost for ever and become a convert to the ideologies of the enemy.

The Nationalists attacked on two fronts. In the first place they wanted to win over the Afrikaans worker and bring him into the ranks of the Nationalist Party, or at any rate subject to Nationalist Party influence. In the second, they wanted to bring about a separation of White and non-White in the trade union movement and in all spheres of employment, so ensuring that the White worker would never be threatened by competition from the non-Whites. The story of the Nationalist conquest of the trade union movement is one of internal subversion coupled, after the Nationalist advent to power in 1948, with direct and blatant government intervention. It is a story which is not yet complete, because there is still a great deal of fight left in the trade unions and in the working class as a whole, though a once mighty and influential trade union movement has been sadly crippled by Nationalist interference in the last thirty years.

With Broederbond backing and guidance, the attack on the trade unions was mounted by the whole host of *volksorganis-asies*, including the Church, cultural and economic movements, political parties, and splinter groups operating inside the trade unions themselves. One of the first shots in the campaign was fired by the Nasionale Hervormde Kerk Algemene Kerkver-gadering of May 1937, which appointed a commission of inquiry into 'Communism and the trade unions'. The commission reported that the South African Trades and Labour Council, the premier trade union coordinating body in South Africa, was working in close collaboration with 'The People's Front', which had been established to counter the fascist menace in the Union, and the Friends of the Soviet Union, both dubbed out-and-out Communist organizations.

'Your commission declares with the greatest emphasis

(1) that Communism is a deadly enemy of the Christian religion . . .

(2) That Communism is a threat to Christian civilization

because it (*a*) propagates a bitter class struggle, and (*b*) agitates strongly for equality between Black and White.'

The commission recommended: (1) that the N.H. Kerk should warn against the danger of Communism; (2) that the Algemene Vergadering should protest very strongly to the government and the Chamber of Mines against the 'closed shop principle', because thereby many Afrikaners in conflict with their consciences were forced to become members of one of the trade unions, namely the 'Mineworkers' Union'; and (3) that the government and the Chamber of Mines should be earnestly requested to leave the miners free to join without any restrictions the Bond van Afrikaanse Mynwerkers because (*a*) the Bond stood on a Christian National foundation, (*b*) it operated outside party politics, and (*c*) would do as much and infinitely more for the workers.

The findings of the commission were set out in a pamphlet entitled *Communism and the South African Trade Unions* by Dr H. P. Wolmarans, which launched a vicious attack on the leaders and methods of the orthodox trade union movement in South Africa and described the Trades and Labour Council executive as consisting largely of Jews and the English-speaking, in the main Communist or Communist-orientated. Once again the main crime of the Communists or so-called Communists was held to be that they advocated equal rights for Black and White. Dr Wolmarans found that this ideology had spilt over into the T.L.C. 'The innocent *boeredogters* [boer, or Afrikaner, daughters], in the Garment Workers' Union have to pay 6d. a week to a central fund, part of which is used to pay a native secretary of the native trade unions.' The Secretary of the Garment Workers' Union was called 'The Communist Jew, Solly [E.S.] Sachs' – a reference which was to prove somewhat expensive for Dr Wolmarans, who ultimately had to pay heavy damages to Sachs for libel. The company which printed the pamphlet, Die Voortrekker Pers, also paid heavy damages, not only to Sachs, but to a number of other trade union leaders who had been defamed.

The pamphlet by Dr Wolmarans referred to a conference of the Federasie van Afrikaanse Kultuurverenigings (F.A.K., the main legal front for the Broederbond) where representatives of all the Afrikaans Churches had been present. 'The congress felt that the next task of the F.A.K. lay in the sphere of industry, where the numbers of Afrikaner workers were steadily growing and where the danger was daily growing that the Afrikaner worker would be led away from the national and religious basis of his people and where many of the trade unions to which Afrikaners belonged were being exploited by conscienceless foreigners to harm the Afrikaners and win them to Communism.' The solution proposed was to organize 'pure Afrikaans trade unions which can protect the interest of the Afrikaner workers on Christian-National lines'.

Dr Wolmarans claimed that shortly after the Bond van Afrikaanse Mynwekers was formed, its membership had been greater than that of the Mineworkers' Union itself. Certain members of the union had then protested to the Chamber of Mines against the formation of an Afrikaans union, and the closed shop had been introduced. As Dr Wolmarans saw it, the mine bosses had shown their antipathy towards the Afrikaner workers by agreeing to this.

The next large-scale attack on the trade unions was launched by the National Economic Conference of the Reddingsdaadbond held at Bloemfontein in October 1939. The Reddingsdaadbond had been the brainchild of the Rev. J. D. Kestell who, appalled by the fact that one-sixth of the White population, mostly Afrikaners, were classed as poor Whites, had issued at the time of the Voortrekker celebrations in 1938 an appeal for a tangible tribute to the memory of the Voortrekkers, declaring that they would be honoured if 'something were done for their "sunken" descendants'. Reddingsdaad committees had been formed in all parts of the country to raise half a million pounds, and the National Economic Conference was held to decide what to do with the money.

The conference was quietly taken over by the politicians, prominent amongst whom were Dr Verwoerd, Dr Dönges, Dr van Rhyn, Dr Hertzog, and Dr Diederichs – all later to be Nationalist Cabinet Ministers. Two main courses of action were decided upon – on the one hand to promote Afrikaner capitalist enterprises (surely something that the Rev. Kestell never dreamt of in his philosophy) and on the other hand to reform the trade unions on Christian-National lines. According to a report in *Die Vaderland* of 6 October 1939:

Dr Hertzog, who spoke on labour organization, pointed out that the trade unions in this country collected £290,000 annually. He wished to embrace these organizations in the objects of the congress and so put an end to the trade unions 'completely ruining the Afrikaner in the cities' . . . he warned against the control of trade unions by foreigners who had considerable financial self-interest at stake. The congress approved Dr Hertzog's proposal that a 'large portion' of the Reddingsdaadfonds should be used for reforming the trade unions.

The conference set up the Reddingsdaadbond to promote the 'economic independence of the Afrikaner'. Among its objects the new organization proposed 'to make the Afrikaans labourer part and parcel of the Nationalist life and to prevent the Afrikaans workers developing as a class distinct from other classes in the Afrikaans national life'. It even established a special labour section, the Chairman of which for many years was Dr Diederichs.

Dr Dönges described the mission of the R.D.B.: 'The foreign influences must be removed from our trade unions, and they must take their place foursquare on a national basis. . . . It is the task of the R.D.B. to keep the Afrikaner worker, in the midst of foreign elements, in his Church, language, and national environment.'

At a later stage the Blankewerkersbeskermingsbond (White Workers' Protection Society) was called into being as an organization functioning specifically in the sphere of labour. Its constitution stated:

The society is founded on the Christian-National traditions of the people of South Africa (a) to study carefully the social problems and evils, especially those that affect the workers' community on the Witwatersrand: to find ways and means to combat those evils and to bring pressure to bear, where necessary, on responsible bodies, so that the necessary measures can be taken to adopt legislation which will promote the best interests of the workers.

Membership was open to 'White persons only who are members of the Protestant Church', and the organization aimed, amongst other things,

(*j*) to support and propagate the undermentioned relationship between European and non-European workers: (1) that there should be a
clear determination of which occupations must be reserved for Europeans and which for non-Europeans; (2) that no undesirable contact
between European and non-European workers should be tolerated in
their employment; and (3) that mixed membership of trade unions of
European and non-Europeans workers shall be prohibited.

Prominent members of the Blankewerkersbeskermingsbond
included Jan de Klerk, present Minister of the Interior, B. J.
Schoeman, later Minister of Labour and present Minister of
Railways, J. du Pisanie, and Dr Diederichs.

These were the main instruments by which the Nationalist
poison was injected into the trade union movement, with special
attention paid to unions in which Afrikaner workers predomi-
nated, but which were not under Nationalist control, such as the
Mineworkers' Union, the Garment Workers' Union, and the
Building Workers' Union.

The campaign against the Mineworkers' Union was stimu-
lated by a donation of £10,000 from a wealthy Afrikaner land-
owner, Mrs Jannie Marais, to rescue Afrikaner miners from 'the
evil materialistic influences of the Witwatersrand'. On 4 October 1936, Die Nasionale Raad van Trustees was formed. It
provided all the funds for the Afrikaner Bond van Mynwerkers
which was established on 7 April 1937, and later changed its
name to Die Hervormingsorganisasie (in die Mynwerkersunie) –
more popularly known as the Reformers – with Dr Albert Hertzog as the guiding spirit.

The Reformers rapidly gained ground amongst the rank and
file of the mineworkers, aided by the bureaucratic methods of the
union leadership which relied upon the closed shop instead of
democratic discussion to maintain its influence with labour. As
with similar leaderships in other countries, an entrenched
trade union bureaucracy is extremely difficult to displace, and
the Mineworkers' Union leaders proved to be no exception.
At times passions ran high. In June 1939, Charlie Harris,
Secretary of the Mineworkers' Union, was assassinated outside
his office by a young Afrikaner, who had no doubt been
convinced by the Reformers that Harris was an enemy of the

volk. The youth was tried for murder and sentenced to life imprisonment.

By 1941 the Reformers had created a situation which could no longer be ignored, and the government appointed a special commission to inquire into the matter. The commission reported itself

fully satisfied that the powers behind the Reformers are much less actuated by an honest desire to reform the affairs and administration of the Union in the sole interests of the mineworkers, and to establish a bona fide trade union along recognized and accepted trade union lines, than by other and less admirable reasons.... The Commission has no hesitation in placing on record its finding that the Reformers and the powers behind them, of which they are the puppets, constitute a subversive movement which is detrimental to the interests of the mineworkers, the mining industry, and the Union of South Africa as a whole.

The commission declared that 'if the Nasionale Raad van Trustees had not been established and not supplied the sinews of war, there would have been no Reformers'. Furthermore it reported that the Reformers had openly declared it their objective, after getting control of the Mineworkers' Union, 'to make a start with the Garment Workers' Union and carry out the same tactics there, after which they would tackle trade union after trade union in the same manner'. The Nationalist offensive against the trade unions was by now in full swing.

The stinging rebuff administered by the commission did little to stem the enthusiasm of the Reformers, and even less to awaken the Union leaders to a realization of the serious threat that faced them. They relied more and more on strong-arm methods, and the good will of the mining bosses, to maintain themselves in power. Eventually in February 1947 the Reformers led some 6,000 miners on strike, not against the mine owners, but against 'the corrupt clique in control of the Union'. After a seven-week stoppage of work, the government ordered elections to be held for officials and also set up a three-man commission to inquire into the administration of the affairs of the Union. Those working under the control of Die Nasionale Raad van Trustees, including D. E. Ellis and Jan Glesiner, amalgamated with an Action

Committee and formed the so-called United Mineworkers' Committee. In 1948 this committee got its candidates elected to the General Council of the Union and thereafter appointed Ellis as Secretary in place of B. Brodrick, who had been sacked following the report of the commission that 'the present seething discontent is in no small measure due to the wrongful conduct of B. Brodrick, Secretary of the Union . . . neither the Executive Committee nor the General Council is free from blame for permitting a paid official to dominate the Union'.

The General Council, acting on the report of its delegates to the Trades and Labour Council conference at Port Elizabeth in 1947, gave three months' notice that it intended to disaffiliate from the T.L.C. because '. . . the T. and L.C. conference is now dominated by Communistic influences and the conference was comprised of a record number of Coloured and native delegates'. After the Nationalist government came to power, an executive meeting of the Union in April 1949 declared several Nationalist Party M.P.s to be 'honorary mineworkers' – Dr Albert Hertzog, Dr N. Diederichs, M. J. van den Berg, de Villiers Visser, Ben Schoeman, Prof. A. I. Malan, Frank Mentz, Dirk Mostert, J. du Plessis and A. J. B. Deysel. The executive committee also announced that 'a vigilance committee is to be formed for closer co-operation with the head committee of the Nationalist Party, to promote the interests of the mineworker. . . . The parliamentary sub-committee consisting of Nationalist M.P.s who will look after the interests of the mineworkers while in Cape Town was also approved by the Council. They have already declared themselves to be prepared to undertake this special task.'

This announcement was received with mixed feelings by the Nationalist politicians, who had for years campaigned to keep politics out of the trade unions. Schoeman later casually denied that he had accepted the position of 'honorary mineworker'. Whether the other members ever agreed to serve in that capacity is not known.

The advent of the Nationalist leadership to power in the Mineworkers' Union did not bring the benefits which the majority of the rank and file had probably expected. In 1951 the government appointed another commission of inquiry, this time to investigate, amongst other things, the purchase of a building, Transafrika House, by the Mineworkers' Union for £176,000, a transaction on which a certain Dr Kritzinger made a profit of £23,000. The commission reported:

We have no doubt that Ellis was promised a reward by Kritzinger if he were to use his influence to bring about the purchase of Transafrika House. . . . We are unable to determine the exact terms of the original promise, as obviously neither Ellis nor Kritzinger will tell the truth on this subject; but it is clear that the interest in the bottle store was given in pursuance of some promise.

The commission suggested that the Union should decide what action to take in the light of its findings. The Union decided to take no action, but in March 1953 Paul Visser, the ex-President of the Union, brought a private prosecution against Ellis on a charge of falsitas. Ellis was found guilty of accepting a bribe and sentenced to eighteen months' imprisonment with hard labour. The conviction was set aside on appeal, however, on the grounds that Visser himself had no title to prosecute.

The echoes of this scandal had hardly died down when a further commission was appointed in 1953 to investigate the Union's financial affairs. The commission had some scathing things to say about the administration of the Union. Yet the same leadership remained in power, and the government never at any time felt it necessary to take steps against it comparable with those it was employing to 'clean up' the non-Nationalist trade unions.

The methods which had been tried so successfully in the Mineworkers' Union were adopted also in the Garment, Building, and Leather Workers' Unions, but with less success, probably because the leadership was more closely in touch with the workers and so less vulnerable than that of the old Mineworkers' Union had been. Tactics reminiscent of those employed by the Nazis were used, particularly against the Garment Workers' Union, which was subjected to all forms of verbal and physical pressure by the Nationalist group in its bid to dislodge the Sachs leadership. Sachs himself was brutally assaulted on more than one occasion, and meetings of the Union were forcibly disrupted by gangs of weapon-wielding thugs. The Nationalists founded a special publishing company to issue their propaganda to the mine, building, and clothing workers, but the company soon fell foul of the laws of libel and went into liquidation, owing large sums of money to a number of trade unionists who had been defamed.

The attack on the Garment Workers' Union reached its climax at a general meeting of the No. 1 branch of the Union held at the Johannesburg City Hall in September 1948, to discuss an arbitration award. In his book *The Choice Before South Africa*, Sachs writes:

> While I spoke on the Arbitration Award the audience listened attentively. Then came, from outside, sounds of great commotion. Suddenly a mob from the street gained forceful access to the meeting by storming the doors and, once inside, blazed a trail of violence: men and women were assaulted, furniture was broken, the loudspeaker smashed, bottles were broken on people's heads, the Arbitration Award was torn up, unbridled threats were shrieked and, from what had been order, chaos was created; and, from what had been tranquillity, terror.

The following morning the Union's President wired the Minister of Justice demanding a public inquiry into the incident. The government, now in the hands of the Nationalists, responded by appointing a commission to inquire, not only into the disturbances at the City Hall, but also into the affairs of the Union itself, including the expulsion and loss of employment of various members, notably leaders of the Nationalist opposition. The commission's report was by no means complimentary to the administration of the Union, but also revealed how the opposition came to be organized by the Nationalists:

> As a result of the expulsion of Mrs Moll and Mrs Nel an Action Committee was established, consisting of members of the three Afrikaans Churches in Germiston. Rightly or wrongly, this Committee deplored the expulsions and felt that a grave injustice had been done. On 6 March 1944, the Action Committee was merged into a larger committee called the 'Breë Kerklike Komitee', consisting of ministers and well-intentioned members. This committee was in turn replaced by the Blankewerkersbeskermingsbond.

The Nationalists, who have never ceased to attack the Anglican

Church for meddling in politics, did not scruple to harness the D.R.C. in their campaign to rid the trade unions of the 'Jewish-Communist' element – personified, in their eyes, by the Garment Workers' Secretary, Solly Sachs, who had done a great deal to uplift the thousands of workers of all races in the industry but who was distrusted by the Nationalists for his parentage and ideology alike.

The Nationalists no doubt hoped that with the commission's report Sachs would disappear from the scene, just as Brodrick had been eliminated from the Mineworkers' Union. But this did not happen, and it was not until sweeping powers were placed in their hands by the Suppression of Communism Act that the Nationalists were able to get to grips with their enemies in the trade union movement. The Act was passed in 1950. Two years later a total of fifty-three trade unionists had been named as Communists. By September 1953, thirty-three of these had been removed from office, and soon afterwards a further fifteen were removed; the Minister simply served notices on them, ordering them to resign, failing which they would render themselves liable to long terms of imprisonment without the option of a fine. Among the victims, in addition to Sachs, were Ray Alexander, founder and general secretary of the Food and Canning Workers' Union, Piet Huyser, secretary of the Building Workers' Union, six other national secretaries, a national organizer, a president and vice-president. The membership of the unions whose leading officers were eliminated in this way totalled 80,000.

On their advent to power, the Nationalists set about the task of revising the country's labour laws in accordance with the policy of apartheid. They had made no secret of their intention to do this. The draft constitution had outlined their plans. Schoeman, later Minister of Labour, speaking in the House of Assembly on 19 March 1942, said:

First, we contend that wage control and wage fixation should be entirely in the hands of the State. Secondly, and this is the most important principle – self-government in industry must be eliminated. . . . Self-government in industry and collective bargaining are things of the past . . . the time has arrived that in the interests of the State, in the interests of employers and employees, self-government in industry and collective bargaining should be eliminated from our economic life. . . .

In regard to the non-Europeans, the unhealthy economic competition which is gradually arising and which will become more and more intense should be entirely eliminated. My party maintains that this can only be done by fixing a definite quota for Europeans and non-Europeans in unskilled, semi-skilled, and skilled occupations in industry.

On 4 July 1944, Schoeman said again: 'There must be changes in the foreign British system, which does not conform to the character and traditions of the Afrikaner . . . the present [labour] system must be destroyed and a new one created. . . .'

On 1 October 1948, the government appointed the Industrial Legislation Commission of Inquiry with comprehensive terms of reference to cover the whole field of labour and race relations in industry, and a specific mandate to report on the desirability of having separate trade unions for the different races and whether existing wage regulating legislation operated as an adequate protection for all races. The commission completed its work with dispatch, and by 1951 its report was in the hands of the government.

In some respects the commission did everything that the government required of it. In others, its report must have been a disappointment. It recommended the establishment of a National Labour Board to coordinate wages and other conditions of employment – but declared that 'the principle of self-government in industry should, subject to certain safeguards, be retained'. It opposed the introduction of general compulsory arbitration in disputes, and stated that no action should be taken to prohibit closed-shop provisions in agreements resulting from collective bargaining. It recommended a form of recognition for African trade unions and even proposed to give them the right to strike in certain circumstances. All this could be regarded as something of a slap in the face for Schoeman, considering his remarks in Parliament only a few years previously.

On the other hand, the commission produced a host of proposals for stricter supervision of trade unions, and recommended that industrial councils, trade unions, and employers' organizations, together with their officials, should be prohibited from taking part in party politics – an obvious hit at the practice of some unions which were affiliated to the Labour Party or supported it in elections. Even the right of a union to issue a publication was to be subject to governmental veto.

Though asked to recommend something like job reservation, the commission failed to do so, stating that it lacked sufficient information to enable it to frame concrete proposals and recommending further study of the subject by the National Labour Board.

But the kernel of the report was undoubtedly the recommendation that 'it should be the policy of the government to achieve the organization of European and non-European workers in separate racial trade unions', even though, the commission admitted, the weight of evidence which had been presented to it 'was overwhelmingly against the introduction of legislation compelling the segregation of the various races into separate unions, and the witnesses who advocated the retention of mixed unions included both employers and employees'. Just how anxious the commission was to find for separate unions may be measured from a study of its findings on the mixed ones. On the one hand it found that mixed unions retarded non-White development. 'Generally Europeans have the leadership of mixed unions, even of some of those whose membership is predominantly non-European, for the purpose of protecting the European standard of living'. But in the next breath it maintained that 'the increasing tendency on the part of non-Europeans to exercise leadership in mixed organizations constitutes an economic threat to Europeans and consequently to industrial peace'. Anyway, whatever the reason, mixed unions were to go. The commission recommended formally that no new mixed unions should be registered and that existing mixed unions should be split on racial lines.

The Trades and Labour Council called a special conference to discuss the report on 12 and 13 January 1952. And this conference expressed itself convinced, that the report and recommendations of the Industrial Legislation Commission of Inquiry are designed not to improve the conditions of the workers, nor to promote industrial peace, nor to increase the national production of the country ... The report and recommendations, if enacted in law, will deprive all workers in South Africa, European and non-European, of the elementary rights of freedom of organization and the right of collective bargaining. . . . The political doctrines enunciated in the report are inspired by Nazi-Fascist philosophy, and so-called economic theories, presented at great length in the report, are merely a collection of anti-Labour doctrines which the enemies of the workers have presented as 'economic science' for generations. . . . Conference rejects the recommendations in their entirety.

The government, of course, adopted those recommendations of the commission which suited it and rejected all the others. In particular, it wanted nothing to do with the recognition of African trade unions in any shape or form. Already in 1951 it had passed the Native Building Workers Act, ostensibly to provide facilities for the training of Africans as building workers, but in the process to establish complete separation between the training and employment of African and non-African building workers. In terms of the Act, no African might be employed as a skilled building worker outside of an African area, while the training and rates of pay for African builders bore no relation to those laid down for non-Africans. The Act extended to the building industry the statutory colour bar which had previously existed only in the sphere of mining.

In 1953 the government passed the Native Labour (Settlement of Disputes) Act, completely outlawing strikes by Africans and establishing a cumbersome machinery for the settlement of disputes. Explaining why he had rejected the recommendation of the Industrial Legislation Commission that African trade unions should be recognized, subject to strict controls, Schoeman, Minister of Labour, declared:

I think the hon. members must realize that if we give that incentive to natives to organize – and we must bear in mind that they are primitive and illiterate natives who have not the faintest conception of the responsibilities of trade unionism, that they are people who cannot even read the constitution of a trade union, who know nothing about negotiation or the industrial set-up of South Africa – if we give them that incentive to organize and they should become well organized – and again bearing in mind that there are almost 1,000,000 native workers in industry and commerce today – they can use their trade unions as a political weapon and they can create chaos in South Africa at any given time. I think that we would probably be committing race suicide if we gave them that incentive.

African trade unions were not outlawed by the Act, but they were not to be recognized and would therefore be unable to use the machinery for collective bargaining provided by the Industrial Conciliation Act. Schoeman said he hoped that as a result of his new measure all African unions would 'die a natural death'.

His strictures on the African workers had been contradicted by his own commission, which had expressed itself 'satisfied that a sufficient number of native workers in commerce and secondary industry know enough about trade unionism to make the recognition of native trade unions a practical proposition, provided suitable measures for the guidance and control of those unions are introduced'. The commission had further added:

Notwithstanding the unsatisfactory features characterizing the native trade union movement, the commission is satisfied that there are a number of unions which are well organized and are conducted on correct lines. The leaders of some of these unions have in the past rendered considerable assistance by advising against, and restraining their members from taking drastic action; they are able to place the case for the workers before wage-fixing bodies, and some of them have shown indications of a measure of ability to negotiate with employers.

Such a pronouncement, however, spelt ruin, not progress to Schoeman, who throughout his career, and especially at the time of the bus boycott in Johannesburg in 1957, used all the forces of the State to smash any sign of resistance and organization by African workers.

'I appeal to employers,' he told the annual conference of the Federated Chamber of Industries in November 1954, 'to use only the machinery of this Act in connexion with native labour disputes and to carry out its intentions and not do anything to embarrass its functioning. I do not want what is happening in

Rhodesia to happen here. . . . Employers must in their own interests stand firm . . . must on no account discuss or negotiate with native political organizations such as the African National Congress.'

The Act provides for the establishment of a Central Native Labour Board, consisting of Europeans only, appointed by the Minister; Regional Native Labour Committees, of which the chairman is a European and the remaining members 'natives appointed by the Minister'; and works committees elected by the workers in any establishment under the supervision of the Native Labour Officer for the area. (Despite the name, 'Native Labour Officer' must be a European, again appointed by the Minister.) The function of a works committee is to be consulted by a Native Labour Officer, who must report to the Regional Native Labour Committee, which must settle the dispute somehow and make a recommendation to the Central Native Labour Board, which in turn must make a recommendation to the Minister, who can do as he pleases, unless the Board is unable to reach a solution, in which case the matter can be referred to the Wage Board.

When he introduced his Bill in Parliament, the Minister proclaimed that it was essential to create machinery and appoint officials 'in whom the natives will have confidence'. Not surprisingly, however, the workers have had no confidence whatsoever in the cumbrous, bureaucratic machinery set up under the Act. By 1955 only four works committees had been established in the whole Union, by 1959 only eight and it is doubtful whether today more than a score are functioning, even on paper, throughout the country. The workers have clung to their trade unions despite every discouragement.

The only section of the Act which can be said to have worked is the one prohibiting strikes, and that has been invoked with unfailing regularity. When a dispute breaks out, the employers have been instructed to send out an immediate S O S to the Labour Department, and in a trice Departmental officials and the police, including members of the Special Branch, descend on the scene. If the dispute has reached the point where the workers have stopped work, the Labour Department officials warn them that they are breaking the law and must return to work immediately. Absolutely no attempt is made to negotiate on the actual grievances or demands of the workers. No undertakings are given. The men are told to go back to work, or else. . . . Not unnaturally, the men often refuse, insisting that they have had good reason to stop working and that they want their demands discussed. This is usually the signal for police to arrest all the strikers on the spot or to launch one of their vicious baton charges. In most cases it can be stated categorically that police and Labour Department intervention has actually prevented the conclusion of a peaceful agreement between the workers and the management, and been the direct cause of the subsequent violence.

Neither force nor blandishments, however, have prevented Africans from going on strike since the Act was passed. In 1960, according to official figures, thirty-three strikes involving 2,199 Africans took place; 364 Africans were prosecuted and 294 convicted. In 1961, twenty-six strikes involving 1,427 workers took place, and in five of these strikes the workers were convicted for striking illegally. Nor do these figures provide an accurate reflection of the true position. Some employers have found out that the swift retribution meted out to strikers is not always beneficial for business. When your entire labour force is removed in police vans to the cells, your factory production comes to a stop; and if hundreds of workers are involved, it is not always possible for the government's labour bureaux to replace them. At Randfontein in 1955, for example, 169 textile workers went on strike and were fined £10 each. The firm employing the workers paid the fines itself, but the court ordered that the money be deducted from the pay packets of the workers, with the entire amount to be paid over a period of eight weeks. Similar examples have occurred elsewhere. The result is that frequently employers are reluctant to use the official machinery for the settlement of disputes because of the disruption it may entail.

Nor do the official statistics of strikes include stoppages which were not due to disputes between employers and employees. In 1960, the year of Sharpeville, for example, tens of thousands of workers took part in a political stay-at-home.

Economic life in the Western Cape, particularly, was almost totally disrupted by the absence from work of the African labour force for between two and three weeks. None of this is reflected in the official figures, since these apparently deal only with domestic disputes of which the Labour Department has been officially informed.

A strike by African workers at Hammersdale in 1959 provided an illuminating insight into the labour policies of the Nationalist government. The owners had closed down their factories in Johannesburg and Durban and opened a factory at Hammersdale – about thirty-six miles from Durban – instead, because they would be able to pay their workers lower wages (in the urban areas the levels are laid down by an industrial agreement which does not cover the rural areas). About 500 workers were employed there at wages ranging from 15s. a week for women to £1 for men, and the labour force included an ex-principal of a school, ex-schoolteachers, and matriculants.

In spite of the low wages paid, there was a surplus of labour in the area, and each day scores of workers seeking employment were turned away. For when the factory was first established at the beginning of 1958, the local Native Commissioner, using the despotic powers vested in him under the pass laws, had blockaded all labour in the area and in the neighbouring Reserves and prevented it from going into the larger industrial centres of Durban, Pietermaritzburg and Pinetown to seek work. The result of the strike was that wages were increased immediately by from 5s. to 7s. 6d. a week; but even at the new level they constitute less than thirty per cent of the monthly figure laid down by the Institute of Race Relations as the bare minimum required by a family of five for the maintenance of health.

Thus the Native Labour (Settlement of Disputes) Act, supported by the pass laws, constitutes the means by which the wages of the African workers are maintained at rock-bottom level. Unions and union officials are hounded, strikes outlawed, and the African worker forced to make do as best he can. Not surprisingly, the vast majority live well below the breadline, even in the urban areas. According to a calculation made by Prof. O. P. F. Horwood of Natal University in November 1960, the average income of nearly 6,000,000 Africans engaged in modern economic activity was little over £50 *per capita* a year, while the average *per-capita* income of occupied persons in the Reserves was between £7 and £13 a year. The professor's figures can be compared with those given by the Minister of Finance in February 1961, when he estimated that the average *per-capita* income of Whites was £410 a year; of Asians, £80 a year; of Coloured, £58 a year; and of Africans, £46 a year.

Nor should government propaganda to the effect that the African standard of living is rising steadily be accepted at its face value. G. C. V. Graham, President of the Midland Chamber of Industries, in a paper presented to a conference of the National Development Foundation in October 1961, stressed that the government's labour legislation was unable to cope with the wage problem. This, he said, was 'amply demonstrated by the fact that the gap between non-European semi-skilled and unskilled wages and that of European wages has been widening since 1945, and that they are, on average, still well below subsistence level'. In consequence of a massive public campaign, African wages in some sectors have risen since then, but it is doubtful if the ratio outlined above has been significantly altered.

The Nationalist government's main assault upon the trade union movement was mounted in the Industrial Conciliation Act which, after being redrafted several times, was introduced in the House of Assembly in May 1954 and, after its second reading, referred to a select committee. The amended Bill was then introduced in the Assembly during January 1956 and became law during the same session.

The Act provided for the creation of separate trade unions, or separate branches of existing unions, for White and non-White workers. After the passage of the Act, no further mixed unions were to be registered, though the Minister was given the power to grant exemptions in instances where the number of White or non-White workers was so small that they could not form an effective separate union. Existing mixed unions were given twelve months to provide (1) separate branches for White and non-White workers; (2) separate meetings for each branch; and (3) an executive committee consisting of Whites alone.

After the expiry of the twelve-month period, no non-White worker would be permitted to attend a branch of White members, and vice versa. Furthermore, no non-White worker might attend or take part in a meeting of the all-White executive committee except to answer a complaint against him.

Should over half of the White or non-White workers in a mixed union wish to break away and form a separate racial union, they could apply in terms of the Act to the Industrial Registrar for registration. The Registrar would then have the power to order the original union to become uni-racial as well. Provision was made for the splitting of assets in the event of the break-up of any mixed unions.

Section 77 of the Act introduced the notorious concept of job reservation – and for this purpose the term 'employee' was deemed to include Africans, otherwise excluded from the provisions of the Industrial Conciliation Act. If the Minister considered that steps should be taken to safeguard the 'economic welfare' of employees of any race in any industry, he was authorized to instruct an Industrial Tribunal set up under the Act to investigate the industry and make recommendations as to whether certain types of work should be reserved for any racial group. The Minister could then accept the Tribunal's recommendation (he could not vary it) and issue it as a determination, but no determination would be binding where an industrial council agreement was in operation, unless the industrial council itself agreed.

Following reverses in the courts over the first determinations promulgated by the Minister, the law was amended, and the industrial council veto abolished, so that the Industrial Tribunal may now recommend job reservation on any basis, and the Minister may allocate jobs to workers of different racial groups without restriction.

In theory, the Industrial Conciliation Act is supposed to be non-racial. The splitting of trade unions and the reservation of work is supposed to benefit the various racial groups equally. In fact, of course, this was never the government's intention. Boasting of his Bill in 1955, the Minister of Labour, Senator Jan de Klerk, said: 'In practice [the Bill] meant that the European's economic position in the industrial world could never be lowered by the non-European. It was also a guarantee that he would never be ousted and that intrusion into his field of work could be prevented.' And this is exactly how it has been employed.

The South African trade union movement has been fragmented by the Bill into its various components. At the end of 1956 there were 184 registered trade unions. Of these fifty-five catered for Whites only, sixteen catered for non-Whites only, and 113 were registered for both White and non-White. Of the 113 trade unions registered as mixed, however, only fifty-nine possessed in fact a mixed membership, the remainder being uni-racial though their constitutions contained no racial restrictions and membership was theoretically open to all.

At the end of 1960 there were 186 trade unions registered. Of these ninety-two catered for Whites, thirty-eight catered for non-Whites, and only fifty-six were mixed, with six of them in the process of splitting. According to the Minister, thirty-one of the fifty-six mixed unions had separate branches and meetings and were controlled by all-White executives. Thirty-three of the mixed unions were predominantly White, and twenty-three predominantly Coloured, with a total of twenty-four possessing fewer than fifty members of the minority group. Six unions had been completely exempted from the provisions of the Act because they had very few members of one or other race, and partial exemptions had been granted to a number of other unions for similar reasons.

According to an investigation conducted by Muriel Horrell for the South African Institute of Race Relations, by July 1961 a further eleven of the mixed unions had divided racially, five were about to do so, and one had de-registered as a result of the 1956 Act. The polarization of the South African working class along racial lines was well under way.

As for job reservation, the various determinations issued up to the end of 1962 reserved for Whites the driving of motor transport vehicles in the Durban municipal cleansing department; reserved for Whites the posts of firemen and traffic policemen above the rank of constable in the Cape Town area, and placed restrictions on the employment of Coloured ambulance drivers and attendants and traffic constables; reserved for Whites the operation of lifts in certain types of buildings in Johannesburg, Pretoria, and Bloemfontein; reserved for Whites all skilled work in the building industry in urban areas in the Transvaal and Orange Free State; prohibited the percentage of Whites, or of Whites and Coloureds employed together, in any unit of the clothing industry from falling below the percentages that obtained at certain dates; reserved for Whites the driving of refuse and night-soil removal vehicles in Springs; laid down that at least eighty-four per cent of the drivers and conductors employed by the City Tramways Company in Cape Town should be White; reserved for Whites the driving of vehicles of an unladen weight of 10,000 lb. or more on the Free State goldfields; reserved for Whites various types of skilled work in the wholesale meat trade.

Two determinations reserving certain types of skilled work in the iron, steel, and metallurgical industry for Whites were suspended until December 1962, because a new industrial council agreement had been made in terms of which considerably higher wages were prescribed for the work concerned. The Minister of Labour said that if wage rates were fixed at a level sufficiently high to attract Whites, then 'the White man, with his superior knowledge, must be able to retain that work against the non-White with his inferior civilization'.

Seven skilled crafts in the building industry were reserved for White workers from 13 May 1963, in certain areas of the Western Cape, where seventy-five per cent of building artisans are Coloured people. Coloured workers now practising these crafts will be allowed to continue with their work in White areas, but no new Coloured workers may be trained.

'This latest form of job reservation has raised no objections from White workers, but a spokesmen for 3,000 Coloured men yesterday described the new determination as "slavery".

'"They are allowing politics to interfere with our bread and butter," he said.' (*Cape Times*, 30 April 1963.)

It can thus be seen that the main preoccupation of the Industrial Tribunal so far has been to safeguard the position of the White workers at the expense of the non-Whites – just as the

Minister promised in 1955. To date not a single job has been reserved for non-Whites anywhere in the Republic.

But perhaps the worst effect of the Industrial Conciliation Act – and, for that matter, of the government's whole labour policy – has been the splitting of the trade union movement into a number of separate and opposing groups based on differences of political and racial outlook.

Until 1947 the Trades and Labour Council was the premier coordinating trade union body in South Africa, representing the vast bulk of organized labour. There were other coordinating bodies operating within a more restricted sphere – like the Western Province Federation of Labour Unions, the Transvaal Council of Non-European Trade Unions, and the railway staff associations – while a number of unions remained independent, affiliated to none of the coordinating bodies. But the T.L.C. spoke for organized labour, and its ranks were open to all unions registered and unregistered alike.

We have already seen how the White Mineworkers' Union broke away from the T.L.C., alleging that it was dominated by Communists and *kafferboeties*.[1] In 1947 there was a further split, following on the defeat of a motion – introduced at the T.L.C. annual conference by L. J. van den Berg of the S.A. Iron and Steel Trades Association and George McCormick of the S.A. Engine Drivers' and Firemen's Association – that African unions be excluded from membership. Delegates from five unions withdrew from the conference altogether, alleging that the slogan of equality for all races emanated from the Communists, resulted in the exploitation of the African, and undermined the position of the White worker. A new organization, the Coordinating Council of South African Trade Unions, came into being with a constitution which debarred mixed unions from membership. A further three unions withdrew from membership of the T.L.C. in precisely similar circumstances during 1949.

The Suppression of Communism Act, under which many trade union leaders were directly threatened, provided the next opportunity to disrupt the T.L.C. Rather than help defend their

1 Literally 'kaffir-brothers', a common term of abuse for those whose attitude to Africans is considered too friendly or liberal.

colleagues who were under attack, the right-wing unions abandoned them to the mercies of the government and withdrew from the T.L.C. to set up the South African Federation of Trade Unions in 1951. The Federation refuses membership to African unions.

Then came the Industrial Conciliation Bill, presenting to the whole trade union movement a threat which was recognized by right and left wing alike. But reactions were very different. The left wanted militant action by the whole trade union movement to defeat the Bill. The right hoped to defeat the danger by compromise. In 1954 the majority of Trades and Labour Council unions joined with the Western Province Federation of Labour Unions to form the South African Trade Union Council. This was the sort of unity for which trade unionists had been working a long time. But it was achieved at a price – the exclusion from membership of African unions and even unions which accepted Africans as members. Thirteen T.L.C. unions refused to accept this bar and joined with the Transvaal Council of Non-European Trade Unions to form the South African Congress of Trade Unions (S.A.C.T.U.), the only trade union coordinating body with no colour bar in any shape or form.

The T.L.C. majority which had helped form the T.U.C. had hoped that by excluding African unions from membership it would be able to win back to the fold the right-wing unions which had broken away and thus present a more united front to the government over the Industrial Conciliation Bill. A few unions did return from the South African Federation of Trade Unions, but for the most part the stratification in the trade union movement persisted, and at no time has it been possible to present a united front on any issue.

In 1957 the South African Federation, the Coordinating Council, and the Federal Consultative Council of the South African Railways jointly formed a South African Confederation of Labour to comprise twelve unions representing approximately 150,000 workers, all except a handful of them White. The basis of their unity is acceptance of the government's racial policies and in particular of the Industrial Conciliation Act.

In the centre stands the South African Trade Union Council,

comprising in 1961 about fifty unions, which together represented some 165,000 workers (110,000 White, 44,000 Coloured, and 11,000 Asian). Under the T.U.C.'s wing at that time was the Federation of Free African Trade Unions, comprising seventeen unions with a membership of 18,000. The T.U.C. approach to politics is pragmatic and opportunist. Its right wing is not very far from the position adopted by the South African Confederation of Labour.

In fact, the Industrial Conciliation Act was the product of cooperation between the Minister of Labour and right-wing trade unionists. In 1953 the Minister appointed a committee of employers and trade unionists to assist him in drafting the Bill. One of the members was George McCormick, Chairman of the South African Federation of Trade Unions, who declared in May 1954:

We accepted the responsibility to assist the Minister in drafting the Bill. The Minister could be excused for thinking that the representatives on the Ministerial Committee expressed the view of their organizations. We made it clear that we were against certain clauses, including Section 77 of the Bill [the job reservation clause]. It could be interpreted that we were in agreement with the rest.

T. C. Rutherford, President of the South African Trade Union Council, giving evidence to the Select Committee on the Bill on 8 March 1955, indicated, however, that 'Clause 77 was inserted in the Bill as a result of a memorandum sent in at the time by our Coordinating Body of Trade Unions. That Coordinating Body represented *inter alia* the South African Federation of Trade Unions and the South African Trades and Labour Council. I was the Chairman.'

The right-wing trade unionists, representing in the main the skilled White labour force, have a lot to answer for at the bar of history. Even when the final terms of the Bill became known, the T.U.C. leadership felt unable to fight it on grounds of principle. It opposed the Bill, certainly, but for the wrong reasons. Reporting on the results of a T.U.C. interview with the Minister, asking for the Bill to be dropped because the Council was against the splitting of the trade unions on racial lines, Rutherford said at a conference of the Boilermakers' Society in 1955: 'An appeal was, therefore, made to the Minister to allow us to keep our organizations intact so as to be able to cooperate with the government in devising ways and means of preventing the ever-increasing native labour force from continuing to menace the European standard of living.' In the interests of preserving White supremacy, providing it was done in 'the traditional way', the T.U.C. leadership was prepared to betray the mass of South African workers. Not surprisingly, the Nationalist government felt that it could safely ignore representations which were not based on solid principle. In insisting on rigid trade union apartheid, it knew that it could rely on the support of the majority of the White workers.

When, at its 1961 conference, the International Labour Office decided, by 163 votes to nil with eighty-nine abstentions, to advise South Africa to withdraw from membership until such time as it abandoned its apartheid policy, the T.U.C. conducted a rapid about-face. At its March 1962 conference it decided to amend its constitution so as to enable African unions to affiliate themselves. It went even further and nominated a non-White, Edgar Deane, to be the South African workers' delegate at the next I.L.O. conference – the first non-White in South African history to fill this role. Once again the reasons for the about-face were mainly opportunistic. The credentials of the T.U.C. delegates had been repeatedly challenged at I.L.O. conferences on the grounds that African unions were excluded from T.U.C. membership. The T.U.C. leaders had reason to fear that unless they eliminated the colour bar from their constitution, they might fall under an I.L.O. ban against the apartheid-ridden South African trade union movement.

The only coordinating body which can claim to be completely non-racial in fact as well as in theory, and which, ever since its foundation has unwaveringly upheld the banner of racial equality, is the South African Congress of Trade Unions, representing about 50,000 workers of all races, the majority of them Africans. S A C T U has closely identified itself with the Congress movement in South Africa, believing that there can be no separation between the struggle for higher wages and the fight for political rights. In consequence, it has incurred the bitter

277

hostility of the Nationalist government, always ready to place obstacles in the way of multi-racial organizations. Its leading officials have been banned, and the organization itself was proscribed for a period of three months in 1961. In terms of the blanket ban imposed on named and banned people under the Sabotage Act, its general secretary and eight other officials were forced to sever their connexion with the organization by 1 February 1963. Furthermore, the government has refused to accept any representations from S A C T U, stating that 'there are recognized trade union federations which are representative of and entitled to speak for organized workers in South Africa. The so-called South African Congress of Trade Unions does not fall within this category.'

*

In her booklet *Racialism and the Trade Unions,* issued by the South African Institute of Race Relations, Muriel Horrell concludes: 'It has become clearly apparent that because of racialism and the disputes caused thereby, labour, at one time a coherent, vigorous force of much significance in South African affairs, is now completely disunited, and has lost the power it once exercised.' The blame for this unhappy state of affairs must be placed where it belongs – on the shoulders of the Nationalist Party, which deliberately imported racialism into the trade union movement as a weapon in its bid for political domination.

14. The Conquest of Economic Power

If there is one sphere in which the Nationalists have not yet been able to triumph as they would wish it is that of the South African economy, in which non-Nationalist elements play a leading role. Yet the economic position of the Afrikaner is by no means as weak as is generally imagined, and the traditional picture of the Boer as a sort of hill-billy character with a vacant expression and tattered clothing is completely out of date. The economic basis of Nationalist power is strong and is growing stronger all the time. Nationalist politicians and economists determine the direction which is taken by the whole economy. The Nationalist control of government is used to bolster Nationalist power and influence in the private sector of the economy.

Traditionally the Afrikaner has been a farmer – the very word Boer means 'farmer' – and the association with the land has dominated the thinking of the Afrikaner since the first settlements were established at the time of Jan van Riebeeck. In the days before mining and industry began in South Africa, farming was, of course, the dominant economic activity. But the industrial revolution through which South Africa has passed in the present century has reduced the contribution of farming to the national income down to about seventeen per cent, though it still constitutes one of the most highly organized and protected industries in the country, and the influence of the farming community in the Nationalist Party is considerable.

The number of farms in South Africa in 1958 totalled 104,093, covered an area of 103,729,316 morgen, and were valued at £1,543,672,077. It has been estimated that some eighty-two per cent of White farmers are Afrikaans-speaking, and the majority of these undoubtedly support the Nationalist Party. It can thus be seen that considerable financial resources were available to the Nationalists when they decided that the time had come to move into commerce, industry, mining, and finance, and challenge the citadels of power previously monopolized by non-Afrikaans elements – the Englishman and the Jew.

Because of his powerful position in the electoral sphere, the White farmer has been able to make successive South African governments dance to his tune. He is assisted in financing his operations by the Land Bank and a whole system of State subsidies and outright grants. He gets his produce delivered on the railways at rates lower than those applicable to mining or industry. He is protected by tariffs from the competition of low-cost food imports from abroad. The government helps him with research and technical assistance. And above all he has been benefited by the development of cooperatives and control boards, which supervise the production, distribution and sale of agricultural products both in South Africa and abroad, so ensuring the best possible return for the farmer.

The first of these control mechanisms to be established was the Kooperatiewe Wynbouwers Vereniging (K.W.V.) set up in 1918 and eventually vested by Act of Parliament with complete control over the whole vine-growing industry. Production is by predetermined quota, to ensure against unwanted surpluses, while the producer gets a fixed price and distribution is wholly entrusted to the K.W.V. If the season has been good, the producer may even get an *agterskot* or final dividend, to convince him that he has been adequately compensated for the surrender of his independence.

Similar control boards were established for wheat and dairy products in 1930, for maize in 1931, for livestock in 1932, and for sugar in 1936. Today, there is hardly a branch of the industry which does not have its appropriate control board. The result is that South African farmers are placed in the position of a highly favoured monopoly. Production and prices are determined, not by the needs of the community, but by the greed of the producers. A helpless population is held to ransom by the farmers, backed by the powerful machinery of the State.

The effects of this system were made mercilessly evident in

1962, when South Africa was hit by an agricultural crisis, because the maize farmers had produced twenty-nine million bags of maize more than they could sell. The 'maize problem' had been created by what the Minister of Agricultural Economics and Marketing, Uys, called an 'explosion' in agricultural production – from forty million bags in 1959 to sixty-one million bags in 1962. It might be thought that such an explosion would have provided cause for joy and celebration, holding out the promise of abundant food for all. There was certainly need enough for the food in South Africa. In the Northern and Eastern Transvaal hundreds of thousands of African tribesmen were suffering from starvation after more than two years of serious drought. A survey conducted by the Gereformeerde Kerk in Vendaland, in the Northern Transvaal, revealed that through lack of food many people, mostly mothers and children, could eat only three times a week. From September 1962 to February 1963, 301 cases of *kwashiorkor*, mostly of children under five, and 1,224 cases of pellagra were treated at five hospitals in the districts of Zoutspansberg and Sibasa alone. The pellagra was not the result of wrong eating habits, as had been alleged by Cabinet Ministers when the situation was first exposed in the Press, but was due to 'drastic famine in drought conditions', said the Kerk report.

At about the same time, Professor J. D. L. Hansen, Associate Professor of Child Health at the University of Cape Town, declared that Coloured and African children in South Africa were dying at fifteen and twenty-five times the rate of White children, with gastro-enteritis, pneumonia, and tuberculosis as the greatest killers. 'Recent studies in hospital showed that it was under-nourished, protein-deficient children who died of these diseases.' (*Cape Argus*, 31 October 1962.)

Yet the government's proposed solution to the 'maize problem' was (a) to export the maize surplus at a price lower than the Maize Board's domestic selling price – why couldn't the price be lowered for the benefit of the local population? – and (b) to restrict production, so that in future there would be no danger of surpluses. The Minister announced that the government was introducing a 'new and revolutionary' scheme for controlling agriculture in the Republic. The scheme would involve production control.

'We are looking for a lasting remedy which will not kill the patient,' he said. But the patient he was thinking of was not the Black child suffering from *kwashiorkor* or pellagra. It was the wealthy maize farmer concerned about his profits. South Africa has also witnessed the destruction of surplus fruit and milk at the behest of control boards in order to keep up prices.

If the profits from farming are based partly on the exploitation of the consumer, they derive even more from the exploitation of the labourer. Approximately one third of the total African population of ten million live on farms in the White areas, while in the Western Province and Natal this labour force is supplemented by several hundred thousand Coloured and Asian workers. There is no wage-regulating machinery for farm labourers, and the level of wages with the conditions of work may vary from farm to farm and from area to area. According to a 1958 survey conducted in the Albany and Bathurst districts of the Eastern Province for the South African Institute of Race Relations, the average annual *family* income was £107. S. J. du Toit, Senior Professional Officer of the Department of Agricultural Economics and Marketing, has given a figure for the central Orange Free State of £176. Professor J. L. Sadie is reported to have stated that the average annual income of African families on farms in the Western Province is £145, and of Coloured families £196. The variations between these figures are considerable, but they all show a standard of living considerably below that of the industrial worker in the towns.

Conditions for farm workers on most farms can be described only as feudal, and have played a predominant role in determining the master-race attitude of Whites to Blacks in South Africa. Most farm owners behave as though they counted their labourers among their personal possessions. Cases of assault by farmers on their workers are frequently brought before the courts, leaving one to guess how many similar cases are not even referred to the police. The brutal conditions prevailing on the potato farms of the Eastern Transvaal have already been mentioned. For all these reasons farmers find it increasingly difficult to secure and retain an adequate labour force. It has been one of the aims of the pass laws and the farm jail system to remedy this deficiency, but even these devices have proved inadequate, and the government has resorted to ever more stringent control and direction of labour in order to ensure that the needs of the farmers are met.

The processes of the industrial revolution through which South Africa has passed have resulted in the destruction of the old system of agriculture, the concentration of agricultural capital in ever fewer hands, and the drift of the Afrikaner to the cities. In 1911, more than eighty per cent of the Afrikaners lived on the platteland; in 1936 the figure had dropped to forty-eight per cent and by 1951 to thirty-one per cent. If later statistics were available, they would undoubtedly show that the proportion had fallen still lower. Part of the accumulated capital of the farmers was invested in farm machinery; the number of tractors on the farms, for example, increased from 20,000 in 1946 to 110,000 in 1960. And part was invested in the new enterprises which the Afrikaner, under the direction of the Nationalist movement, had started to launch in the towns.

PRIVATE NATIONALIST CAPITAL

The attempt of the Afrikaner to establish himself in industry and commerce was a by-product of the whole Nationalist movement whose course has been traced in this book. Apart from small retail shops, the first enterprise of any significance founded by Afrikaners was Die Nasionale Pers, owners of the Nationalist newspaper *Die Burger*, which was started in 1915 with Dr Malan as the first editor. This was followed by the establishment of the two insurance companies of SANLAM and SANTAM in 1918. Appeals were made to the *volk* to invest in 'their own' institutions, but progress was slow.

The next big spurt in Afrikaner economic development occurred in the 1930s as a direct result of the Broederbond's activities. According to statements by the former secretary of the Broederbond, I. M. Lombard, it was the Broederbond which gave rise to the founding of Volkskas, the Afrikaner banking

house, in 1934. The Broederbond raised £1,000 for the repatriation of the Argentine Boers, £3,000 for loan bursaries to the
Afrikaner medical faculty in Pretoria, and £3,000 for an Afrikaans
engineering faculty at Stellenbosch. The 1930s also saw the
entry of the Afrikaner into the urban distributive trades with the
setting up of Uniewinkels and Sonop in Bloemfontein.

The greatest achievement of the Broederbond in this sphere,
however, was the holding of the National Economic Conference
in 1939 at which the Reddingsdaadbond was formed. We have
already seen the steps taken by this conference in connexion
with the capture of the trade unions (see chapter 13). Of even
greater importance was the conference decision to launch an
economic movement which would harness the resources of the
Afrikaner community for the development of an Afrikaner
capitalist class. Dr M. S. Louw, managing director of
SANLAM, proclaimed: 'If we want to achieve success we
must use the technique of capitalism, as it is applied in the most
important industry. We must establish something like the
finance houses of Johannesburg.' He was reported to have
linked this with the original objective of the Reddingsdaadbond
by saying that 'the real aim was to strengthen also existing
businesses and to found and build up new Afrikaner undertakings which would give employment to Afrikaner boys and
girls'.

Progress after the 1939 conference was steady, if still un-
spectacular. Before the Second World War the Afrikaners controlled 1,200 factories, including building and construction
works – three per cent of the total. According to the Afrikaanse
Handelsinstituut the Afrikaner's share had doubled to six per
cent by 1949, and the number of institutions had grown to
3,385, employing 41,000 people. But eighty per cent of the
undertakings were one-man businesses and only two and a half
per cent were registered as public companies. There was nothing
to show in heavy industry.

In commerce there was a substantial improvement of the
Afrikaner's position. Whereas before the Second World War
almost all businesses in the country towns were in the hands of
the English-speaking, the Jews, or the Indians, by 1949 the

Afrikaner controlled twenty-five per cent of all commercial undertakings. Three quarters of the 10,000 trading concerns then in his possession had been established or taken over in the ten years since the Economic Conference was held. During the same decade the Afrikaans financial houses had increased their stake from five to seven and a half per cent of the total.

Nevertheless, the advance was largely relative. In 1945 there was only one Afrikaner company with a capitalization of £1 million, whereas there were 116 companies on the Johannesburg Stock Exchange with at least that capitalization.

The Nationalists' great opportunity came with the capture of State power in 1948. There was one wing of the Nationalist Party, led by extremists like Dr Albert Hertzog, who felt that the best way to promote the Afrikaner cause was to use government to gain control of the country's whole economy at one fell swoop. 'I am satisfied,' said Dr Hertzog in April 1949, 'that for all those who look to the future of South Africa there is only one solution, and that is that, irrespective of any other key industries, the gold mining industry should be nationalized by the State.' Nationalist political power, however, was still too precarious for such rash ventures, and Dr Hertzog was repudiated by the Prime Minister, Dr Malan, himself, who announced that 'the government contemplated no sweeping measures such as the nationalization of the gold mines'. Nevertheless, the idea of nationalization or some form of direct State control has remained in the background of Nationalist economic thinking, to be put on view from time to time as a threat whenever non-Afrikaans big business shows signs of proving recalcitrant.

Meanwhile, the Nationalist political and business leaders entered into an alliance which has proved extremely beneficial to both over the years. The spectacular progress of Afrikaner capital since 1948 has been due partly to the direct placing of government contracts with Nationalist firms, partly to the association of Nationalist capital with State capital. In *Die Afrikaner in die Landsekonomie*, Professor J. L. Sadie explains:

With a party in power consisting of an overwhelming majority of Afrikaners we find further a willingness in undertakings to seek cooperation with Afrikaner businesses, partly apparently because it is believed that the latter have easier access to authority. In the final instance the contribution of the government to the economic life by the establishment of undertakings such as Iscor, Sasol, Foskor, Escom, and the Industrial Development Corporation has created opportunities by which the Afrikaner could obtain experience in the function of management; opportunities which he would otherwise not have had.

State control over a certain sector of the economy is common to a number of capitalist countries, but in few has it progressed as far as in South Africa, where the State owns or controls land and forests, post, telegraphs and telephones, railways and airlines, broadcasting, and a host of other public services. In addition, the State has entered the field of private industry in electric power generation (Escom), printing, the manufacture of arms and ammunition, the production of iron and steel (Iscor), heavy engineering (Vecor), insecticides (Klipfontein Organic Products), oil, gas and chemicals from coal (Sasol), and fertilizers (Foskor). The State has also launched the Industrial Development Corporation, which has become, together with private capital, a permanent shareholder in a host of industries, like the Zwelitsha textile mill in Kingwilliamstown; the National Finance Corporation, to provide short-term loans for development; and the Fisheries Development Corporation, to build up a modern fishing industry.

Not all these projects were sponsored by the Nationalist government. Some of them, like Iscor, date back to the first Nationalist government of General Hertzog. Some of them were born of the needs of the United Party government during the war, when imports were scarce and the country had to look to its own resources. But undoubtedly the most significant development of State capital has taken place since 1948, when the Nationalist advent to power resulted in a dwindling flow of capital from abroad. After the Sharpeville shooting of 1960, indeed, the flow was reversed, and capital started to flee the country until controls were imposed to stop it.

In these circumstances, there has been a steadily increasing tendency for the State to take the initiative in economic development. While the hesitancy of private capital has led to a slowing down in the rate of increase of the national income (the average net increase in the national income per head of population between 1952 and 1960 was a bare 1·4 per cent), the State has been forced to come forward with grandiose schemes to stimulate economic activity and prevent the collapse or indefinite stagnation of the economy. In recent years the threat of an international boycott and the United Nations resolution of 1962, which called for the application of sanctions against South Africa in protest at the policy of apartheid, have still further strengthened the government's desire to develop its resources and make itself independent of foreign supplies wherever it can.

In a series of articles for *Fighting Talk* during 1962 analysing the relationship between Nationalist capital and State capital, G. Fasulo estimated the total assets controlled by State capital in 1960 as somewhere in the neighbourhood of £1,500 million. And if the assets controlled by subsidiaries and firms in partnership with State capital were added, the total would be considerably higher. By comparison, the assets of the Oppenheimer empire, the largest private investment holding in South Africa, total £1,000 million. The total of foreign capital invested in South Africa is approximately the same as the total of State capital, but because it is split up among many institutions, its political and economic impact is by no means as great as that of State capital, which is wholly under the control of the Nationalist government. It has been estimated that civil servants and employees of State capital number about one fifth of the White population, constituting with their families a majority of the electorate. Fasulo commented: 'All the Nats have to do is keep the dependants of the State happy and they can remain in power indefinitely so long as there is no major extension of the franchise.'

Development plans announced for the various branches of State capital include £270 million for Iscor between 1960 and 1972; £80 million for Escom; £50 million for telephone services up to 1966; £30 million for Sasol; and £225 million for the gigantic Orange River scheme. By comparison, the development plans announced by private industry are modest in the extreme.

Furthermore, the whole direction which is being taken by the South African economy is calculated still further to strengthen the hold of State capital at the expense of the private sector. It

287

is now established government policy that future industrial development should as far as possible take place, not in the existing built-up industrial areas, but in the areas bordering on the African Reserves. The reason for this is partly political – the government wants to avoid further immigration of Africans from the Reserves into the 'White areas', fearing the consequences of an increase in the size of the African working class in the midst of the White population; and partly economic – the cost of labour in the border areas is far lower than that prevailing in the towns. Industry as a whole, however, has opposed the border industry plans and has been reluctant to commit itself to schemes which it believes have no basis in economic reality. To prove its point, the government has had to undertake the initial capital investment, totalling £57 million spread over five years, in the way of road and rail construction, the provision of light and water, housing and related facilities, without which any sort of industrial development is impossible.

In February 1963 the government announced that it intended spending £22½ million on capital investment during the next ten years to promote textile industries in border areas which would provide employment for 3,000 Whites and 25,000 to 30,000 Africans. 'Basic facilities and housing will be provided, Bantu labour will be trained, income tax allowances will be made and protection will be granted', stated a Press summary of the report of the Permanent Committee for the Location of Industry and the Development of Border Areas tabled in the House of Assembly.

In 1962, proclaimed the report, the State gave assistance for the development of thirteen industries in areas bordering on the so-called 'Bantu homelands'. Five instances of financial assistance approved totalled some £2½ million. The Industrial Development Corporation also invested about £150,000 in border industries. Wage concessions were made to two industries which received financial support. Seven income tax concessions, totalling about £13,000, were granted on investments in border areas of about £437,500.

In other words, every inducement is being held out to persuade industrialists to move into the border areas; and in most instances when they do move in, the State moves in as well, as a partner or supervisor. The economic power of the Nationalists is strengthened all the time.

Regional development, it might be thought, is a commendable project to which no one could have any reasonable objection. But the border industry schemes are based on the super-exploitation of cheap African labour. In an analysis of the 'Potential in the Undeveloped Areas' contained in Fact Paper No. 35, *South Africa's Industrial Potential*, issued by the State Information Office in May 1957, Dr F. W. Quass points out:

> The ratio of non-Whites (mainly natives) to Whites in the main industrial areas of the Union is 2:1. It is evident that this development scheme (on the borders of the Reserves) envisages a greater proportion of Bantu employment, namely 5:1. This will result in a considerable reduction of labour costs and is regarded as a major factor in making the scheme possible and economical.

A hint of the savings that industrialists will be able to make by employing more Black labour is offered by Dr Quass.

> Consideration must be given to the aspect of *housing of all employees, both White and Bantu*. The average cost of a house for Whites is set at £2,500. The cost of Bantu houses is put at £100, but this represents only the cost of the building materials per unit as the Bantu are encouraged to build their homes themselves. (This gives a sense of ownership and pride, which unfortunately is sadly lacking amongst the Bantu of the locations near White cities.)
>
> The average salary of skilled Whites is set at £900 per annum plus free housing, light, water, sewage and garbage disposal, medical services, etc. For unskilled White workers and apprentices the average salary is calculated at £600 per annum with all the above allowances and free services. Bantu would receive *initially* £90 per annum plus free housing and services. Where practicable the Government would provide schools and other educational facilities for both Whites and Bantu.

Dr Quass is not entirely unaware that he is advertising a shameful state of affairs.

> In overseas countries such relatively low wages for the Bantu as suggested above may appear as selfish exploitation, yet Bantu living

independently in the Reserves have comparable incomes, and close on a million Bantu migrate from the neighbouring British and Portuguese territories to the Union in search of work for less than this wage.

To appreciate adequately the cynicism of the government's attempts to attract industrialists to the border areas, one must bear in mind that it is the same government which enforces job reservation to protect the White worker – and which in this scheme goes behind the back of the White worker to the employers and canvasses an industrial development based on the dilution of White labour. Moreover, most of the employers who have opened up border factories have been supporters of the Nationalist government, thus demonstrating that the profit interests of the Afrikaner middle class are pursued – with the backing of the government – in complete disregard of the 'civilized labour' policy which the Nationalists officially proclaim to be essential for the preservation of White supremacy.

But South Africa still has a long way to go before its Bantustans and border industries can be regarded as economically viable. This was one of the points made at a conference of the Nationalist-orientated South African Bureau of Racial Affairs held at Pretoria in June 1963.

Delegates were told by Dr A. J. Visser, an industrialist, that there are 7,000,000 Africans living in and near the Reserves, but that only 56,000 of them are employed in industry. Factories on the border of and in the Transkei provide jobs for only 756 of the 1,400,000 Africans in East Griqualand, Tembuland, Pondoland, and other Reserves in the area. Natal, with 28,000 of its 2,000,000 Africans in the Reserves employed in industry, is the most advanced of the provinces in the development of border industries.

The Transvaal stands in most need of more intensified industrialization on the borders of the Reserves, according to SABRA. Of the 2,500,000 Africans living in or near African areas, only 15,000 are working in factories. The gross production of border industries in the Transvaal amounts to £9,000,000 a year – less than two per cent of the industrial output of the province.

JOBS FOR PALS

The Nationalists have used their State power to benefit Nationalist private industry. They have openly given State contracts to private Nationalist firms. For example Verwoerd's publishing houses (Dagbreekpers and Hayne & Gibson) received government contracts worth £1½ million between 1960 and 1962. Advertisements were placed in Nationalist newspapers to an extent out of all proportion to their relative circulation. A recently formed diamond-prospecting company with a share capital of £1,250,000 has obtained, through the Nationalist investment company of Bonuskor, an important concession on the coast of South-West Africa from the Nationalist-controlled Administration of South-West Africa. The company obtained the concession in the face of strong competition from De Beers and allied American interests.

Two of Escom's biggest power stations are built next to coal mines owned by Federale Mynbou, a Nationalist mining concern, which is accordingly guaranteed a long-term market for its coal. Federale Volksbeleggings, a Nationalist investment house, is to finance a synthetic rubber plant using raw materials from the State firm Sasol, and the rubber firm has full government backing to guarantee it a market.

In his article for *Fighting Talk* on Nationalist capital in October 1962, G. Fasulo wrote:

This Broederly assistance from public funds is made easier by a system of interlocking directorates which has been built up between Nat capital and State capital. For example, Dr H. J. van Eck of the State firm I.D.C. [the Industrial Development Corporation] is a director of SANLAM.[1] Dr M. S. Louw of SANLAM has been appointed head of the government's new Coloured Development Corporation. . . . Mr C. H. J. van Aswegen, general manager of SANTAM, has been appointed a director of the State-owned National Finance Corporation. . . . Mr J. G. van der Merwe is a director of Voortrekkerpers and of Massey Ferguson, the big agricultural machinery firm, in which Federale Volksbeleggings has a large investment, and of the State firms Iscor and Klipfontein Organic Products (KOP). In addition the State capitalist firms and State

1 The largest Afrikaner insurance company.

departments are used as a training ground for Nat business managers.

An indication of how greatly this State aid assisted Nat capital is provided by SANLAM which had assets of £3½ million in 1939 and £10 million in 1949 which rocketed to £90 million by 1961.

In July 1962, the magazine *Tegniek* listed the ten biggest Afrikaans financial institutions and their assets as follows:

Volkskas (in round figures)	£99,000,000
SANLAM	90,000,000
Trust Bank	41,500,000
Saambou	32,500,000
SANTAM	12,500,000
Sentrale Finans-Korporasie	10,000,000
Bonuskor	8,000,000
African Homes Trust	7,750,000
Federale Volksbeleggings	7,500,000
Federale Mynbou	4,000,000
Total	£312,750,000

This total did not include the assets of the various industrial or commercial subsidiaries of the group. The biggest industrial concerns under Nationalist control, like the cigarette and liquor firms controlled by Anton Rupert with assets worth £55 million, are not listed. Thus the total extent of Nationalist capital is considerably higher than the figure given by *Tegniek*. Moreover, though still much smaller than non-Nationalist capital, it is increasing at a much faster rate. Above all, it is firmly associated with State capital and accepts the basic economic and political doctrines of the Nationalist government.

The bulk of farming capital, an expanding sector of private industrial and commercial capital, and a complete monopoly of State capital – these constitute the economic basis of Nationalist political power. It is a powerful weapon, directed purposefully and ruthlessly by men whose ideology includes State direction of the country's economy in the interests of Afrikanerdom and the maintenance of White supremacy. The Afrikaner has come a long way economically since 1948, yet he still feels that he has a long way to go.

In 1952 the Afrikaanse Nasionale Studentebond paper *Werda* estimated that in Johannesburg only 1·5 per cent of the 70,679 Afrikaners had an income of £1,000 and over (the figure for the English was given as ten per cent) while fifty per cent were earning less than £600 (English, forty per cent). Of the 3,282 persons with an income of £3,000 and over, only eighty-one were Afrikaners.

Later figures were given in the pamphlet by Professor Sadie already quoted. In 1957 he claimed that the Afrikaner was responsible for £334 million or twenty-six per cent of the £1,284 million in the private sector of the national income. This had to be compared with the fact that Afrikaners constituted fifty-seven per cent of the total White population (assuming that the non-White contribution to the national income was negligible). Professor Sadie pointed out that, while Afrikaners were responsible for three quarters of the income from farming, outside of this sphere their share of the national income was only fourteen per cent. In mining they controlled only one per cent of production. The total personal income of Afrikaners was £425 million, or forty-four per cent of the personal income of all Whites in South Africa. The average Afrikaner earned £260 a year in comparison with £435 earned by the non-Afrikaner.

The share of the Afrikaner has undoubtedly risen since then, but still has far to go before the Afrikaner himself is likely to feel that he controls the economy of the country to the extent that his numbers warrant. However, there should be no doubt that this is the ultimate aim of the Nationalists, and that they will pursue it with the same concentrated attention they have devoted to their affairs ever since the thirties. Nor should there be any doubt that their ideal is the creation of a corporate State on the Fascist model, with the interests of capital and labour coordinated by allegedly impartial organs of the State staffed by the Broederbond *élite*. This ideal was outlined in the draft republican constitution published during the war. The growing State-controlled sector of the economy gives more than a hint of the shape of things to come.

Indeed, it will be impossible for the Nationalists fully to implement the policy of apartheid so long as a major sector of the economy lies beyond their control. Apartheid, with its emphasis on racial separation and the retention of migratory labour, runs directly counter to the needs of secondary industry, which requires a trained and stable labour force for its proper development. Even in mining a considerable body of opinion, headed by the Oppenheimer group, wants an end to the old compound system of labour and the creation of a permanent urban African proletariat. These sectors of the economy are precisely the ones in which the Nationalists are most weakly represented. For ideological as well as economic reasons, the Nationalists will spare no effort to subdue them and compel them to conform at last to the demands of the State.

Since the National Economic Conference of 1939, the Nationalists have been able to advance from a position of great weakness to one of great and increasing strength. Time and the fruits of office have not mellowed them. Today they stand poised for their final assault on the remaining bastions of economic power, the conquest of which promises to bring with it the fulfilment of the Afrikaner dream.

POSTSCRIPT: A new development which is likely to have far-reaching repercussions in the political sphere was the link-up announced in August 1963 between the Afrikaans mining company, Federale Mynbou, and the giant Anglo-American Corporation in the formation of a £11 million new company, Main Street Investments. This was followed by the announcement on 20 September 1963 of the appointment of Mr T. F. Muller (managing director of Federale Mynbou) as managing director of the £37,500,000 General Mining and Finance Corporation, and of Mr W. B. Coetzer (chairman of Federale Mynbou) as a director of the Corporation. These developments reflect not only the spectacular development of Afrikaans capital in the sphere of mining, but also the increasing willingness of its competitors to come to terms with it.

15. Iron and Blood

Throughout the years of its reign the Nationalist government has provoked ever-increasing hostility with every attempt to implement its policy of apartheid. The rigid, merciless dogmatism, the blindness and brutality of Nationalist doctrine and administration have become anathema to the overwhelming majority of the world's population, as witnessed by the rising tide of resistance at home and the growing pressure for the application of international sanctions, recommended by the 1962 General Assembly resolution of the United Nations. On all sides the Nationalists feel themselves threatened, their future endangered, by a multitude of perils ranging from international Communism to Sunday sport. The struggle to maintain their 'traditional way of life' in the face of foreign influences and intervention becomes daily more desperate.

In the 1830s, faced with a similar situation, the Afrikaner could load his family and belongings on to his ox-wagon and trek away into the distance, turning his back on his enemies and seeking security in the vast almost-empty spaces of the interior. Today he can trek no more. He must turn and face his dangers, answer the challenge of his day, as best he can, relying on the spiritual and material resources that lie to hand.

The tragedy of the South African situation is that the Nationalist government has adopted a position from which it cannot retreat without destroying the very basis of its power. Nationalist rule means Nationalist domination over all other sections of the population, White and non-White alike. Not only the African, the Coloured, and the Asian, but also the White non-Afrikaner must accept the consequences of Afrikaner hegemony. The presence of two English-speaking members in the Nationalist Cabinet does not alter the fact that the character of the government and the administration is overwhelmingly Afrikaans. The very factors which have helped to make Nationalist Afrikanerdom the power that it is automatically exclude participation by non-Afrikaners, who cannot share the emotionalism and mystique on which the Nationalist thrives. The African understandably cannot share the Afrikaner's feelings about the Battle of Blood River. The English-speaking cannot join with the Afrikaner in bitterly condemning the British conquest, and even the Voortrekker Monument outside Pretoria fails to arouse his enthusiasm. Thus the Nationalist can never weld a united nation out of the various peoples of South Africa. Nor does he intend to do so. His perpetual emphasis on race is designed to fragment South Africans into their component parts, for it is through the disunity of the non-Afrikaners alone that the Afrikaner can retain his supremacy. 'Unity is strength,' proclaims the official motto on the South African coat of arms. The theory and practice of the Nationalist government pursue precisely the opposite direction.

The racial exclusiveness of the Nationalist is at once his strength and his weakness. According to the 1960 census, the population of South Africa is composed as follows:

African	10,807,809
White	3,067,638
Coloured	1,488,267
Asian	477,414
Total	15,841,128

Of the White population, perhaps 1,750,000 are Afrikaners, and it is on their unity that the Nationalist government depends for the maintenance of its power. They constitute a majority of the electorate, and for as long as they respond to Nationalist leadership, Nationalist power is secure – electorally. It is the rise of forces which cannot be channelled through the ballot-box that in recent years has presented the greatest challenge to the survival of Nationalist rule.

To meet this challenge, the Nationalist government has resolved to rely mainly on force, to strengthen the army and the police so that they are capable of meeting any attack from inside or outside the country. And meanwhile the government hopes against hope that its Bantustan policy will serve to head off African nationalism and divert it into channels which are harmless to White supremacy. There is no possibility of compromise under Nationalist rule. The alternative to apartheid is integration, and to the Nationalist integration means death.

Nevertheless, the forces working for integration remain tremendously strong. Economically, White and Black in South Africa are interdependent and are becoming more so with every passing year. White supremacy, after all, depends upon the existence of Black labour; and it is Black advancement within the framework of an industrial society, Black acquisition of skills and knowledge, that lie behind the political challenge presented by Black nationalism in its various forms to White overlordship. To hold back Black advancement for as long as possible, the Nationalist government has evolved the policy of apartheid, to keep its subjects separate from one another in sealed compartments, to prohibit Blacks from acquiring skills which threaten White dominion, above all to prevent unity between Black and White in any sphere. For such unity – political, social, or economic – spells the ruin of White supremacy, and within that supremacy the end of Afrikaner rule. From this fear derives the fantastic apparatus of laws designed to prevent contact between Black and White at any point except in the workshop. From this fear derives in particular the ferocity with which the government has pursued all forms of multi-racial political association. As the challenge has grown, and South Africa's peoples have asserted with mounting strength their common humanity, so the Nationalist reply has become increasingly brutal – culminating in the Sabotage Act and the General Law Amendment Act of 1963, which have converted South Africa into a blatant police state. Today the South African opposition listens for the knock on the door at midnight. The security of the individual has gone. The flow of prisoners detained without trial has begun with a trickle – a bare twenty-seven people taken within three weeks of the gazetting of the General Law Amendment Act – but who can doubt that in the course of time it will become a flood?[1]

PREPARATIONS FOR WAR

Not even the Nationalists believe that the laws they have placed upon the statute book can pacify the nation. They know that they are provoking violence, and they are preparing to meet the violence, whether from inside or outside the country. Enormous sums are being spent to bring the army and police force up to combat level.

The Nationalist government believes that in any crisis which may overtake it, it cannot rely on support from any except the other White supremacist powers of Southern Africa. The United Nations General Assembly resolution in 1962, calling for the application of sanctions against South Africa, may not yet have led to much in the way of practical action. But it has left the Nationalist government with no illusions. Should an attack be launched, South Africa will stand alone. The assistance which can be offered by Portugal and Southern Rhodesia is precarious – they are burdened with their own security problems. South Africa's powerful friends in the West – Britain and the United States, who are responsible for approximately seventy per cent and thirteen per cent respectively of the £1,500 million invested from abroad in South Africa – would hesitate to antagonize the Afro-Asian powers by coming to Verwoerd's aid and would prefer to operate behind some sort of United Nations screen as in the Congo. Naturally enough the Nationalists are not prepared to look to such intervention for their security. They prefer to rely on their own strength, and their own strength is considerable.

1 By the end of June 1963, the total of persons detained under the General Law Amendment Act of 1963 was approaching the 200 mark, and more men and women were being detained every week. A further 176 men and women were being detained in the Transkei under the notorious proclamation 413 of 1960 (see page 176). Persons detained under the General Law Amendment Act of 1963 are held under the ninety day no-trial clause and are allowed no visitors (except for urgent business transactions), no reading or writing material, no extra food, no cigarettes or tobacco, no comforts of any description. They are kept in solitary confinement for 23½ hours each day, the remaining half-hour being allocated for 'exercise'. These stringent conditions are clearly designed to 'break' the prisoners and get them to confess or provide information which will enable the police to draw others into the net.

The South African Police Force – constantly referred to as 'our first line of defence' – consists of 26,000 men, one half of whom are non-Whites. The Whites are armed with every variety of modern weapon, backed with armoured cars and troop carriers; the non-Whites carry only sticks and assegais. Since the Poqo scare, a police reserve has been established in all centres consisting of White civilians who receive training to assist the police in times of emergency. The total number of people in the reserve is unknown, but there are believed to be several thousand. In the 1963 budget, spending on the police increased by more than £2,500,000 to an all-time record of £22,500,000. The Special, so-called 'Security' Branch has undergone enormous expansion and now constitutes almost a force within a force. Several thousand pounds are devoted annually to police 'secret services'.

The expansion in the army has been even more spectacular. Speaking at the Free State Congress of the Nationalist Party in Bloemfontein in September 1961, the Minister of Defence, J. J. Fouche, proclaimed: 'I can give any power contemplating an attack on South Africa the assurance that we will fight. We will fight until the blood rises to the horses' bits, and I can tell you that the blood won't be on the bits of our horses only.' Translated into action, this bloodthirsty prediction has resulted in a complete reorganization and expansion of South Africa's armed forces. In 1961 government expenditure on defence rose by £14 million to £35,750,000; the 1962 budget brought a further increase to £60 million, more than the highest war-time expenditure on the South African forces. In 1963 this phenomenal figure was pushed even further, by £5 million to £65 million. 'Indications are,' reported the *Cape Argus* of 22 February 1963, 'that defence spending during 1963–4 will be even higher.'

In his budget speech the Minister of Finance confirmed this prediction. There were no prospects that defence spending would decrease in future years, he declared. The nation 'would be called on to pay this premium on our policy of national security on a considerable scale for some years to come'.

Huge increases in defence spending include money voted for aircraft, aircraft stores, service and equipment, which increased

299

by £5 million compared to 1962. Expenditure on bombs, aircraft and ammunition rocketed from £40,000 to a spectacular £3 million. The costs of making munitions practically doubled to £12 million.

An analysis of the budget showed that more than one fifth of total expenditure was ear-marked for national security. By contrast with the millions being spent on defence and the police, only £12 million was voted for Bantu Education. Brawn, not brain, is first priority in South Africa today.

The South African Army consists of a permanent force of between 20,000 and 25,000 men, backed by a Citizen Force which was expected to train 60,000 White youths between 1962 and 1966. In addition there is an air force equipped with jet fighters, turbo-jet transport, and long-range coastal reconnaissance aircraft and helicopters. Much of the expenditure in the 1963 budget was due to the fact that the South African Air Force was beginning to take delivery of costly modern aircraft which had been ordered and first payments on which had fallen due. These included Lockheed Hercules C130 heavy transport aircraft and French Mirage IIIc jet-fighters capable of flying at twice the speed of sound, some of which had already arrived and were in use in the country. Still to come were the supersonic Blackburn Buccaneer naval strike aircraft and an undisclosed number of Canberra bombers. Neil Marten, British Parliamentary Secretary to the Ministry of Aviation, told the House of Commons in May 1963 that at least fifty companies employing a total staff of 135,000 were engaged in the manufacture of aircraft and equipment for South Africa. South African orders represented one year's employment for 25,000 men – 13,000 in the aircraft industry, 4,000 in electronics, and the rest in ancillary industries.

Considerable expansion is also taking place in the South African Navy, based at Simonstown, the use of which is guaranteed to Britain in time of war under the Simonstown agreement. The South African government wishes to place itself in a position to repel any likely attack launched by land, sea, or air. It is undoubtedly in earnest when it maintains that such an attack is possible. It is in no position, of course, to withstand an assault from any of the major powers, but it does not believe such an assault to be likely. More to be feared, in its opinion, is an attack by some combination of the Afro-Asian powers, to repel which it has built up by far the strongest military force on the African continent.

Behind the lines of the regular army stand the citizen commando units, based in the main on the rural areas and staffed overwhelmingly by Afrikaners. This is an all-purpose force mostly directed at the suppression of internal unrest, but capable of use in war. All in all, the Minister of Defence claimed in Parliament on 3 June 1963, that he could put 140,000 uniformed men into the field if the necessity should arise. Judging by the performance of the South African armed forces in two world wars, this is by no means an overestimate.

The government's greatest fear, of course, is that it will have to meet an attack on all fronts at once, launched by both internal and external forces. With this in view, police command boundaries have been re-defined to coincide with the army commands, and a high degree of cooperation has been built up between the army and the police force. Both army and police units were used in the suppression of the Pondo revolt in 1960 and 1961, while army and naval units took part in the patrolling of the Cape Peninsula during the disturbances of March 1960.

The Algerian war has provided in the government's view an example of the sort of warfare that South Africa must expect, a combination of internal insurrection and aggression from beyond the borders of the country. 'A re-appreciation of the situation and a careful study of the course of events in Algeria have shown that the possible major task for the South African defence force is likely to be one of conventional warfare against lightly armed forces of aggression,' said Erasmus, former Minister of Defence, in November 1959. 'Attacks by subversive elements can best be beaten off by fast, lightly armed security forces.' A military mission was sent to Algeria to study the methods adopted by the French in the course of their campaigns there.

A key role in the Algeria struggle was played by Tunisia, used as a base by the Algerian Army of Liberation and immune from reprisals by the French. To prevent such a situation from developing in relation to South Africa, the government has taken steps to seal off all the frontiers, especially those common to the Protectorates. A total of thirty-six police control posts is to be erected immediately, and a further sixteen later on, to prevent the illegal entry of Africans into the Republic – and the flight of refugees away into the outside world. Eighteen of these posts are planned for the Basutoland border, nineteen for the Swaziland border, and fifteen for the Bechuanaland border. In addition, a helicopter patrol may be introduced. A considerable section of the border is being fenced. Army camps have been set up in the Transvaal at Zeerust, forty miles from the Bechuanaland border, and at Middelburg, near the borders of Swaziland and Moçambique.

Fears that the international campaign to stop the supply of weapons to South Africa may prove successful have led the South African government to step up the production of arms and ammunition in South Africa itself. A French armaments firm that produces rocket missile components for NATO, Le Carbone, has established a factory on the Reef. A French armoured car, the Panhard A.M.L., is to be built under licence on the Reef for the army. The Belgian automatic F.N. rifle is now manufactured in South Africa and is gradually replacing the old ·303 as standard equipment for the troops. Mortars, bombs, and revolvers are made by South African industries. Recently it was announced that Oppenheimer's African Explosives and Chemical Industries were to build three new armaments factories for government contracts at a cost of £10 million. The trend of government thinking was revealed by Dr Andries Visser, a member of the South African Atomic Energy Board, who declared some time ago that South Africa should begin manufacturing atom bombs for use against 'loud-mouthed Afro-Asian States'. Any intention to do so was denied by the Chairman of the Board, but an unnamed scientist was quoted by the *Rand Daily Mail* (12 January 1962) as saying: 'It is within the bounds of our resources to make an atom bomb.'

There is no inherent reason why South Africa should not ultimately make its own atom bomb. It would give her dominance in a continent which she fears, and a standing in international affairs which she does not rate at present. It would be in line with present government policy to make South Africa self-sufficient in every possible sphere, so as to become invulnerable to outside pressure. South Africa is at present engaged on plans which will culminate in the construction of an all-South-African motor-car. It has been a consistent theme of Nationalist policies right from the time of the first Hertzog government that South Africa should develop her own industrial capacity to the utmost, in order to reduce to the minimum her dependence on the resources of unsympathetic powers.

In their more megalomaniac moments, the Nationalists see themselves as the saviour of Western (i.e. White) civilization from the menace represented by the advance of the Afro-Asian peoples to independence and nationhood. The transfer of power from the metropolitan countries to the colonies is denounced as a betrayal of the White man and an encouragement to the forces of barbarism. In his 1963 New Year message, Verwoerd referred contemptuously to the 'ducktail' nations of Africa who dared to criticize the policies of the Nationalist government and, while unable to maintain stability in their own countries, worked for the downfall of the only stable power in Africa. Similarly, Foreign Minister Eric Louw, after the summit meeting of independent African States at Addis Ababa in May 1963, referred to the participants as 'bum and beggar' nations. Appeals are constantly made to White South Africans to remember their destiny, not only in relation to the affairs of their own country, but in the international arena as well.

But race-dominated South Africa cannot perform the role allotted to it by the Nationalists so long as it forms part of the international comity of nations. Contact with other peoples brings in its train contact with other ideas, subversive concepts of humanism and tolerance which run counter to the doctrines of apartheid. Hence the attempt to cut South Africa off from the free flow of ideas by censorship; hence the withdrawal from the Commonwealth, now regarded as being in pawn to the non-Whites. There is not a single diplomatic representative of South Africa in any of the newly independent African States. The last tenuous link with the rest of the world is maintained through the

United Nations, and even that might not last for long. As far back as 1952 Dr Malan announced that the United Nations had proved 'a hopeless failure' because it had 'failed to preserve world peace'. He proclaimed that South Africa had the 'indisputable right to withdraw from the United Nations' and would exercise that right 'if the United Nations continued to meddle with the Union's domestic affairs'. If UNO should go further than pass pious resolutions, there is no doubt of what the South African reaction would be. She would quit, just as she quit the Commonwealth, and regard it as a triumph for Afrikaner Nationalism that she had done so.

The Nationalist government wants to be strong enough, and free enough, to do with the South African peoples what it likes. Military force, it believes, gives it the strength; isolation, the freedom. Behind the corrugated iron curtain, it will continue to implement the inhuman policy of apartheid for as long as it is able.

BANTUSTAN

While on the one hand the Nationalist government prepares to resist change by the increasing use of force, on the other hand it tries to head off the demands of Black nationalism by offering the concept of Bantustan.

Dr Verwoerd, the Prime Minister, and de Wet Nel, Minister of Bantu Administration and Development, maintain that the seeds of the modern concept of Bantustan were always contained in the Nationalist policy of apartheid. That may or may not be true, because no one has yet been able to establish clearly what either apartheid or Bantustan really means.

The African Reserves are generally understood to comprise thirteen per cent of the total area of South Africa, but this is only the total area that was promised under the Native Trust and Land Act of 1936 in return for the removal of the Africans from the common voters' roll. In fact this promise has never been fully implemented. Speaking in the Assembly on 10 June 1963, de Wet Nel admitted that, of the prescribed quota of 7,250,000 morgen, only 5,065,593 morgen (or seventy per cent) had been acquired by the end of 1962. The balance of land still to be acquired for Bantu occupation amounted, therefore, to 2,184,407 morgen. Meanwhile, African franchise rights on the separate roll were completely abolished by the 1959 legislation to which reference has already been made, so that none of the promises incorporated in the 1936 Acts have been kept.

Shortly after he came to power, Dr Malan told the House of Assembly on 16 August 1948:

... Nor does our policy of apartheid mean that we are going to eliminate all the natives who are at present in the European areas and who came here to work, and that we are going to send them all to their own Reserves. That is a caricature of our policy of apartheid. There is no one on this side of the House who has ever advocated a policy of that nature, nor is it contained in our written policy of apartheid, our election manifesto.

Clearly, then, for the politicians, apartheid did not mean total separation of the races by means of a partition which, however inequitable, would at least guarantee to each group independence and complete self-government. What then could it mean except a continuation of the old segregation policies, with a greater emphasis on White domination? Horizontal but not vertical separation of the races, with the White man firmly in control? And the first crop of Nationalist laws, with the emphasis on measures of harsh one-sided discrimination, seemed to confirm that this was in fact all that apartheid meant.

For some in the Nationalist ranks, however, this was not enough. The present suppression of the black man could only be justified if something were offered in return, even if only a vague prospect for the future. From the Dutch Reformed Church and SABRA (the Afrikaner counterpart of the South African Institute of Race Relations) came rumblings which could not be ignored. In 1950 the Dutch Reformed Church (N.G.K.) at a meeting of its Federal Council came out for a policy of territorial and political separation and urged the government to put it into effect as soon as possible.

Even a newspaper like *Die Transvaler* supported the idea of partition and wrote in September 1955:

... Territorial separation ... must have the result that the Europeans will have to perform all their labour themselves. This great ideal will have to be realized if European civilization is to be upheld in the southern point of Africa. It implies that the Europeans will have to resign themselves to great sacrifices. At the same time let it be stated now honestly and frankly that the majority of Europeans have not awakened to the realization that this is the only manner of rescuing civilization here. The conception that the European is above such forms of labour and that the non-European is meant for this is so deeply rooted in them after three centuries that they apparently cannot imagine another state of affairs.

Die Transvaler was right. The majority of Whites were not prepared to consider for a moment doing without Black labour. As Dr Malan declared on 12 April 1950, one might support total separation if it were practicable, but it was 'impracticable under present circumstances. Our whole economic structure is to a large extent based upon non-White labour.'

When Strijdom succeeded to office as Prime Minister, he repeated that total territorial segregation might be the ideal, but that in practice it could not be carried out, because the tens of thousands of people who were using the labour of Africans and Coloureds would never agree to it.

Even de Wet Nel told the 1955 Congress of the Jeugbond that the idea of Bantustan should be rejected since it was as dangerous as integration. He predicted that as a result of Nationalist laws South Africa would become steadily Blacker over the next twenty years, but that thereafter the tide would turn.

The Tomlinson Commission, especially appointed to investigate whether Bantustan was a practicable proposition, estimated that if the Reserves – totalling, when the full quota of land has been purchased, only thirteen per cent of South Africa, with the remaining eighty-seven per cent in non-African, mainly White hands – were developed to full capacity, they would accommodate 10 million Africans by 1987, of whom 2 million would be dependent on wages earned in the European areas by 500,000 migratory workers. But that would still leave an estimated 6 million Africans living in White South Africa, half of whom would be on the farms and half in the towns. The report envisaged the establishment of industries in the Reserves and a ten-year expenditure of £100 million on development. The government quietly pigeon-holed the report, announcing that it was not prepared to admit White capital into the Reserves at any price and refusing to finance development on the scale recommended by the Commission.

It may be noted in passing that the Tomlinson Commission assumed in its calculations the incorporation as further Reserves of the British High Commission territories of Basutoland, Swaziland, and Bechuanaland, claim to which was revived by Verwoerd in his speech to the Nationalist Party congress in Pretoria on 3 September 1963. The Commission also acknowledged that tribalism was a bar to modern economic and industrial development, though Nationalist Bantusan policy is based on a revival and entrenchment of tribalism.

What then is left of the concept of separate development? Stripped of all verbiage and illusion, it means simply this: that in return for limited rights of self-government in the Reserves, the Africans are to lose all rights in the remaining White areas of South Africa, where they will enjoy the status only of 'temporary sojourners'. Two Acts passed during the 1963 session of Parliament make these Nationalist intentions crystal clear.

The first is the Transkei Constitution Act, which sets out to 'confer self-government on the Bantu resident in or deriving from the Transkei', the largest and most developed of the Reserves. As the wording indicates, the Act not only applies to Xhosa-speaking persons in the Transkei, but to all so-called Transkei citizens, defined in the Act as including:

every Xhosa-speaking Bantu person in the Republic, including every Bantu person belonging to any associated linguistic group who normally uses any dialects of the language spoken by what is commonly known as the Cape Nguni, providing such person does not belong to any Bantu homeland other than the Transkei or fall under the jurisdiction of any other regional or territorial authority or council or any other self-governing territory.

Transkei citizenship also covers every 'Bantu person' born in the Transkei, every 'Bantu person' who has been domiciled in the Transkei for at least five years, and every Sotho-speaking 'Bantu person' in the Republic who derives from or is generally regarded as a member of any of the Sotho-speaking tribes resident in the Transkei.

Thus Xhosa-speaking Africans who were born in, say, Cape Town and have never set foot in the Transkei will also be regarded as Transkei citizens under this Act. The implications of this are far-reaching. The Transkei Legislative Assembly set up under the Act is given the power, for example, to impose direct taxation on citizens of the Transkei, whether resident in or outside the Transkei. Furthermore, laws made in the Transkei may apply to Transkei citizens whether resident in or outside the Transkei. And Transkei citizens who break Transkei laws may be prosecuted not only in Transkei courts but also in the courts of the Republic. The Act states:

Any proceedings under any law made by the Legislative Assembly may, in so far as such law applies to citizens of the Transkei who are resident outside the Transkei but within the Republic, be instituted against any such citizen in any competent court having jurisdiction in the area within which such citizen may be or may not be resident.

Thus the Transkei Legislative Assembly may pass a law in Umtata, the capital of the Transkei, and some Transkei citizen born and brought up and resident in Cape Town may be hauled before the court in Cape Town for having contravened it. This provision of the constitution is bound to cause intense friction and even outbreaks of violence by the urban Xhosa, most of whom are hostile to Bantu Authorities and particularly to the Matanzima clique which is tipped to hold considerable power when the Act is implemented and the first Cabinet established. The Legislative Assembly is to consist of the four Paramount Chiefs, the sixty chiefs holding office in the nine regional authority areas in the Transkei, and forty-five members to be elected by the registered voters of the Transkei. (Every citizen of the Transkei over twenty-one or a Transkei taxpayer over eighteen will be eligible for the vote.)

Thus government paid and appointed chiefs will always constitute the majority; the elected members of the Transkei Assembly will always be in the minority. This is the self-government in his own area for which the African has had to sacrifice his right to representation in the central legislature of the Republic.

The Transkeian Legislative Assembly will have power to make laws in connexion with: direct taxation of Transkeian citizens, whether within or outside the Transkei; Bantu Education; agriculture; the establishment, administration, and control of inferior courts; the appointment, powers, duties, and functions of justices of the peace and commissioners of oaths and members of the public service in the Transkei; the protection of life, persons, and property and the prevention of cruelty to animals in the Transkei; the control of such portion of the Police Force as may have been sanctioned by the Minister of Justice of the Republic; public works and irrigation; the control of municipal and local authorities; and a variety of similar minor matters.

Xhosa is recognized as an additional official language in the Transkei, which is also given its own national anthem ('*Nkosi Sikelel'i-Afrika*) and flag to be flown side by side with the flag of the Republic.

At a time when other metropolitan powers are liquidating their colonies in Africa, the South African government is attempting to create them. For there are important limitations on the powers of the Transkeian legislature. Not only will it fall under the dominion of the Republican government, especially in matters pertaining to defence, internal security, and foreign affairs, but it will also have no control over Whites resident in the Transkei, who will remain citizens of the Republic and will not be eligible for the franchise in the Transkei. No White man will be subject to the laws of a Black government and no White man will be hauled before a Black court. Multi-racialism will be tolerated as little in Bantustan as in the Republic itself.

If these powers fall short of real self-government, Verwoerd justifies them on the grounds that they are, at least, a step in that direction. But how far is he prepared to go? Does the Bantustan policy really envisage the establishment of genuinely independent African States in the Reserves? Can it be accepted that that is the aim of the Nationalist government?

The answer is a categorical 'No'. In an article he wrote for the magazine *Optima* in March 1959 the Secretary for Bantu Administration and Development, Dr W. W. M. Eiselen, declared: 'The utmost degree of autonomy in administrative matters which the Union Parliament is likely to be prepared to concede to these areas will stop short of actual surrender of sovereignty by the European trustee, and there is therefore no prospect of a federal system with eventual equality among members taking the place of the South African Commonwealth.'

Similar declarations have been made by Nationalist speakers, including the Minister for Bantu Administration and Development, De Wet Nel, during the debate on the Transkei Constitution Bill in the 1963 session of the Assembly. Here is a quotation from the *Cape Times* of 20 March 1963: 'Fritz Steyn, Nationalist M.P., said yesterday that the Transkei would have a long wait for sovereign independence – if it were ever attained at all. He firmly rejected suggestions that it was government policy to encourage sovereign independence for the Transkei and other Bantustans.'

Even Dr Verwoerd, in his policy speech on 10 April 1961, in which he indicated that the Bantustans could develop into 'separate Black States', clearly stated at the same time: 'This is not what we would have preferred to see. This is a form of fragmentation which we would rather not have had if it was within our control to avoid it.'

The Prime Minister blamed the pressure of forces outside South Africa for the decision of the government to embark on the Bantustan experiment at all. 'In the light of the forces to which South Africa is being subjected, there is, however, no doubt as to what must be done in the course of time.'

Which still leaves a doubt as to whether 'separate Black States' mean the same thing as 'sovereign independence' – a doubt which the Prime Minister has never been willing to resolve.

Even let it be presumed, however, that sovereign independence is a possible outcome of the present Bantustan policy, and that the Nationalist rank and file are slowly being conditioned to accept this. The government will delay as long as possible the grant of eventual independence, but is prepared to accept the inevitable if it should be left with no alternative. Its attitude can be summed up as: 'Better separate Black States than Black majority rule in an integrated South Africa.'

The probability is that Verwoerd himself is not unduly disturbed about the creation of a number of Black States round the borders of South Africa. His aim is to divide the African people on ethnic lines, and he hopes that it will prove impossible for the separate small ethnic Black States to unite in common action against White South Africa.

The 1960 census divided the African population according to tribal origin as follows:

Xhosa	3,423,000
Zulu	2,959,000
Northern Sotho	1,122,000
Southern Sotho	1,089,000
Tswana	863,000
Tsonga	366,000
Swazi	301,000
Venda	195,000
Southern Ndebele	162,000
Northern Ndebele	47,000
Other	280,000
Total	10,807,000

Two thirds of these peoples live in the White areas, and only one third are resident in the Reserves. In what way then, reasons Verwoerd, could separate Black States based on these ethnic groups threaten the existence of White South Africa? They would be too poor to compete economically, and too feeble militarily to mount any sort of attack against the armed forces of the Republic. If they should seek outside aid, Verwoerd has made it clear, the South African government would immediately intervene. Outside interference would not be tolerated. The 'separate Black States' would still be the colonies of White South Africa. Basutoland is nominally independent of South Africa at the moment, yet Basutoland constitutes no sort of problem for South Africa, since it is wholly dependent on the Republic for its economic existence. The Basotho people have an undeveloped agricultural economy, and half the Basotho population must seek employment in the Republic to survive. Were South Africa to close its frontiers, Basutoland would face immediate starvation. Such independence the Republic is prepared to concede – if it has to – to its own Bantusans.

That such is, in fact, the vision of the Nationalist government is confirmed by the companion to the Transkei Constitution Act, the Bantu Laws Amendment Bill introduced by the Minister of Bantu Administration and Development during the 1963 session of Parliament. This 139-page Bill was described by the Minister of Information, English-speaking Frank Waring, at a Press conference in February as designed to remove points of friction between the authorities and the African people. When the Press complained, after examining the Bill, that it was nothing of the sort, the Minister blandly admitted that he had not read the Bill at the time he had held his Press conference on it. No clearer indication could have been given of the real function that Waring performs in the Nationalist Cabinet.

The fact is that the Bill turns the whole African population into homeless wanderers in the land of their birth. The last few remaining rights of Africans in the urban areas are stripped from them. Mercilessly the government maintains that the Africans must look to their 'homelands' for their political and economic development; in the White areas they will be admitted only to supply the labour needs of the White economy, preferably on the basis of migrant labour. It is contrary to government policy that African family groups should be permitted to establish themselves in the urban areas.

Under the Bill, no African has an automatic right of residence anywhere in an urban area and can be shunted around at the pleasure of any minor government official. Previously any African who had been born in an urban area and worked there continuously, or who had worked for one employer for ten years or for more than one employer for fifteen years had an automatic right of residence in an urban area, and could be removed only by order of the Minister or the Governor-General acting under the Native Administration Act.

Under the new Bill this safeguard is abolished. Any African

can be 'endorsed out' of town by any officer in charge of a labour bureau, who can grant or refuse permission for residence in an urban area at will. The labour officer can refuse to sanction the employment or continued employment of any African in his area, and can cancel – for a variety of reasons – any contract of employment entered into with an African.

If the African refuses to submit himself for medical examination, or if, on examination, he is found to be suffering from any disease considered to be dangerous to public health, he may be expelled from his work, and even from his birth-place. The government's cure for disease is not medical treatment, but ejection from urban society. The victim can take his disease back with him to 'his own area', so long as the White community is saved from contamination.

A labour bureau official can also refuse to sanction the employment or continued employment of any African 'if it is not in the interest of either the employee or the employer or both or in the public interest that the relative contract of service should be entered into or that it should be allowed to continue'. The agreement of the Secretary for Bantu Administration and Development is required, but this can hardly be regarded as an effective safeguard against drastic administrative action, since both public officials are pledged to carry out the policy of the government.

A labour bureau official may also prohibit any African from working on his own account or as an independent contractor or as a casual labourer save under such conditions as may be prescribed. (It is already government policy that no African should be allowed to run more than one business in an urban area, and that no African should be allowed to open a business in an African location if the needs of the people can be satisfied from an existing White business.)

Conditions for the entry and residence of African women in urban areas are further restricted. Men, even married men, are preferably to be housed in single quarters. Family life is as far as possible to be confined to the Reserves.

The Bill sets up what are described as 'depots' for each labour bureau, and Africans may be detained in these depots

without trial, both while seeking work and while awaiting repatriation if they have been endorsed out of town. The mere
murmur of a labour bureau official will be enough to decide
whether or not an African is locked up or released. So-called
'youth centres' for the reception of Africans from the ages of
fifteen to twenty-one years are also to be established. The Bill
does not limit the period for which an African may be forced to
remain in such depots or centres, but states baldly:

Any Bantu who is refused permission by a municipal labour officer
to take up or be in employment in a prescribed area or whose contract
of service has been cancelled by such officer, may be referred to a
depot, if such a depot is available, or to the district labour officer in
whose area the local labour bureau concerned is situated, and the
officer in charge of such depot or such district labour officer may offer
such Bantu suitable work either in his area or in any other area or
may, with due regard to the family ties or other obligations or com-
mitments of such Bantu, require such Bantu and his dependants to
leave such prescribed area within a period specified by him.

Persons who qualify for permanent residence in an urban area,
as has been indicated, will lose this privilege, but the Bill
specifies that they shall not be ordered to leave a prescribed
area 'unless other suitable work, either in such prescribed area
or any other area, is offered to such Bantu'.

Certain classes of Africans (presumably doctors and the like)
may be exempted from the control of a labour bureau official
'provided that the onus of proof that he falls within such class
shall be upon the Bantu concerned'.

The government may also declare certain areas or occupations
closed to Africans, who will thereupon be removed from
employment in those areas or occupations. This is apparently to
prepare the way for the wholesale removal of Africans from areas
like the Western Cape, and the banning of Africans from occupations where they might compete with other races. Furthermore,
the authorities may determine that the number of Africans
employed in a certain area or occupation shall not exceed a
certain level. If they do, the 'surplus' Africans may be removed 'provided that Bantu born in the prescribed area shall
only be so removed after all the other Bantu, who in the opinion

of the Minister are surplus, have been removed from that area'.

One of the most dangerous sections of the Bill is that dealing with the treatment of so-called 'idle or undesirable' persons. An 'idle' person is defined by a number of clauses, one of which is that he 'has been discharged from employment for any reason personal to himself on more than three occasions over any period of one year'.

An 'undesirable' person is, *inter alia*, anyone who has been convicted of any offence involving public violence, any offence under Sections 10, 11, 12, or 13 of the Riotous Assemblies Act, Section 2 of the Criminal Law Amendment Act of 1953 (outlawing defiance campaigns), the Unlawful Organizations Act of 1960 (banning the A.N.C. and P.A.C.) and Section 21 of the General Law Amendment Act of 1962 (the Sabotage Act).

An African arrested as 'idle or undesirable' must be brought before a Bantu Affairs Commissioner within seventy-two hours. The Bantu Affairs Commissioner, if he finds him 'idle or undesirable', may then, amongst other things, order him to take up employment or be sent home, or order him to be detained in any rural village, settlement, rehabilitation scheme, retreat, or other place indicated by the Secretary in the Reserves, and per-form such labour as may be indicated by law.

Thus an African who has already served a prison sentence for any of the offences listed, for public violence or incitement or sabotage or carrying on the affairs of the A.N.C. or P.A.C., may arbitrarily be sentenced to a further period of detention. In addition, the Bantu Affairs Commissioner can order any 'idle or undesirable' African not to enter or remain in any area except with the written permission of the Secretary for Bantu Administration and Development.

A provision of the Bill which is likely to cause the most bitter resentment among White South Africans is the one de-claring that no householder may have more than one full-time servant accommodated on his premises, and that even this permission may be withdrawn if suitable alternative accommoda-tion is available in a location. In their anxiety to prevent the towns from going Black, the government is even prepared to demand 'sacrifices' from its own supporters!

This, then, is the reverse side of the Bantustan medal. So-called 'self-government' in the Reserves is to be paralleled by the conversion of the entire African population into migratory labourers, who will have no rights at all in the White areas and who will be shifted from one place to another, herded into camps, subjected to a multitude of administrative restrictions and penalties to suit the labour requirements of the White-dominated economy. Citizenship rights in Bantustan are to be paid for by the complete loss of citizenship rights in the rest of the country.[1]

What this Bill will mean in terms of human suffering, the separation of parents and children, husbands and wives, the destruction of family life, cannot be measured. And more appalling even than the provisions of the Bill itself is the concept that lies behind them – that these crimes can be perpetrated against the African people because they are not the same as Whites, because they do not deserve the same consideration and respect, because they are barbarians living barely above the level of animals.

1 On 4 June 1963, the Deputy Minister of Bantu Administration, M. C. Botha, announced that since the government did not wish to press contentious legislation at the tail end of the session, it would not proceed with the full 145-clause Bantu Laws Amendment Bill but would consider only a shortened thirty-three-clause measure. The remaining clauses will presumably come up for discussion during the next session of Parliament.

16. The Rot

This is the real horror of the South African situation – that as a result of the Nationalist government's policy of apartheid, *herrenvolk* attitudes of separateness and superiority are becoming ever more firmly entrenched in the White community. Appalling crimes are committed against the non-Whites, particularly the Africans, and are tolerated because, after all, 'they are not the same as us'. The Nationalist claim that race relations have never been better is demonstrably false. For the most part there are no race relations at all. With the persecution and virtual outlawing of all the multi-racial political and social organizations, the exclusion of non-Whites from the 'open' universities, the constant growth in the apparatus of segregation, White and Black seldom meet except as master and servant. For many non-Whites the most significant contact with Whites is with an official who, at worst bored and contemptuous, at best harassed and burdened with the administration of hateful laws, projects the worst possible image of the White supremacist. The overwhelming majority of the White population lead a soft and sheltered existence, completely unaware or careless of the countless cruelties endured in the locations on the other side of town from their own garden suburbs.

South Africa is not yet Nazi Germany, with its concentration camps and gas ovens. But the attitude of mind which produced such inhumanities in Nazi Germany is there, and it needs only the whiff of a crisis for White South Africa to throw aside its remaining civilized pretensions and grasp in a frenzy of panic at any weapon for preserving its privileges. If there are not yet street gangs and private armies, it is because the police have so far proved a very adequate first line of defence. Let the South

African armed forces, police, and soldiers show signs of being unable to cope with rebellion, and a ferocity will be unleashed by White South Africa which will make the atrocities of the O.A.S. in Algeria pale into insignificance. Speaking on Republic Day, 31 May 1963, the Minister of Justice, Vorster, declared: 'We have reached the stage in our national life where we realize more and more that there are times in a nation's history when not only reason must speak but blood as well – and that time is now.' No more sinister pronouncement was ever made by any of the leaders of Hitler's Nazi government at the height of their power.

Meanwhile, the crimes that are being committed in the name of White supremacy are debased and debasing enough: the deliberate educational stunting of the non-White peoples to hold back their development; the banning, jailing, banishment, and executions of political opponents; the destruction of family life; the mass removals of population.

Alexandra Township, that one square mile of overcrowded African slum just to the north of Johannesburg, is changing fast. There used to be some 100,000 people living there. In the last five years 43,000 Africans have been moved. A further 20,000 must still go, leaving a population of about 30,000.

This is not just slum clearance. Ultimately it is planned that Alexandra Township should be a dormitory location, consisting of barracks for 'single' men and women working in the northern suburbs of Johannesburg. And meanwhile the population is removed by massive and never-ending police raids. Men and women, husbands and wives, parents and children are caught in the net and swept off to the police station if they are not in possession of permits. At the Bantu Commissioner's Court they are charged, sentenced to imprisonment, and then deported. If they are lucky, some of the victims will escape jail, but will still be ordered to leave the urban area, for the overcrowded starving Reserves.

Mrs Tshabalala of Sixteenth Avenue, Alexandra, was arrested on 20 January 1963, as she sat outside her house, breast-feeding her baby. She was sentenced to a fine of £15 or forty-five days' imprisonment. She served the term in jail as she could not pay the fine. In prison she found twelve other women with babies serving sentences ranging from one to three months each. The babies were crying and the jail authorities demanded that the mothers part with their children, but the women refused. Later it was decided that the children should be taken from their mothers if they were old enough to walk. Mrs Tshabalala was able to keep her child because it was still too young. But what happened to the other children? Welfare workers have come across tiny children left stranded and alone in their homes at Alexandra after both parents had been swept off in police raids.

Mr Mndaweni of Fourteenth Avenue, Alexandra Township, was also arrested in January 1963 and sent to jail because he did not have a permit. One week later his wife was arrested. She was not given a chance to arrange for her children, but was bundled into a van. The children, left behind with nobody to look after them, disappeared the next day. A reporter of the newspaper *Spark* inquired what had happened to them. A search for the children began, but they could not be found.

The government is clearing the Africans out of the Western Cape because they constitute a danger to White civilization there and in any event must not be allowed – in the ethnic pattern of South Africa – to compete with the Coloured workers. Again there is the same story of broken homes, of wives and children separated from husbands, of thousands of married men forced to live in single barracks, with the 'surplus' Africans endorsed out of town and forced to return to the Eastern Cape. On 27 February 1963, it was reported in the *Cape Argus* that the Chairman of the Native Affairs Committee of the East London City Council had appealed to the government to stop endorsing Africans out of the Western Cape, because they were merely piling up in their thousands on the outskirts of East London and creating a dangerous situation there.

'A great many Africans were not only unemployed but were reaching a state of unemployability because they no longer had the strength to labour or because they had been out of work for so long that they had lost the skills by which they had previously earned a living.'

These atrocities would never be tolerated if the victims were

White, for Whites have votes and must be considered. The non-Whites have no vote and can be ignored – until their anger explodes. A riot breaks out, or sabotage takes place. Amongst a section of the Whites there is then a wringing of the hands and a desire to mend their ways before all is lost, but the majority harden their hearts. Fierce new laws are passed, and the police get even tougher in their handling of suspects.

Here are reports which have appeared in the South African Press during recent months:

On rail sabotage charge: Indians Allege Torture by Police. . . . H. Wolpe, for four of the men, and R. N. Bhoolia, for Nanabhai, told H. S. Bosman that they were instructed that Vandeyar was hit and kicked at Langlaagte police station 'and there appears to be a consider-able possibility that some of his ribs are broken'. Also at Langlaagte police station, a wet sack was tied round Nanabhai's head and twisted until he was choking. Electric charges were applied to wires attached to the big toes of Chiba and Jassat by the Railway Police at Park Station and they were suspended upside down by sacks tied over their bodies and were struck to the ground and pulled up by the hair. Van-deyar was told he would either sign a confession this afternoon or be subjected to further physical violence by this afternoon, the defence alleged. (*Cape Argus*, 19 April 1963.)

Torture by Electric Shock, court told. . . . Allegations that electric shock torture was used on two men charged with being members of an illegal organization were made by J. Kudo in the Cape Town Magis-trate's Court today. . . . 'Unorthodox methods have been used and the men have burn marks on their little fingers which they say were caused by electric shocks.' (*Cape Argus*, 22 April 1963.)

Accused Alleged Assaults. . . . Allegations that some of the thirty-seven alleged Poqo members, including several students from native high schools, had been assaulted by the police to extract information, and were being detained in 'shocking circumstances' were made by A. Chaskelson, their defence counsel, when the thirty-seven appeared before H. S. Bosman in the cells of the Johannesburg Magistrate's Courts yesterday on charges of arson. (*Cape Argus*, 8 May 1963.)

Third Degree Methods in East London. . . . One night they [the police] awakened W. Bongco at his home and after searching his house took him to the police station where they used strong-arm tactics to elicit information about the firearms they are searching for. They handcuffed him and hung him up against the wall. Then they assaulted him, some using sjamboks and others pulling him by his sexual organs. Bongco fell unconscious and they untied him. When he recovered they trampled on his face and kicked him with their boots, using obscene language. They were mad with anger, some crying and shouting that if Bongco continued to be stubborn they would take him to the bush and shoot him dead as one who was escaping from custody. At this time blood was already oozing from their victim's ears. After some rest they resumed their work and, squeezing him by the neck, gave him hard blows which rendered him partly deaf. He went unconscious again and this time they took him to shower in his clothes and washed him before they could release him. . . . Today Bongco is in bed at the Frere Hospital as a result of the beatings of the police. A charge of assault has been laid. (*Spark*, 14 March 1963.)

Similar cases of assault were reported from Port Elizabeth during the period that sabotage cases were being investigated there. Usually there are no witnesses, and courts are reluctant to disbelieve the police version of what happened. Justice Bekker declared, when the case of the Indians came before the Supreme Court: 'It is unnecessary for me to return a verdict on the alleged assault as it is not relevant to the issue and it is impossible to state from the evidence that the accused were assaulted by the police after their arrest.'

Yet reports of this type of assault are now so frequent that it is wilful to ignore them. It was not so long ago that the same sort of bestiality was reported from Algeria, and the allegations, at first denied, were eventually proved to be true. The French, who had themselves been the victims of Nazi atrocities during the war, were now committing the same crimes against the Algerians. And for the same reason. The Nazis had treated the French as racial inferiors; the French treated the Algerians in the same way. And in South Africa it is the same story. The *herrenvolk* attitude lends itself to cruelty and sadism because the victims are regarded as being different, inferior. Just as carelessly as one swats a fly one can torture a Jew, or a kaffir. The cult of difference leads straight to the cult of violence and death.

Most White South Africans would probably wax indignant at any suggestion that they are conniving at the torture or ill-treatment of non-Whites. Like the Germans who claim that they never guessed the significance of the columns of smoke rising from the chimneys of the Nazi crematoria, they will spread their hands out and say: 'But it's not true', or 'we didn't know'.

For many, this excuse may even be partly valid. The isolation of one community from the other makes it possible for many Whites to go through life without thinking that anything very wrong happens around them. The mass removals of people from one area to another, the endorsements out of town and the breaking up of homes, the beatings in police stations, the arrests and imprisonments – all happen to other people, not to the Whites. Announcements that so many Poqo members have been sentenced to death or executed can be accepted without a murmur because none of one's friends or relations will be involved. One need never be haunted by the thought, 'There but for the grace of God go I', for by law one cannot be placed in the same position. The difference comes to be accepted as permanent, immutable. The concept of change is rejected as not merely undesirable, but impossible.

This, certainly, has been the tradition of the past, but it is a tradition which is becoming ever more difficult to maintain. As the years of Nationalist rule take their ever mounting toll, the facts cry out with ever more strident urgency. Apartheid is a horror which can no longer be hidden or denied. The whole world condemns and execrates it; the United Nations General Assembly has called for the imposition of sanctions to end it. When the time comes for the settling of accounts, White South Africa will have to bear its full burden of guilt and atonement.

When the time comes. . . . this is the outstanding question in South Africa today: when will the time come when apartheid can be abolished and a new society produced in which discrimination will be outlawed and all men and women will enjoy equal rights and opportunities? When will Nationalist rule be ended? How long can the Verwoerd government survive?

There is no easy answer. As this book has set out to explain, the Nationalist government is powerful, not merely in the possession of a well-equipped and disciplined army and police force, but by virtue of its firm political foundation. This is not a cluster of old-time colonialists or settlers who can be ejected from the continent the moment that the protection of some metropolitan country is withdrawn. The Nationalist roots go deep into history, and Nationalist policies enjoy the support of a substantial section of the White population. Afrikanerdom maintains itself in power through its own independent strength, without requiring the aid of foreign troops. The Nationalists are not the colons of Algeria, who could retain control only for as long as the French were prepared to deploy an army of 500,000 men to protect them.

Nor is the White population outnumbered to anything like the extent that it is elsewhere in Africa. The Whites constitute only one fifth of the total population, it is true, but the remaining four fifths do not constitute a homogeneous group. The proportion of Africans to non-Africans is only two to one – by far the lowest in the continent. In Algeria it was nine to one, in Southern Rhodesia it is fourteen to one. Elsewhere the proportion of Whites to the total has been insignificant, and Black power, once aroused, has been overwhelming.

Consideration of these facts explains why the liberatory movement in South Africa, though enjoying the longest history of struggle and in some ways the most advanced level of ideology and organization, has not made the same spectacular progress as elsewhere in the continent. The reality of White power must never be overlooked. If a measure of non-White leadership, ability, and struggle is wanted, it may be sought in the record of the ever more vicious counter-measures to which the Nationalists have had to resort in order to maintain White supremacy. It is above all non-White pressure which has reduced South African government to the level of rule by arbitrary decree and imprisonment without trial. And the pressure is growing all the time.

There are those who feel that Verwoerd, like Franco, can maintain himself in power indefinitely. This, however, is to ignore the history of the last fifteen years, not only in South Africa, but throughout the world. When the Nationalists came to power in 1948, there were only two independent Black countries on the African continent – Liberia and Ethiopia. Today the whole continent is Black with the exception of the White supremacy states at the southern tip. The tide of emancipation that is sweeping through the Afro-Asian countries, far from abating in the course of time, is growing in intensity. In May 1963, the summit meeting of independent African States resolved to do its utmost to speed up the liberation of the African peoples in the Portuguese colonies, Southern Rhodesia, and South Africa. Pressure for the implementation of the United Nations sanctions resolution is steadily mounting.

This is not to suggest that the liberation of the South African people will come from outside the country alone. It will not. But the struggle of the South African people cannot be seen in isolation from the world-wide struggle of the dependent peoples for freedom and independence. With each citadel of colonialism that falls, the position of the White supremacists in Southern Africa becomes more exposed. The Nationalist government finds it ever more difficult to implement its policies and maintain its economy on an even keel.

Speaking in the House of Assembly on 26 March Dr Verwoerd claimed that there was peace and order in the country – thanks to the work of a strong police and defence force. 'On the other hand,' he proclaimed, 'nobody will deny that a crisis exists in South Africa . . . All over the world there is a crisis. One sees this in the United Nations, in developments in Africa and in threats to South Africa by agitators. These agitators will not be able to achieve anything, but it is a time pregnant with trouble. The government will continue to take the necessary steps to preserve peace and order. . . .'

Dr Verwoerd made it clear that the Nationalist government would not surrender. 'If it becomes necessary to combat Communism and the deeds which flow from Communist agitation, I will not hesitate to place the security of the State and its citizens above technicalities . . . in the ordinary administration of justice.' To maintain White supremacy, in other words, he is prepared to abrogate the rule of law altogether. And certainly the laws placed on the statute book have led South Africa a long way on that road.

Yet the sharper that the crisis becomes, the less the Nationalist government will be able to solve the problems of the country. The Nationalists themselves admit that they cannot succeed unless they enjoy the collaboration of the substantial majority of all sections of the population. But that goodwill is being more and more consciously withdrawn, both by the non-Whites and by a growing number of Whites.

To those who assert that the Nationalists have the right to protect themselves against the use of violence by terrorists and saboteurs, let it be pointed out that White rule is in itself an act of violence against the non-Whites, arbitrarily deprived of the franchise. The democratic doctrine that there shall be no taxation without representation has long been flagrantly violated in South Africa. Today the taxed and unrepresented masses are resolved at last to have their say.

The stage is set for a massive conflict in South Africa. And no one can confidently predict how this conflict will be resolved. But one thing is certain: the scope of the conflict and the amount of damage that is caused will be determined, not only by the strength of the participants in South Africa itself, but by the influence which world opinion can bring to bear upon the situation. That the policy of apartheid constitutes a threat to world peace is self-evident and has already been acknowledged in United Nations resolutions. The discrimination perpetrated against people of colour by the Nationalist government is bitterly resented by non-Whites throughout the world. The more Nationalist repression is intensified, the greater will be the urge for others to intervene.

It took a world war and the loss of 30 million lives to dispose of the Nazi menace – simply because those who had the power refused to use it in time to stop Nazism from overrunning Europe. Let us hope that the cost of ending apartheid will not be so great. There are those, both inside and outside South Africa, who have the power to stop it. Now is the time for all men to take action, so that the cost in life and resources of establishing a democratic order in South Africa may not exceed the bounds of reason, and make the task of reconstruction infinitely more difficult.

A new South Africa, based on freedom and equality for all, is struggling painfully to be born. Who has a right to refuse his help?

Index

327

Two other books in the
Penguin African Library are described on the
following pages

Two recent additions to the Penguin African Library

SOUTH WEST AFRICA

Ruth First

South West Africa has recently stepped into the news and may any day seize the headlines. This book, by a well-known South African journalist, is the first concise yet comprehensive survey of the reasons why South West Africa is today one of the most vital areas of the African continent.

Ruth First traces the course of over eighty years' economic and political exploitation of the African population by a succession of white powers, from the original British and Dutch traders to the Nationalist régime begun in 1948. She shows how the African majority has been progressively deprived of lands, political representation, and the means of full economic development. But she argues also that the ironic tragedy whereby a League of Nations mandate became an instrument of oppression may yet become a source of hope. The U.N. Trusteeship Committee, the International Court of Justice, and South West Africa's shared frontiers with Angola, Northern Rhodesia, and Bechuanaland may help the territory and turn it into the Achilles' heel of *apartheid*.

EAST AFRICA: THE SEARCH FOR UNITY
Kenya, Tanganyika, Uganda, and Zanzibar

A. J. Hughes

For two generations the climate, scenery, and sporting life of Kenya have attracted a stream of wealthy white settlers – pioneers who peopled the White Highlands, planted new crops, opened mines, helped to officer the King's African Rifles, and silently to their surprise generated the native opposition which culminated a few years ago in the Mau Mau insurrection.

Today we see Kenya committed to the principle of federation with Tanganyika, Uganda, and Zanzibar – neighbours with very different histories. Such an imaginative experiment could have the profoundest consequences for the whole of Africa. Nyasaland and Northern Rhodesia might be drawn into the orbit of such a force, which could well set the political style for the rest of the continent.

The author of *East Africa* has spent several years as a political correspondent in East Africa and as an official of one of the nationalist parties. In his account of the histories of these diverse countries he underlines the boldness of this political venture. Whilst Kenya was a British colony, Uganda was made a Protectorate – an area of indirect government – in 1890. Zanzibar, like the coastal ports of the mainland, is largely Arabic in character, and Tanganyika, before the Mandate, was German territory.

This is the first full survey in one volume of the histories and politics of this part of Africa. It graphically outlines a brave and crucial political experiment.

*For a complete list of books available please write to
Penguin Books whose address can be found on the back
of the title page*